Revisiting Richardson

TRANSITS
LITERATURE, THOUGHT & CULTURE, 1650–1850

A landmark series in long-eighteenth-century studies, *Transits* publishes monographs and edited volumes that are timely, transformative in their approach, and global in their engagement with arts, literature, culture, and history. Books in the series have engaged with visual arts, environment, politics, material culture, travel, theater and performance, embodiment, connections between the natural sciences and medical humanities, writing and book history, sexuality, gender, disability, race, and colonialism from Britain and Europe to the Americas, the Far East, the Middle/Near East, Africa, and Oceania. Works that make provocative connections across time, space, geography, or intellectual history, or that develop new modes of critical imagining are particularly welcome.

Recent titles in the series:

Revisiting Richardson
Rebecca Anne Barr and Bonnie Latimer, eds.

Charles Johnson's "General History of the Pyrates" and Global Commerce
Noel Chevalier

British Romanticism and Prison Reform
Jonas Cope

Prolific Ground: Landscape and British Women's Writing, 1690–1790
Nicolle Jordan

Consuming Anxieties: Alcohol, Tobacco, and Trade in British Satire, 1660–1751
Dayne C. Riley

The Part and the Whole in Early American Literature, Print Culture, and Art
Matthew Pethers and Daniel Diez Couch, eds.

Teaching the Eighteenth Century Now: Pedagogy as Ethical Engagement
Kate Parker and Miriam L. Wallace, eds.

Women and Music in the Age of Austen
Linda Zionkowski with Miriam F. Hart, eds.

For more information about the series, please visit bucknelluniversitypress.org.

Revisiting Richardson

Edited by
REBECCA ANNE BARR AND
BONNIE LATIMER

BUCKNELL UNIVERSITY PRESS
LEWISBURG, PENNSYLVANIA

Library of Congress Cataloging-in-Publication Data

Names: Barr, Rebecca Anne, editor. | Latimer, Bonnie, editor.
Title: Revisiting Richardson / edited by Rebecca Anne Barr and Bonnie Latimer.
Description: Lewisburg, Pennsylvania : Bucknell University Press, [2025] | Series: Transits : literature, thought & culture, 1650–1850 | Includes bibliographical references and index.
Identifiers: LCCN 2024040375 | ISBN 9781684485666 (hardcover) | ISBN 9781684485659 (paperback) | ISBN 9781684485673 (epub)
Subjects: LCSH: Richardson, Samuel, 1689–1761—Criticism and interpretation. | English literature—18th century—History and criticism.
Classification: LCC PR3667 .R48 2025 | DDC 823/.6—dc23/eng/20241214
LC record available at https://lccn.loc.gov/2024040375

A British Cataloging-in-Publication record for this book is available from the British Library.

♾ The paper used in this publication meets the requirements of the American National Standard for Information Sciences—Permanence of Paper for Printed Library Materials, ANSI Z39.48-1992.

bucknelluniversitypress.org

Distributed worldwide by Rutgers University Press

CONTENTS

Revisiting Richardson

INTRODUCTION

Rebecca Anne Barr and Bonnie Latimer

In June 2021, one year into the COVID-19 crisis, *The Rambling* published an entire issue devoted to responses to Samuel Richardson's *Clarissa* (1747–1748). More usually a text consigned to undergraduate reading and doctoral programs' qualifying exams, *Clarissa* emerged, in these eight essays, as neither an academic text nor a historical document, but as a peculiarly contemporary resource. This eighteenth-century novel was a "go-to" read of the pandemic. As "a novel of lockdown" whose "heroine careens from one state of confinement to another," Richardson's gargantuan text emerged as a touchstone that calibrated and mediated contemporary readers' sense of their own understandings of bereavement, surveillance, community, and political misinformation.[1] "Our Clarissa Quarantine," as Deidre Lynch called it, attests to not merely the aesthetic endurance of the novel, but also its immediacy and relevance, its capacity to conjure seemingly limitless reinterpretation.

While Richardson had "something of a critical moment in the early 1980s," attracting scholarship by feminist, Marxist, and deconstructionist critics, scholarly work on the Richardsonian corpus has continued steadily since then.[2] Since 2010, the Cambridge Edition of the works of Samuel Richardson has provided further impetus for new research on his writings by updating the scholarly editions of all his works and making his correspondence accessible to readers in all its voluminous complexity. The present collection seizes upon the opportunities provided by this and other recent work in the field to both take account of dominant approaches since 2010 and to showcase new voices and fresh frameworks for reading Richardson in the future. In this introduction, we assess the critical field during the past decade or so before turning to new, overlooked, uncharted, or unexpected histories of Richardson and Richardsoniana—fresh paths out of past conversations that the collection hopes to illuminate.

RICHARDSON AND THE CRITICS, CA. 2010–PRESENT

The great intervening fact of the past decade in Richardson studies has been the publication of the Cambridge Richardson (2011–2022). Its value to the field is hard to overstate. Broadly, the Cambridge project is the fruit of an approach to Richardson that has deep roots in a tradition of eighteenth-century literary criticism, one that flourished particularly in the decades of the 1990s and the 2000s. This approach offers a thick, nuanced, and sometimes incredibly granular view of Richardson's texts, their circumstances of production and consumption, and the networks of print culture surrounding them. It owes much to previous scholarship in histories of the book and of material culture and has resulted in some of the most incisive critical work on Richardson in recent decades.[3]

Alongside the Cambridge project, there is another set of critical approaches to his work, one that sees Richardson as consistently, perhaps peculiarly, amenable to the preoccupations of current literary and political theory. But both sets of approaches share recurrent concentrations of interest and lines of enquiry, clustering around the nature of authorship, gender relations, and power, and how possible or productive it is to read Richardson in our own moment, asking what acts of reconstruction, projection, and imaginative amplification this might entail. The present volume interrogates and develops these ideas, suggesting that they are at the heart of the most important critical conversations in Richardson studies in the 2020s. But *Revisiting Richardson* also pushes the conversation further, embracing perspectives that centralize critical race studies, historical and queer masculinities, and digital and conceptual writing and identifying new, overlooked, or misconstrued forebears and descendants of Richardson. Throughout, we also revisit and consider recent dominant methodologies in the field, keeping in constant view how the types of evidence we adduce when reading Richardson result in new and divergent perspectives on his work.

From its opening volumes, the Cambridge Richardson project represented a renewed engagement with Richardson as a political agent, cultural commentator, and mover and shaker in the world of 1730s–1750s print culture. This is a descendant, in part, of earlier painstaking and highly illuminating scholarship, such as Keymer and Sabor's *The "Pamela" Controversy* (2001). This comprehensive reconsideration of the explosion of print culture ignited by Richardson's first novel picked out responses that ranged from odd and opportunistic, like Charles Povey's *The Virgin in Eden* (1741), to those with more enduring cultural significance, such as Carlo Goldoni's operatic version of the novel from the early 1750s. Their achievement was, in part, to drive home the messy complexities of Richardson's relationship to the book trade, with his acute awareness of the contemporary marketplace, evinced most clearly in his frustrated responses to John Kelly's spurious continuation *Pamela in High Life* (1741). Keymer and Sabor's success in unsettling lazy critical shorthands for Richardson's position (*Pamela* versus *Shamela*; Richardson as a coterie writer for ladies) was cemented by their 2005 *"Pamela" in the Marketplace*, which, despite the focus of its title, in fact productively decentered Richardson to focus on the Grub Street milieu in which he actually operated, suggesting that Richardson must be understood in terms of a print landscape that eighteenth-century scholarship of previous decades might more naturally have associated with Pope and Swift. Their work typified a highly productive critical strain that kept in sight both intense textual focus but also wider market and material realities, modulating into finely tuned textual and editorial scholarship. Such work characteristically and consciously rethought Richardson as a printer, correspondent, and book trade operator, but also retained a sense of the implications of such revisionism for reconsidering the period's ideas of authorship more widely. It is from this milieu that the Cambridge Richardson emerged.

Publication of the Cambridge project began in 2011 with volume 2; Albert Rivero's excellent edition of *Pamela*, was first to press, followed in subsequent years by volumes on *The Early Works* (2012), edited by Alexander Pettit, and Rivero's edition of *Pamela in Her Exalted Condition* (also 2012). At the time of writing, the last volumes of the *Works* have just been released: E. Derek Taylor, Melvyn New, and Elizabeth Kraft's 2022 edition of *Grandison*. In parallel, the press also published the first-ever comprehensive, modern scholarly edition of Richardson's correspondence, rectifying a remarkable gap in the field. Prior to this, of course, scholars had often relied either on John Carroll's slim Clarendon Press version of the *Selected Letters* from 1964, widely available in university libraries in the United Kingdom and North America, but representing a highly compressed selection of material, or possibly on Barbauld's *Correspondence of Samuel Richardson* (1804), which also appeared in a Cambridge Edition in 2011. Even fewer scholars have accessed directly Richardson's manuscript letters, archived in folios in the National Art Library at the Victoria & Albert Museum, but also found in Duke Humfrey's Library at the Bodleian in Oxford University, such as swaths of his correspondence with Thomas Edwards, and elsewhere in over a dozen significant archives globally.

A governing principle of the Cambridge volumes is a return to origins: a focus on first editions, extensive recontextualization, the clearing up of dubious attributions, and the revaluation of seemingly minor works and relationships.[4] For instance, Rivero's edition of *Pamela* used the original text that hit the public on November 8, 1740. The *Works* consistently have an eye on the moment the text hits the market, but also on its immediate legacy and context. In a similar vein, Alexander Pettit's edition of the *Early Works* offers a superlatively detailed exploration of the textual history of *The Apprentice's Vade Mecum* (1733), previously available in a modern edition only in a 1970s Garland facsimile version or an Augustan Reprint Society version of 1975. Pettit combines this with judicious speculation on the possibilities of expanding Richardson's canon to include *The Infidel Convicted*

(1731). The methodological underpinnings of the *Works* encourage focus on Richardson's status as a book trade insider, but also on the nature, boundaries, and implications of his authorship, which emerge in the Cambridge volumes as simultaneously pioneering and pastiche, intensely political and trimming. A major achievement of the Cambridge Richardson is its unsettling focus on the detail and complexity of Richardson's and his contemporaries' idea of him as an author and producer of books.

The *Correspondence* takes a similar methodological tack. Christine Gerrard's 2013 volume of Richardson's exchanges with Aaron Hill's family, for example, attempts to reconstitute the spontaneous and adventitious aspects of familiar correspondence by including, for instance, writing shared with Richardson by Hill's daughters Urania, Astrea, and Minerva; Peter Sabor's 2016 volume includes Lady Bradshaigh's annotations on *Clarissa*. With gestures such as these, the project motions toward—and embodies the impossibility of—attempting to interpolate ourselves into the initial moment of receipt and reading. That sense of seeking an irrecoverable instant is one that animates and frustrates these volumes. The *Correspondence* follows the organizational pattern first laid down by Richardson, according to which clusters of letters are grouped by correspondent or by their relation to a particular novel rather than strictly chronologically, allowing the reader to attend to the organic growth of relationships and conversations. By organizing and publishing the totality of his immense epistolary archive in this way, the Cambridge project adds to our sense of the literary network undergirding the fiction's imaginative and moral project—and in so doing, it also implicitly transforms the notion of authorship that has dominated work on not just Richardson but many other authors. The material presented by the Cambridge Edition bolsters Hilary Havens's model of "networked authorship," which understands writing through relationships between a "principal figure" and "contributing author figures . . . [who are] continually entering and exiting."[5] The dual appearance of the *Works* and *Correspondence* add new dimensionality to prior critical discussions of Richardson's conception of and experiment with the material book and to the subtle valences and evolutions of his political thought.

Unsurprisingly, the Cambridge Richardson has catalyzed new scholarly possibilities. The project forms either a rubric or a bellwether for many of the most recent significant critical treatments of Richardson, some of which stem from and overlap the grand project. Louise Curran's *Samuel Richardson and the Art of Letter-Writing* (2016) foregrounds Richardson's letters as objects of interest in their own right, considering them not as adjuncts to the novels or even as commentaries on them, but rather as their own sites of creativity and the development of ideas. Her study is particularly useful for the sharp focus on women correspondents as authors, addressing the somewhat two-dimensional views found in Richardson scholarship of preceding decades and again resetting our notions of how authorship can be thought about in this period. Sabor and Schellenberg's *Samuel Richardson in Context* (2017) also emerges in part from the Cambridge Richardson; as its title suggests, it guides readers in relation to a host of areas of culture in thirty-seven short essays by major scholars in the field. The collection opens with a familiar but highly productive concentration on book history, reception history, and textual scholarship, with essays from Hilary Havens on "Editions," Norbert Schürer on "Transnational Print Trade Relations," Pat Rogers on "Editing," or Eve Tavor Bannet on "Readers and Reading." The latter sections move into cultural and social history, with chapters on "Religion" by E. Derek Taylor and "Politics" by Howard Weinbrot. The collection makes accessible some of the richness and detail implicit in the exhaustive scholarship undertaken for the weightier *Works* and *Correspondence*, but also draws together the key thematics of Richardson scholarship from the 2010s noted above.

The stimulating effects of the Cambridge project on Richardson scholarship of a different tack can be seen in "Mediating Richardson," a 2017 special issue of *Eighteenth-Century Fiction* edited by Louise Curran and Sören Hammerschmidt. The Cambridge project is one starting point for their collection, but they also go on to consider recent work on authorship more generally, noting scholarship on how economic, legal, and cultural forces bear upon individual authors, but also how authorship itself may be understood as "networked, dispersed, or mediated." Drawing upon both the history of mediation and upon recent interest in coterie and group authorship, Curran and Hammerschmidt's introduction positions novels generally as offering "excavation sites as well as laboratories" to explore and experiment with literary production and readerly engagement.[6] In so doing, they open up a different plane upon which Richardson's work can be situated for critical consideration. Their collection probes Richardson's relationships and legacies, but also considers how Richardson himself becomes a kind of discursive token, accruing differing meanings in the contested afterlives of his novels. For instance, while Bethany Wong's essay studies how Richardson deploys theater in *Pamela II* and the risks this opens up, Teri Doerksen focuses on Anna Meades's *William Harrington* as offering a vicariously "Richardsonian" experience that allows us to think anew about what Richardson came to mean in the years immediately after his death. In a similar manner to Havens's work, already cited, the *Eighteenth-Century Fiction* special issue draws upon two dominant approaches in the field to bring a new urgency to the interrogation of how we can and should read Richardson now.

Curran and Hammerschmidt's special issue interrogates the particularities of our own positions as readers of Richardson in the early twenty-first century and resurrects issues of gender, sexuality, and their relationship to selfhood that have recurred in conversations around Richardson since his own day. Notably, Kathleen Lubey's essay on "Sexual Remembrance" reconsiders the rape of Clarissa, arguing against its "ineffability" and insisting that the "black transaction" is part of a continuum that denies women the possibility of consent, agency, and personhood. Lubey reads the novel "pornographically," insisting on the link between the narrative's many violations of Clarissa's will and the final penetration by Lovelace.[7] Lubey's essay is part of an important trend of treating Richardson's works as paradigmatic sites for complicating ideas of consent, states of mind, and intentionality. While Richardson's *Pamela* was once the case study for the representation of subjectivity itself in twentieth-century literary criticism, the past decade has seen critics challenging the limitations and critical presumptions of the "interiority thesis."[8] *Clarissa* has played a special role in this re-evaluation. In *Reason and Religion in "Clarissa"* (2009), E. Derek Taylor grapples with earlier accounts as he reads the novel alongside Richardson's understanding of the providentialist thought of John Norris, construing God as a "master plot" that Lovelace fails to foil, and ultimately revealing the "tragic potentiality" of human freedom, which here remains merely hypothetical. Understanding similar questions through a very different rubric, Sandra Macpherson's *Harm's Way: Tragic Responsibility and the Novel Form* (2010) shows how the legal concept of strict liability (in which individuals are culpable for harmful effects irrespective of their intentions) intensifies the novel's sense of retributive justice by minimizing the moral importance of subjective intent. Macpherson polemically declares that *Clarissa*'s sense of injustice is profoundly distinct from "the claims of a person individuated by the contingencies of her experience and by her capacity to give an account of herself that differs from her social emplotment."[9] In *Actions and Objects from Hobbes to Richardson* (2010), Jonathan Kramnick similarly pries apart interiority and intention, diagnosing Lovelace's attempts to engineer or infer Clarissa's consent from external appearances as consistent with a philosophical position that largely regards volition as produced by circumstance.[10] Such work shows how the theoretical preoccupations of the 1980s and early 1990s, from Eagleton to Castle to Warner, have been transformed by more recent commentators. The "struggles of interpretation" found in such cultural and literary theory offer a parallel, though sometimes overlapping, path to the histories of material culture, the book, the print trade, and reading that mark the Cambridge project.

The question of women's agency and how it can be conceptualized is an especially rich theme in those considerations that work with current literary and political theory. Both Peter DeGabriele's *Sovereign Power and the Enlightenment* (2015) and James Smith's *Samuel Richardson and the Theory of Tragedy: "Clarissa"'s caesuras* (2016) centralize these considerations.[11] DeGabriele shows how *Clarissa* interrogates the "external limits of selfhood" and their vulnerability to arbitrary power. Using Locke and Hume's materialist theories of contiguity, solidity, and annihilation alongside Agamben, Derrida, and Esposito, *Sovereign Power* argues that Lovelace's violent desire to penetrate Clarissa is a fantasy of power in which his "sovereign touch" will produce a "relationship of propriety" between two bodies in the absence of consent. Smith's monograph thinks about tragic form and *Clarissa*, although through a very different lens to Macpherson's legal framework, bringing the novel into contact with Benjamin, Agamben, Lacan, and others. Like both Castle and Eagleton before him, Smith focuses on the "Mad Papers" as an exemplar of the ruptures caused by desire and its violence. Reading these fragments as a form of found poetry, Smith anticipates the contemporary poets who are Amelia Dale's focus in the present collection: contemporary writers who draw on Richardson's texts for their own purposes.

The generative immobility that Smith uncovers in Clarissa also forms a focus for two other recent significant studies, both of which demonstrate Richardson's continuing centrality to studies of the novel as genre: Stephanie Insley Hershinow's *Born Yesterday: Inexperience and the Early Realist Novel* and Wendy Anne Lee's *Failures of Feeling: Insensibility and the Novel* (both 2019). Like Lubey's article, these works testify to the formative influence of Frances Ferguson's "Rape and the Rise of the Novel" in rethinking Richardson's politics of gender, genre, sexuality, and narrative.[12] In *Born Yesterday*, Clarissa's role as a perpetual novice provides a fresh perspective on Richardson's seemingly bleak novel. Hershinow casts *Pamela* as an illuminating example of the ways in which the "Teflon goodness"[13] of youthful characters are markers of the midcentury "novel's formal innovation" rather than aesthetic failures or accident.[14] In her reading, Pamela's naïveté grants her moral authority immune from skepticism and imports a transformative idealism into this supposedly realist genre. Clarissa Harlowe's otherworldly vision likewise remains fundamentally untouched and unaltered by the grim events of the novel (unlike, perhaps, her exhausted and jaded readers). *Born Yesterday* provides insight into the ways in which Richardson's adolescent heroines are poised at the crux between universal type and characters with interiority. Hershinow's account builds on Deidre Lynch's *The Economy of Character* (1998), which argues that flat characters were currency for readers negotiating the anxieties of the new consumer culture, to show how transitional figures such as Pamela Andrews were both less impressionable and more "generative," "transformative," and resilient by virtue of their very inexperience.[15] *Born Yesterday* thus provides a convincing account of why Pamela "could provoke powerful changes in those around her, while remaining little changed herself."[16] Using "inexperience as both a moral coordinate and a model of character," Hershinow reads *Clarissa* as a text that "subordinates empiricism to the level of subplot," thus loosening the realist epistemology that has frequently defined the form.[17]

Lee's *Failures of Feeling* interpolates *Clarissa* into a longer literary history of emotions. Lee uses critical dissatisfaction with the novel as an opportunity to investigate what Richardson's fiction does, rather than what it doesn't do. Like Scott Paul Gordon in *The Power of the Passive Self* (2002), Lee understands Clarissa's adamantine, unlikable character not as an accident, but as a deployment of the moral power of insensibility—the unsympathetic "picture of perfection" a purposeful alienation effect. Lee reframes that supposed *ur*-text of sensibility as a novel that exploits the "perverse logic" of insensibility: after all, she notes, "nothing incites the passions like dispassion."[18] Lee embeds Richardson's works in early modern history and philosophy of emotion, and beyond to the anomie of twentieth-century fiction. Clarissa's obduracy leads to Melville's disaffected Bartleby, providing a linkage from the eighteenth-century novel to Sianne Ngai's genealogy of affect.[19] Brilliantly summating Frances Ferguson's account of rape as a new theory of the novel, Lee calls the genre a "self-cancelling form, whose double purpose is both to construct and to eradicate the inner life"; the heroine's "lack of personal development" is here a vibrant and stimulating "formal value."[20] The late 2010s, then, produced not only the vast triumph of the Cambridge project but a strand of critical work that interrogates anew the core structural elements, purposes, and intentions of the novel form, resituating Richardson's fiction within current considerations of aesthetic and philosophical values and the possibilities of the genre itself.

Looking back at the 2010s, then, one might say that Richardson has had another "critical moment": but what now? In the wake of the trenchant revaluations of his forms, plots, politics, and effects discussed above, what is left to say? The present volume approaches Richardson from the vantage point of the little known, the niche, the historically overlooked, as well as the sharply contemporary: these essays consider minor works, odd echoes, modern adaptations, and perverse readings. In so doing, we seek new insights on questions of authorship, gender, selfhood, and the possibilities open to us and to future readers of Richardson.

THE CHAPTERS AND THEIR THEMES

At the outset, *Revisiting Richardson* considers Richardson's work in still-overlooked contexts to reappraise his authorship as a novelist and how this was understood by his legatees, immediate and recent. In chapter 1, Bonnie Latimer focuses on Richardson's underdiscussed *Apprentice's Vade Mecum* (1733) in order to make visible the generic conventions of popular didactic writing from which his fictions both diverge and borrow. Revisiting the *Vade Mecum*, a work often dismissed as "derivative," shows how Richardson is invested in the potential of the young and their moral futures. Didactic writing also provides a blueprint for the kinds of reading that Richardson's fictions promote and indeed rely upon for their moral impact: repeated attention to a text, and its modeling, followed by self-directed action. Latimer suggests that this slight text signposts Richardson's later political concerns with moral reform of male manners, but also the need to extract the *Vade Mecum* from "a matrix of value derived from novels" and assess it within the tradition in which it was written. Taking a different tack on Richardson's relation to novelness, Samuel Rowe (chapter 5) offers a sadeian—even sadist—Richardson, whose long narratives are propelled by what he designates "the persecutory plot"—the sexual machinations of villains rather than the static goodness of his heroines. Rowe responds to Margaret Cohen and Carolyn Dever's call for a newly "binational account" of the novel by uncovering a Richardsonian Sade: imaginatively invested in the desires of persecutors, roused to love virtue by watching her suffer and succumb to evil. Narratologically, Rowe contends, Richardson's "inertial theory of virtue" makes plot impossible without a persecutor.

Yet inertia can prove strangely compelling. In chapter 9, E. Derek Taylor argues that Richardson's most seemingly inert character—Sir Charles Grandison—has had a more extensive influence on subsequent fiction than previously reckoned. Taylor traces transmutations of the good man in the work of Henry James and Ford Madox Ford and the golden-age detective fiction of Dorothy Sayers. In twentieth-century American fictions Sir Charles's virtue becomes tragic, his forms of feeling sentimental and sexual rather than chaste and authoritative. In *The Good Solider*, the good man "disrupts, rather than heals, the world around him, and his best intentions almost never have salubrious effects." Taylor's contention that more "engrossed readings" of Richardson remain to be discovered is borne out by Amelia Dale's "Conceptual Richardson" (chapter 4), which investigates what "contemporary citational poetry does with Richardsonian epistolarity." Dale focuses on Nicholas Nace's *catch-words* (2017), which recasts Richardson's printerly tags as poetry, combining book history with conceptual writing. In Trish Low's *The Compleat Purge* (2013), Dale goes on to contend, Richardson's novels provide a rich repository of traumatic narrative and confessional voices, sampled alongside other eighteenth-century texts by Eliza Haywood and John Cleland. Mixing pornography with print history, novel criticism with post-conceptual poetry, Dale's chapter suggests the complexity of Richardson's legacy and the need for scholarship to attune to new, strange, and experimental remediations of his work.

The tripartite relationship between disorderly sexuality, gendered social norms, and individual emotional and ethical experience has long been understood as sitting at the heart of Richardson's fictions. Two chapters in the present volume address such topics in *Pamela* and its much-maligned sequel, *Pamela in her Exalted Condition*. Heather Ladd (chapter 3) questions whether Richardsonian conjugality offers women any pleasure—in the form of happiness—at all. Ladd shows how Richardson's heroine, despite the promise of "virtue rewarded," continues more unhappy than content in her socially elevated role as wife. The novel's marital dynamics create what Ladd identifies as a gender "happiness gap" between Mr. B and his long-suffering wife. For Richardson's heroines, "moral goodness" seems to be inextricable from trial and domestic suffering, even within the apparent success and safety of bourgeois marriage. Likewise, Declan Kavanagh (chapter 2) characterizes the heterosexual marital unit as more precarious, and more incipiently queer, than previous readings have suggested. For Kavanagh, Mr. B and Pamela's domestic security remains shadowed by the disruptive forces of libertine homosociality. *Pamela*'s marriage plot is not merely the establishment of a heteronormative space of domestic union but also the creation of heteronormative time. Richardson's *Pamela* contrasts temporal regularity and order with the anarchy and waste of the unreformed bachelor, with Pamela's domestic labor including the production of stabilizing order.

In her 2013 monograph *Making Gender, Culture, and the Self in the Fiction of Samuel Richardson*, Bonnie Latimer argued that his *History of Sir Charles Grandison* was "the most sophisticated, subtle and intellectually compelling of [all] his novels."[21] Interest in *Grandison*, alongside a sense of its importance for understanding the implications of Richardson's work, has grown. Two chapters focus on this final novel, both using a presentist prism to explore its unsettling gendered moral vision. Rebecca Anne Barr (chapter 7), writing on the "misogynist anger" at the core of Richardson's "good man," argues for the sadistic component of *Grandison*'s chaste hero, finding revisions of his character in Elizabeth Inchbald's *A Simple Story* and Charlotte Brontë's *Jane Eyre*. Sir Charles and the figure of the male virgin emerges as a surprisingly oppressive yet beguiling figure for later women writers, casting a long literary shadow from the eighteenth-century novel to contemporary romance. Sarah Berkowitz (chapter 8) argues that the magnetically static character of Sir Charles prompts "readers to prioritize imaginative speculation about relationships." Extending Ruth Perry's narrative of the triumph of the conjugal family over the consanguineal, Berkowitz shows how *Grandison* is peculiarly productive of erotic and affinal investment. Its conduct book mainstay sponsors "a fantasy of community" that retains male hierarchy while endlessly expanding to incorporate new members.

This community is also tacitly Protestant, English, and *white*—not only explicitly nationalized but tacitly racialized. As the collection seeks to push forward new ways of thinking about Richardson that merit further development, this point is crucial. In chapter 6, Kerry Sinanan uncovers *Clarissa*'s colonial underpinnings—the Harlowes' wealth as new, "trade" money, references to galleys—before demonstrating how Lovelace's descriptions produce Clarissa not simply as a virtuous woman but as a virtuous *white* woman, culminating in the fantasy, both terminal and salvific, of her rising as a "transparent white" angel from her black coffin. The binaries that structure Lovelace's rhetoric around the heroine, Sinanan argues, are inherent to the novel itself, which creates Clarissa as an imperial product. Noting that Clarissa is rarely discussed in terms of her imperial function, Sinanan explores what happens when we consider Clarissa as a white woman, suggesting that the famously fragmentary nature of her narrative (and, at times, her consciousness) in fact produces and calls attention to her real, underlying, impermeable *intactness*. In so doing, Sinanan develops a dimension to

Richardson studies found in the work of Laura Doyle and others, but also extends long-standing critical discussions of the female self in Richardson's work, revisiting questions of how it is possible to approach female experience. In considering Clarissa's fragmentations, Sinanan compares Richardson's representation and recuperation of his heroine through narrative and book form to the fugitive mentions of an enslaved young girl, Abba, in the Thistlewood archive, reflecting on the perceptual difficulties and ethical snares in glimpsing and imagining her experience. Sinanan's attempt to "gather what has never been gathered" alongside a new reading of *Clarissa* draws attention to the role racialization plays in Richardson's work and in the preoccupations of literary criticism itself: asking us to revisit the critical field and ask what is missing, what has been lost, and how new methodologies might shift our understanding of the literature.

NEW DIRECTIONS FOR RICHARDSON STUDIES

The essays in this collection are rich and various, treating figures from Henry James to Dorothy L. Sayers to Trisha Low. As a whole, the collection offers not definitive positions but a series of prompts to action, spurs to further thought, and nudges to read differently and more widely in relation to Richardson. But certain strong themes do emerge from the essays, disparate as they are—topics that represent extensions of current critical preoccupations. Chief among these is gender. Until around a decade ago, it was Richardson's modeling of virtuous femininity in distress that critics tended to focus on. Important work by Tassie Gwilliam, Elaine McGirr, Erin Mackie, and others illuminated the gendering of men and historical modes of masculinity in the Richardsonian corpus.[22] The essays presented here suggest a further critical development in thought about men and masculinity in his work. Several of the arguments in this collection reconsider the idea of virtuous masculinity. Latimer's chapter traces some of Richardson's earliest engagements with masculinity in the form of his writing for apprentices, a population that often stood in discursively and metaphorically for "youth" in general, particularly boys and young men. In this analysis, Richardson's address to apprentices becomes simultaneously an engagement with real, historical adolescent boys such as Thomas Verren Richardson, but more interestingly, a means of imaginatively projecting a reformed nation, buoyed by both expanded trade and elevated morals. In a sense, these quasi-fictional boys, striding toward a future that is now long in the past, represent the earliest antetypes of Richardson's famous (or notorious) "Good Man," a figure that also assumes central importance in the chapters by Rebecca Anne Barr and E. Derek Taylor.

Barr's dissection of the moral and erotic power of the male virgin sees his moral supremacy as sentimentalism charged by misogyny. Like Latimer, Barr is interested in the forging of political consensus and the consolidation of political power, but from a different angle, predicated upon the programmatic humiliation of women in Richardson's last novel. Barr's argument further disrupts *Grandison*'s vision of its own protagonist, advancing a recent tendency in the field to read Sir Charles with a skeptical eye. Barr identifies the female abjection that surrounds the male virgin Dorriforth and St. John Rivers as the ambivalent legacies of Richardson's novel. Taylor, too, uncovers a forgotten Grandisonian lineage, expanding the "circumscribed purview" of Sir Charles's influence as a model of masculinity that peculiarly captures not only the spirit of his own age but also certain qualities and narrative trajectories. For Taylor, later writers interested both in the idea of male virtue and in some of Sir Charles's pet projects extrapolate from Richardson's novel, interrogating the solutions Richardson proposes in his ending through both reappropriation and subtle ironization. Taylor's connection of the good man to the "superman" of the later nineteenth and early twentieth centuries posits another kind of influence that traces Grandisonian resonances in such far-removed characters as Lord Peter Wimsey, the alternately odd, charming, and controlling protagonist of Sayers's Harriet Vane series.

All three of these chapters unpick, in different ways, what is meant by male mastery in the fullest sense of the word. So, too, do Samuel Rowe and Declan Kavanagh. Rowe's focus on how we can read Richardson's "strong, manly" characters in perverse and unexpected ways locates them as propagating an unexpectedly "dark lineage," responsible for the persecutory plots seized upon by Sade. Advancing arguments notably made by scholars such as Laura Hinton in the 1990s, Rowe probes Richardson's male characters as antetypes of "the devil without," the Sadean sexual tormentor, in a way that has implications for reading not only Lovelace but perhaps Richardson's other male characters, too, from Hickman to Mr. B and even Sir Charles, that modest rake.[23] Mr. B is the subject of Kavanagh's analysis, usefully bringing Richardson's earlier fictions into a discussion that sometimes focuses too exclusively on his mature work. Kavanagh brings to bear upon *Pamela* the idea of "queer temporality" as a means of thinking through the structures of domestic routine deployed by Mr. B to segregate himself from the alternative masculinity embodied in "rakishness" and to stabilize, fix, and control his vastly more intelligent wife. Sarah Berkowitz's study of kinship in *Grandison* identifies another modality of male mastery of the domestic sphere, developing work on family in the wider field from Naomi Tadmor, Ruth Perry, and others, to explore the characterological functions of the seemingly infinitely expanding sentimental family. Berkowitz helps to resurrect the novel's sheer popularity, but also implicates it in wider discourses around midcentury understandings of the bounds and functions of the family. In this way, her study chimes with others in the collection that revalue *Grandison*'s influence, such as Taylor's and Barr's; like Dale's, Latimer's, and Rowe's, it expands also what we might think of as the Richardsonian canon.

The collection also continues to centralize and advance conversations around the possibilities of female subjectivity, especially interrogating the feasibility and implications of claims to a coherent selfhood. Sinanan, as discussed above, productively reframes old questions of intactness and integrity, asking us what we really mean when we invoke such terminology, and pushing us to think about the wider ramifications of centering such ideas as criteria of value at all. In chapter 3, Heather Ladd foregrounds how Richardson's early work alienates the essential qualities of the heroine's emotional experience from her, re-creating personal "happiness" as a property that is, for women, peculiarly detachable from themselves, prone to appropriation and weaponization by others. Ladd's focus on how *Pamela* both extracts and reproduces cultural norms of female selfhood links her chapter to Amelia Dale's. Dale uses the digital transvestitism of slash fiction written by female fans to resurrect questions about the female "agonized writing 'I.'" The ironizing, skittish distancing of female articulations of sexual desire implicit in slash pulls early digital forms of writing from the 2000s into a continuum with Richardson's fictions, both characterized by yet-unresolved questions on the possibilities of writing female individuals.

In chapter 4, Dale reframes the concept of authorship, understood in the broadest sense, by analyzing Richardson's relation to the contemporary digital moment. What "authorship" signifies in regard to the Richardsonian corpus is increasingly understood as complex; as we have already noted, critics of various hues have sought to deepen and shift our understanding of what authorship means in relation to Richardson. A professional printer who wrote in moments snatched from the demands of his work, Richardson also cultivated women's writing—both in the extended scribal coteries that characterize his correspondence and by ushering work into press—and procured the creative input and critical labor of male and female correspondents alike. Some of these contributions were already visible to readers in the form of paratextual puffs, introductions, and forewords written by associates of the author. The profoundly networked form of authorship revealed by the Cambridge presentation of the correspondence in particular dovetails with the creative usages of Richardson's work Dale locates in contemporary poetry. Richardsonian epistolarity is revealed as itself inherently citational: its scribal borrowings and artifactual presentation form part of a post-print nostalgia. Many post-digital readers of Richardson will have encountered his works through immaterial facsimile on *Eighteenth-Century Collections Online* or on other digital platforms. In the online era, Richardson's digital corpus is both radically fungible (due to the affordances of cut and paste and optical character recognition) yet simultaneously archaic and nostalgic, a new storehouse of strange narratives and old tropes. In our networked world, Richardson's writing is reborn digitally: divested of the authorial ownership he strove to assert. Didactic editorial hectoring is muted by historical distance and media difference. Yet, even this reminds us of Richardson's description of his readers as "if not authors, carvers."[24] Just as *Pamela*'s pseudonymity left it open for unlicensed continuations, Dale shows how the new digital context frees readers as potential co-creators, able to inventively mine Richardson's fictions for reimaginings.

It is such reimaginings, both creative and perverse, that form the core and impetus of this volume. In drawing together these essays we have surveyed, interrogated, and advanced current questions central to Richardson scholarship and mobilized live approaches to his work. Many of these preoccupations and methodologies have insufficiently examined potential; the essays here find new play, new plasticity, in the critical concepts that have dominated the conversation over (roughly) the past eventful decade of Richardson studies. The essays ask, what types of evidence, what legacies, what frameworks and connections can we productively take into account when reading Richardson today? And, indeed, what responsibilities do we have? Which areas merit revisitation and challenge, in terms of unsettling our own scholarly categories, but also in terms of ethical imperatives that transcend academe? As the *Rambling* volume with which we began implies, reading Richardson in the 2020s is not simply a scholarly exercise in more firmly situating his texts in a static past. Instead, acts of engagement with Richardson's work are now, as always, implicated in discussions of the novel form and how we can understand his particular place within its history and present. This collection sets out some of the key areas that matter for reading Richardson—not just in the decade past, but in that to come.

NOTES

1. Deidre Lynch, "'Nothing of Body': Our *Clarissa* Quarantine," *The Rambling*, June 11, 2021, https://the-rambling.com/2021/06/11/issue11-lynch/.
2. Judith Pascoe, "Before I Read *Clarissa* I Was Nobody: Aspirational Reading and Samuel Richardson's Great Novel," *The Hudson Review* 56, no. 2 (2003): 239–253, 242–243.
3. Important studies under this banner include Janine Barchas's *Graphic Design, Print Culture, and the Eighteenth-Century Novel* (Cambridge: Cambridge University Press, 2003), Christopher Flint's *The Appearance of Print in Eighteenth-Century Fiction* (Cambridge: Cambridge University Press, 2011), and various essays by John Dussinger (inter alia, Dussinger, "Samuel Richardson's 'Elegant Disquisitions': Anonymous Writing in the *True Briton* and Other Journals?," *Studies in Bibliography* 53 [2000]: 195–226; Dussinger, "'Stealing in the Great Doctrines of Christianity': Samuel Richardson as Journalist," *Eighteenth-Century Fiction* 15 [2003]: 451–506; Dussinger, "Fabrications from Samuel Richardson's Press," *Papers of the Bibliographical Society of America* 100 [2006]: 259–279). Strong examples of the intersection of material cultural history with Richardson studies include Kathleen Oliver, *Samuel Richardson, Dress, and Discourse* (Houndmills, UK: Palgrave Macmillan, 2008); Lynn Shepherd, *Clarissa's Painter: Portraiture, Illustration, and Representation in the Novels of Samuel Richardson* (Oxford: Oxford University Press, 2009); Karen Lipsedge, *Domestic Space in Eighteenth-Century British Novels* (Houndmills, UK: Palgrave Macmillan, 2012).
4. In this, the Cambridge Richardson drew on an extant tendency in the field, typified in important work such as Darryl Domingo's essays on Richardson's allusions and his use of

indexes and abridgements, as well as work by commentators on Richardson's relationship to particular aspects of material culture, such as work cited above by Lipsedge, Oliver, Shepherd, and others. Darryl P. Domingo, "'Well Observed by the Poet': Elias Brand and Richardson's British Ancients," *Eighteenth-Century Fiction* 24, no. 4 (2012): 597–622; Darryl P. Domingo, "Richardson's Unfamiliar Quotations: Clarissa and Early Eighteenth-Century Comedy," *Review of English Studies* 66, no. 277 (2015): 936–953.

5. Hilary Havens, *Revising the Eighteenth-Century Novel: Authorship from Manuscript to Print* (Cambridge: Cambridge University Press, 2019), 2.
6. Louise Curran and Sören Hammerschmidt, "Mediation, Authorship, and Samuel Richardson: An Introduction," in "Mediating Richardson," special issue, *Eighteenth-Century Fiction* 29, no. 2 (2016): 121–129, 123.
7. Kathleen Lubey, *Excitable Imaginations: Eroticism and Reading in Britain, 1660–1760* (Lewisburg, PA: Bucknell University Press, 2012).
8. Sandra Macpherson, *Harm's Way: Tragic Responsibility and the Novel* (Baltimore: Johns Hopkins University Press, 2010), 16.
9. Macpherson, *Harm's Way*, 16.
10. Jonathan Kramnick, *Actions and Objects from Hobbes to Richardson* (Stanford, CA: Stanford University Press, 2010).
11. Peter DeGabriele, *Sovereign Power and the Enlightenment: Eighteenth-Century Literature and the Problem of the Political* (Lewisburg, PA: Bucknell University Press, 2015); James Smith, *Samuel Richardson and the Theory of Tragedy: "Clarissa"'s caesuras* (Manchester: Manchester University Press, 2016).
12. Frances Ferguson, "Rape and the Rise of the Novel," *Representations* 20 (Autumn 1987): 106, http://doi.org/10.2307/2928503.
13. Stephanie Insley Hershinow, *Born Yesterday: Inexperience and the Early Realist Novel* (Baltimore: Johns Hopkins University Press, 2019), 3.
14. Hershinow, *Born Yesterday*, 47.
15. Deidre Shauna Lynch, *The Economy of Character: Novels, Market Culture, and the Business of Inner Meaning* (Chicago: University of Chicago Press, 1998); Hershinow, *Born Yesterday*, 9.
16. Hershinow, *Born Yesterday*, 27.
17. Hershinow, *Born Yesterday*, 29, 34.
18. Wendy Anne Lee, *Failures of Feeling: Insensibility and the Novel* (Stanford, CA: Stanford University Press, 2019), 1.
19. Sianne Ngai, *Ugly Feelings* (Cambridge, MA: Harvard University Press, 2005).
20. Lee, *Failures of Feeling*, 60, 90.
21. Bonnie Latimer, *Making Gender, Culture, and the Self in the Fiction of Samuel Richardson: The Novel Individual* (Farnham, UK: Ashgate, 2013), 3.
22. Tassie Gwilliam, *"The Good Man, Alas!": The History of Sir Charles Grandison and the Triumph of Masculinity in Samuel Richardson's Fictions of Gender* (Stanford, CA: Stanford University Press, 1993), 111–160; Elaine McGirr, "Manly Lessons: 'Sir Charles Grandison,' the Rake, and the Man of Sentiment," *Studies in the Novel* 39, no. 3 (2007): 267–283; Erin Mackie, *Rakes, Highwaymen, and Pirates: The Making of the Modern Gentleman in the Eighteenth Century* (Baltimore: Johns Hopkins University Press, 2009), 59–70.
23. Laura Hinton, "The Heroine's Subjection: Clarissa, Sadomasochism, and Natural Law," *Eighteenth-Century Studies* 32, no. 3 (1999): 293–308, https://doi.org/10.1353/ecs.1999.0017.
24. Richardson to Johannes Stinstra, in *Selected Letters of Samuel Richardson*, ed. John Carroll (Oxford: Clarendon Press, 1964), 296.

1

CITIZENS OF THE FUTURE

The Apprentice's Vade Mecum in Context

Bonnie Latimer

"It is a dry performance," Richardson wrote resignedly of his own *Moral and Instructive Sentiments*, "Dull Morality, and Sentences, some pertinent, some impertinent . . . I cannot expect much from it."[1] Richardson's hesitations around the *Sentiments* have been treated with faint derision: after all, despite his insistence that it was only an "ingenious Gentleman" (perhaps Solomon Lowe) who prompted him to his labor, when did Richardson ever need encouraging to go back over his own work? As John Dussinger points out, Richardson's studiously humble attitude to the *Sentiments* has been taken as "mere fishing for compliments," although Dussinger himself more kindly reads it as evidence of "serious reservations."[2]

There is a third way, however. Richardson is writing in a well-established genre—the demotic enchiridion or collection of moral sayings—with its own tropes, one of which is the preface apologizing for the unformulated, tedious nature of the following collection. In 1748, for instance, Charles Palmer noted ruefully that his extracts had been "originally collected for a private, and not a public use"; James Mauclerc claimed that he had only "copied out, at first confusedly and promiscuously" "what Reasons and Arguments he found to make the greatest Impression on his Mind"; Sir John Fielding offered in extenuation of his volume of extracts that "'Twas in . . . retirement I collected the opinions, sentiments, and examples of virtue contained in these sheets."[3] As well as seeing Richardson as prey to vanity or uncertainty, we might also read this often-cited letter as drawing on a set of generic conventions. That genre, however, like other instructional genres of the period, is often imperfectly visible to scholars working today. This may have implications for how we read his work as a whole.

From the mid-1990s, scholars have broadened studies of Richardson, interrogating the author's relations to print culture and the book trade, his understanding of authorship and intellectual property, his status as an innovator, and his engagements with fashion, portraiture, theology, and more.[4] Catalyzed by the appearance of the Cambridge Richardson project, important collections and monographs published since 2011 have given an even richer sense of how we might read his oeuvre contextually.[5] Despite this refreshing new work, I suggest that a crucial area of eighteenth-century culture that remains insufficiently interrogated in relation to Richardson is popular didactic writing, a tradition pervasive in the period and yet too easily sidelined by critical comment. The present chapter focuses on one area of the educational tradition, the apprentice guide, relating it to one of Richardson's earliest identified works, *The Apprentice's Vade Mecum* (1733). Building on the exhaustive work done by Alexander Pettit in his edition of the text, and on John Dussinger's extensive scholarship, this discussion fleshes out literary traditions against which the *Vade Mecum* might be read.[6] *The Apprentice's Vade Mecum* often warrants a merely introductory mention or footnote in wider discussions of Richardson's novelistic work.[7] By concentrating on the text and its contexts, however, this chapter offers a minor provocation to try and read his work against different traditions and according to different rubrics of literary value. I suggest that reading Richardson's early educational works in terms of their participation in popular didactic traditions generates new insights into these texts, how they are intended to be read, and their meanings. Further, this approach may also help us to reconsider what it even means to talk about Richardson as a "didactic" writer, interrogating the often-pejorative connotations of that term. Throughout, I contend that situating Richardson's work in a set of derivative generic traditions should not result in reading his didacticism only as a pale precursor of his later, superior, novelistic writing; instead, it has implications for reading all of his oeuvre.

THE APPRENTICE'S VADE MECUM AND ITS CONTEXTS

The Apprentice's Vade Mecum was published in late 1733, although postdated as 1734 on the title page. It was trailed by various journals with which Richardson was involved, including the *Weekly Miscellany* and the *Daily Journal*.[8] A generic advice text, it appeared between two lesser texts addressed by Richardson to apprentices he knew—his 1732 letter to his nephew, Thomas Verren Richardson, and his "Rules and orders to be observed by the members of this chapel" (1734).[9] As John Dussinger shows, the *Vade Mecum* comprised shreds of Richardson's own texts and recycled elements of others' work, including his avuncular letter *The Infidel Convicted* (1731), *The Seasonable Examination of the Pleas and Pretensions* (1735), and John Leake's *The Scholar's Manual* (1733).[10] Its reception was modest compared to his novelistic success, of course, but it continued to be advertised until at least 1744.[11] Part I consists of a commentary on the standard indenture for apprentices, generally supposed to be a Richardsonian innovation in the apprentice guide genre. Part II represents a derivative narrative guide for apprentices, written by Richardson but based on and at times leaning on other, related texts (part II will be the substantial focus of this piece). Part III offers "brief Cautions against Scepticism and Infidelity," drawn from *The Infidel Convicted* (itself a mishmash of unattributed quotations) and Leake's *Scholar's Manual*.[12] Richardson's writing for apprentices also reached posterity another way—a version of the letter to his nephew was gifted to apprentices of the Company of Stationers into the twentieth century.[13]

The Apprentice's Vade Mecum is written in the context of discursive uncertainties around apprenticeships and apprentices. Looking across the shift from the early modern to the modern periods, apprenticeship was changing. The apprenticeships familiar in Richardson's time had been formalized in England in an act of 1563. Between the mid-sixteenth and early nineteenth centuries, traditional apprenticeships altered in character, with formal binding becoming less relevant and with the rise of a larger journeyman class in evidence.[14] Peter Earle's classic *The Making of the English Middle Class* describes the traditional outlines of apprenticeship: the premiums paid by parents or families, the system of trial or "liking," and the formal procedures and oaths involved in binding an apprentice, including the indenture explicated in the *Vade Mecum*.[15] Apprenticeship has its own substantial historiography, largely lying in the fields of social and economic history. Ilana Ben-Amos estimates that "about 1,400 youths began apprenticeship terms every year in mid-sixteenth-century London" and that the total apprentice population of the capital at this time was about 10 percent of its inhabitants; by the early eighteenth century, the numbers of apprentices had increased to some 30,000, making apprentices a "sizeable and visible sector" of the population.[16] Tabulating exact numbers is difficult, and naturally figures differ between regions and cities, but Ben-Amos's estimations are broadly supported by other scholars; Patrick Wallis's re-evaluation of the economic historiography of apprenticeship puts nonagricultural apprentices at 7.5 to 10 percent of the labor force in the early eighteenth century, and another recent survey estimates that 10 to 40 percent of London's adult males had at some time been apprentices and that England-wide, about 6.5 percent of teenaged males would travel to London to start an apprenticeship.[17] The cost of premiums varied widely, with as little as £1 recorded in some provincial areas, to £10–12 for less desirable trades in London, up to over £1,000 plus bonds of security for prestige trades in the capital.[18] Apprentices were often bound far from home; Ben-Amos notes that "the evidence suggests that most apprentices barely knew the people to whom they were apprenticed," and also emphasizes the "difficulty involved in adapting to apprenticeship" caused by the sudden enjambment of adult and adolescent strangers under a single roof.[19] We can see such worries surface when Richardson mentions his nephew's "unpolished roughness of behaviour" or when the *Vade Mecum* notes with the voice of weary experience that "Repetition [of instructions] is a tedious and irksome thing" (*AVM*, 40).[20]

Apprentices certainly did face challenges. Recent scholarship concludes that apprentices were older than previous accounts had suggested; binding often occurred around age fifteen or sixteen, meaning, as Patrick Wallis powerfully argues, that apprentices' labor had economic value to their masters from early on in their terms.[21] This labor, however, might consist in menial work, a common complaint. Ben-Amos believes that apprentices frequently occupied the bottom rung of a household's social ladder, leading to a "sense of humiliation." Francis Kirkman's picaresque memoir recalls his apprenticeship to a scrivener being marred by "Petty Services": "clean[ing] the Shooes, carry[ing] out the Ashes and Dust, sweep[ing] the Shop, cleans[ing] the Sink . . . draw[ing] the Beer . . . fetch[ing] up Coals, and Kettles . . . go[ing] of all errands, and carry[ing] all burthens."[22] Due in part, perhaps, to such clashes, apprentices often did not complete their terms; Wallis notes that many apprenticeships appear to have finished early, partially due to mortality, sickness, and disability on either side of the contract, but also to apprentices' wishing to dissolve their bonds.[23] The unreliability of apprentice bonds is lamented in the literature of the period: Thomas Tryon gloomily suggested that "Of all the Youths that Yearly come up to *London*, to be Apprentices to *Merchants*, *Drapers*, *Silk men*, &c. there is not one in twenty that serves his time out, or lives on his Trade," uncharitably attributing this to "the effects of those Poysonous Weeds of Pride and Arrogance, their Parents sow'd in them in their Childhood."[24] Perhaps more realistically, *The Apprentice's Vade Mecum* subtly emphasizes the possibility of the master's behavior causing a dissolution of the bond, imagining him sabbath-breaking, having "flagrant" "Infirmities" that must be overlooked, and having a "severe, or morose" temper (*AVM*, 35, 39, 41). Whatever the causes of apprenticeships' failing, they did, and Peter Earle argues that even of those who did complete their terms, many would never become masters of their chosen trades.[25]

RICHARDSON AND APPRENTICE GUIDES

Beyond the historical realities, the apprentice was also a stock figure of popular culture—a folk hero such as Dick Whittington or the "famous prentice" Aurelius, but also a generic type of disruption and misrule.[26] J. A. Sharpe notes that "youth" was generally framed as subject to "sensuality, disobedience, levity, wantonness, idleness, excess, envy, ambition, and mocking of elders or authority more generally," and that this was a life stage in which "individuals would be shaped by good or bad influences which might normally be expected to leave a decisive impression upon their characters for the rest of their lives."[27] The apprentice as a figure becomes a locus for representing those problems associated with "youth," with "'the apprentices' or more often 'prentices' appear[ing] frequently as a generic term [that] sometimes means what it says but quite often [is] synonymous for youth in general."[28] Mihoko Suzuki describes how, from the Elizabethan period, the apprentice is popularly linked "with vagabonds and masterless men as criminal elements threatening the social order with violence," while Anne Wohlcke suggests that Georgian apprentices were discursively lumped in with "servants, soldiers, and other young men," representing "an ominous and unpredictable force if authorities failed to contain them."[29] Daniel Defoe opined that what apprentices really needed to learn was "subjection to their masters."[30] Such concerns abound in imaginative literature, but may even have influenced actual regulatory practice, lengthening the terms of apprenticeships in an effort to control "potentially disorderly youths."[31]

The charges drawn against apprentices ranged from the vanilla—Kirkman's master accused him of being "proud, idle, negligent, cross" and of working for others outside the terms of his bond—to the riotous and beyond.[32] The popular ballad *The Loyal London Prentice* imagines a Cavalier youth, "Devout" but given to drinking, loud singing, and debt.[33] Even the soberest apprentice literature sees apprentices as subject to voracious sexuality; following the terms of the indenture, which forbad "fornication," R. Campbell cautioned parents of prospective apprentices that "Women is another strong Temptation to Apprentices. . . . The Blood runs warm in their young Veins, and they are naturally prone to gratify the new-grown Appetite."[34] In popular imaginations, the apprentice often becomes a figure of topsy-turvy sexual fantasy, his sociopolitical aspirations intertwined with (in Alexander Pettit's wonderful phrase) a "salvific hypergamy."[35] A case in point is the ballad *An Amorous Dialogue between Iohn and his Mistris*, which frames the social mobility of apprentices through cuckoldry, with "the man" becoming "the master, the Prentice the Dad," as "Iohn" turns to "handling my mistresses ware" instead of the shop wares.[36] The apprentice-as-criminal, too, is a recurrent figure. George Barnwell, Jonathan Wild, and Jack Sheppard are prominent examples—as Jones DeRitter points out, the two latter started their careers as runaway apprentices.[37] The *Vade Mecum* is typical when it adjures apprentices prophylactically to read "the *Dying-Speeches* of unhappy Criminals" (*AVM*, 32). Sensationalist broadsheet literature takes the apprentice as a stock figure in gory torture and homicide cases, such as the 1668 recounting of Thomas Savage's mindless murder of a serving maid, or the 1676 account of a mistress's attempt to burn her husband's apprentice to death for divulging her extramarital affairs.[38] In such cases, the apprentice's knowledge of intimate household secrets enables and adds piquancy to the scandalous events.

A substantial proportion of literature written to and about apprentices was, of course, what we would now term didactic literature. An early apprentice guide is Edward Coote's 1597 *English School-Master*. This text claims to be directed to apprentices, but they remain in practice undifferentiated from its other advertised audience of schoolboys. Coote supplies useful knowledge such as directions on pronunciation, mnemonics, didactic rhymes, a glossary of difficult words, and a template for forming letters. In this vein, too, is Richard and John Dafforne's *Apprentices*

Time-Entertainer Accomptantly (1640), which is divided into a sort of accountant's catechism, model accounts, and a blank practice account book. Post-Restoration, apprentice guides tend toward narrative advice, a tradition that includes *The Apprentice's Vade Mecum*. Guides such as Caleb Trenchfield's *A Cap of Gray Hairs for a Green Head* (1671), Nathaniel Crouch's *Apprentices Companion* (1681), and William Smythies's *Advice to Apprentices* (1687) contain standard adjurations, revealing the tensions around the apprentice's presence in the household. For instance, Crouch warns against answering back to one's master (or even talking in his presence!), while Trenchfield notes that a "talkative humour should be avoided."[39] Comparably, Richardson's *Vade Mecum* cautions against "idle Prating and Talkativeness" (*AVM*, 30). Crouch lays down strictures on "Servants Apparel" in relation to the apprentice, and Trenchfield offers "a caution against Intemperateness and fantastickness in Apparel" since "'tis not rare to see those persons exposed like Owls, to the ridiculous wonder of sober men, strut along, as if they drew after them the admiration, and not the laughter, of those that see them."[40] One is reminded of Richardson's comic flight about the fopling apprentice with his wig "*plaister'd* rather than *powder'd*, and appearing like the *Twigs* of a *Goosebury-Bush* in a *deep Snow*; his Shoulders also crusted or iced over with White, as thick as a *Twelf-Cake*" (*AVM*, 32–33). Following the standard indenture, all of them, including Richardson, inveigh against lying, scoffing at religion, breaking the sabbath, idleness, and carelessness with the master's goods, with other common cautions including care in the choice of company and the avoidance of plays.[41] These indicators of the low-level but continuous annoyance of a strange teenager in one's household are the true keynotes of the apprentice guide, and of apprentice literature generally. They surface in texts as diverse as John Ayres's model copybook of 1688 through to the scandalous ballads and broadsheets, which often link the bloodiest crimes directly to a relatively minor household infringement such as staying away from church on a Sunday or not returning from an errand on time. The murderer Thomas Savage starts by sabbath breaking, and the narrator sagely notes that "Youthful extravagancies have commonly bad consequences," and several versions of the Barnwell myth have him first encountering Millwood when he is out without his master's knowledge.[42] (The *Vade Mecum* similarly imagines an inexorable descent from "bad habits of speech" to "Drunkenness, Whoredom, Theft, Robbery, Murder, and the Gallows" [*AVM*, 32].) By contrast, the "valiant London prentice" Aurelius, who ends by combating "Gyant-like" Turks, begins rather more humbly by "not omitting any thing that might please or be for his Masters Interest," in a formulation that might have come directly from Crouch or Trenchfield.[43] These tropes persist throughout texts such as the 1700 *Apprentice's Faithful Monitor* and R. Campbell's 1747 *London Tradesman*. Taken together, they speak to the culture's deeper qualms over nascent capitalism, shifting patterns of labor, the status and power of "youth," and the populist disruption inherent in London's periodic riots.[44] They seek, in their different ways, to address these broader, troubling shifts by keeping within due bounds the ductile figure of the apprentice.

The Apprentice's Vade Mecum is deeply steeped in this tradition. The derivative nature of the *Vade Mecum* is clear when comparing its most apparently original section, part II, closely with a text such as *The Apprentice's Faithful Monitor.* Unlike parts I and III, part II is neither obviously cribbed from other texts nor published elsewhere. However, it is still heavily dependent on existing writing in genre of apprentice guides. The *Faithful Monitor*, as a comparator, is a pamphlet of three pages, initially published in 1700, but then reprinted just before the appearance of the *Vade Mecum*, in autumn 1733. Alexander Pettit has shown that Richardson fretted about this incipient rival. The preface to the *Vade Mecum* refers to the *Faithful Monitor* as "a piece that seems calculated to promote the same Design" as the *Vade Mecum*, but defensively distances Richardson's production from this ill-timed rival (*AVM*, 8). There *are* substantial differences between the two—the first and third parts of the *Vade Mecum* do not trespass upon the *Faithful Monitor*'s territory, and the total length and elaboration of the *Vade Mecum* much exceed the earlier production. That said, there are distinct similarities between the second part of the *Vade Mecum* and the *Faithful Monitor*. The *Monitor* begins with an adjuration based on Ephesians 6:6, admonishing the apprentice to serve his master "not with *Eye-Service, but with Singleness of Heart.*" Comparably, article IV of the *Vade Mecum* cautions against "Eye-Service and Idleness" (*AVM*, 29).[45] The *Monitor* discusses the importance of obeying directions quickly, of using time to the master's benefit, avoiding bad company, not lying to cover a fault, maintaining duty to parents and God, and keeping the sabbath. With some excursions, this is the same ground covered in part II of the *Vade Mecum*'s articles IV, IX, X, XIV, XV, and XXIV. The *Monitor* closes with a caution on the value of reputation in trade, mirrored in the discussions of friendship and advantage that conclude part II of the *Vade Mecum*, where the apprentice is enjoined to become "a Credit to Trade in general" (*AVM*, 36).[46] Although not directly copied, part II is heavily dependent on existing tropes, structures, and rhetoric within the genre.

CITIZENS OF THE FUTURE IN *THE APPRENTICE'S VADE MECUM*

Richardson's engagement with the genre, however, is not limited to the reproduction of rote cautions. Richardson's apprentice addressee was originally a real boy—but one who, in the text's evolution from the initial letter to Tom Richardson, morphed into an ideal figure that could be used to limn out a morally reformed society.[47] In this, Richardson drew on and developed a tendency latent in apprentice literature. Much apprentice literature seemingly lumps apprentices in with servants, characterizing the state of apprenticehood as servile, and not envisaging a life beyond. Texts from Coote's Elizabethan tract, cited above, to Abraham Jackson's

Pious Prentice (1640), through Trenchfield in the 1690s and Nicholas Zinzano's *Servants Calling* (1725) address themselves promiscuously to "servants and apprentices." Crouch describes the state as "a genteel Servitude," and Trenchfield recommends even an animalistic servility to the apprentice: "For as we love Mettle in Brute Creatures, and take Delight when Dogs or Horses shew their ready motion at our Whistle or Chirrup; so there's nothing we take more Pleasure in, than a diligent or willing Servant."[48] At first glance, then, we might generalize to all apprentice literature Jones DeRitter's insight that Lillo's *George Barnwell* encourages those who "choos[e] not to rock the boat" and "represents a conscious attempt to create a cult of dependence."[49]

In fact, though, apprentice literature as a genre contains glimmerings of something more ambitious: as well as a figure requiring chastening, stabilizing, and keeping within bounds, the apprentice can represent both a future man and future manhood, or even a speculative and ideal polity. *The Prentises Practise in Godlinesse* (1608), an early example of such literature, frames apprenticeship as a time of moral choices that will come to inform the rest of the apprentice's life.[50] Defoe noted that "if a young man . . . passes over the season for such improvement, he very rarely ever recovers it."[51] Zinzano framed "the Time of his Subjection" as determining the apprentice's "succeeding Course of his Fortunes."[52] That sense of the apprentice as trembling on the threshold of his own future is found woven throughout the genre. Francis Kirkman remarks, "All the good or ill fortune of my life depended upon my serving this eight years," and generally, "he that is an Apprentice at present, in short time [is] out of his time, and then he is a Companion for his Master, and it may be a better man than he."[53] Trenchfield's final chapters imagine the apprentice's future life as a master, setting up in trade and managing his own servants, and Campbell addresses the apprentice as a future husband.[54] Wallis et al. characterize the adolescent apprentices of this period as not mere riotous boys bound to grudging or exploitative masters, but "thoughtful agents in their own economic destiny," "on the path to acquiring the skills and income that would allow them to establish an independent household of their own"—or, as Carol Houlihan Flynn puts it, "the apprentice is always preparing to become someone different, something more."[55] Seen this way, the apprentice becomes a figure for talking about future men, and the interest in "stabilizing" them transforms from a quasi-punitive urge to an aspirational shaping of the next class of masters.

It is within this strain of thinking, common to apprentice guides of the period, that we should read *The Apprentice's Vade Mecum*'s investment in futurity. Like many apprentice texts, Richardson's manual emphasizes that the moral effects of choices made during apprenticeship will last until "the End of Time, and for ever"; the guide's advice pertains "during the whole Course of his future Life" (*AVM*, 27, 25). Unlike the original letter to Tom Richardson, though, which emphasized the nephew's "future livelihood and well-being in this world," the *Vade Mecum*'s ambition stretches beyond the individual destiny to the collective.[56] Abandoning the "Master," who is apparently party to "the Degeneracy of the Times, and the Prophaneness and Immorality" of modern society, the text turns instead to "the Servant, who when he comes to be Master, in his Turn, may contribute to amend the Age." It is easy to see Richardson as disingenuous when he remarks shortly after that he knows of no other texts "that are peculiarly calculated to instruct Young Men in the particular Duties of an Apprentice." As the preceding discussion establishes, there were many extant discussions of apprenticeship, and it beggars belief that Richardson was not familiar with them (as Alan Dugald McKillop notes drily, "His pretensions to originality . . . were exaggerated").[57] He is right, though, that they tend to confine themselves to (at furthest) the future life of the individual apprentice. By contrast, Richardson's preface to *The Apprentice's Vade Mecum* addresses the text generally to "the Class of Young Men who are about being apprenticed," seeking to influence "the Minds of Youth" at large, in pursuit of "the Good of the Community in this great Trading Kingdom," a class of people "on whose Industry and Labour the Welfare of the Whole almost intirely depends" (*AVM*, 5). Interestingly, the puffs printed when the *Vade Mecum* appeared gloss it as addressing itself both to apprentices, but also to the "young *Tradesman*"; the reviewer's summary of Richardson's arguments flits between apprentices and tradesmen more generally.[58] The different parts of the *Vade Mecum* may draw on different tracts, written by different people and printed at various junctures, but the language of its brief preface unites the subsequent, disparate text into a political statement in support not only of trade but of a "reformed" and morally harmonious society to be realized in the near future. Here, we might relate the *Vade Mecum* to Lovelace's mock utopias and Sir Charles Grandison's ideal estate community, which both (in their different ways) figure forth the future regulation of male desires and the establishment of a reformed and peaceable polity.[59] Richardson's writing is invested throughout his life in imagining utopian communities, and this may be an early instance of this tendency. Following this line of thought, the *Vade Mecum* can also be read against the more fantastical apprentice fictions, which characterize the apprentice as the surprising agent of future political change. The apprentice mob in *The Loyal London Prentice* (1681) will be responsible for the stability of the monarchy; William Smythies mistily imagines the elevation of the most disenfranchised through the apprentice system when he describes "the great Estates with which poor *Orphans, Hospital-boys, Beggar-boys, Foundlings*, and such like, have been blessed."[60] The "valiant London prentice" Aurelius becomes the representative of British interests abroad when he travels as a factor and subsequently settles into the mercantile elite as Lord Mayor of London, reprising the Whittington myth. *The Apprentice's Vade Mecum* is in some respects far removed from such fantasies, but I suggest that Richardson shares their sense of the apprentice's agency in the establishment of a morally improved collective order. This imperative may be understood through Paul Griffiths's insight that apprentice culture generally was characterized by "a long tradition of collective action" with an interest in righting wrongs and establishing justice.[61] Read this way, we can see the *Vade Mecum* as both an early text in Richardson's political thought and one in conversation with a distinct generic tradition, compared to his novelistic texts.

DIDACTICISM, DERIVATIVENESS, AND READING RICHARDSON

This might lead us, finally, to reflect on how we value *The Apprentice's Vade Mecum* (a minor, derivative work) and perhaps, by extension, eighteenth-century popular didactic writing more generally. In common with Richardson's other non-novelistic writing such as the paraphernalia surrounding his novels, this is a text that demands to be read in different ways than a novel, and to be valued according to a different rubric, too. As I have suggested elsewhere, Richardson's para-novelistic writing, such as the *Moral and Instructive Sentiments*, requires a reading methodology based around rereading, comparison, selectivity, and self-application. In that essay, I also contended that we should consider Richardson's ideal novel reader as one who reread and self-applied moral precepts.[62] That earlier discussion focused largely on collections of moral sentiments and enchiridions. Here, I extend that argument to apply to Richardson's engagement with apprentice literature. Barbara Benedict's seminal study *Making the Modern Reader* (1996) argued that literary anthologies "stimulate readers to compare, judge, and thus rank the separate items" excerpted to comprise the anthology.[63] David Allan has similarly seen commonplace books (in a sense, a species of personal anthology) as involving a comparable exercise of selection and comparison.[64] If such arguments represent a scholarly consensus about how to read anthology-type texts—that is, if there is general agreement that such texts require an active engagement—I suggest we should extend this to other forms of eighteenth-century didactic writing, too, and, in particular, apprentice literature. Richardson clearly intended for his apprentice texts to be reread and deeply considered. He exhorted his nephew to "transcribe these lines, and keep them by you for your better observation," and to "copy out fair these articles."[65] Less explicitly, but along the same lines, the *Apprentice's Vade Mecum* explicitly demands an "attentive Reader."[66]

Generally speaking, seventeenth- and eighteenth-century didacticism often envisages the gaining of knowledge through repeated exposure. To take simply one well-known example, Richard Allestree's seminal *Whole Duty of Man* directs the reader to con "one of these chapters every *Lord's Day*, [so that] the whole may be read over thrice in the Year."[67] (A similar pattern is found in many texts—to instance one Richardson knew well, Leake's *Scholar's Manual*.) This represents a more generalized understanding of how learning works: repeated attention to a model.[68] However, several species of didactic writing then imagine such rote learning to be followed by more self-directed action. Guides on epistolarity and books of model letters are a good example of this, as are collections of moral sentiments or enchiridions. Apprentice guides, too, can assume this movement from memorization to action: Abraham Jackson adjures his apprentice reader to "read over againe and againe these directions following, which I have gathered for you to be put in practice . . . by this meanes you shall make them so familiar unto you, as that you shall not be to seeke for directions how to behave your selfe."[69] The *Vade Mecum* comparably urges its apprentice reader to "*conclude the Boy*, and *begin the Man*; and act up to the new Character which you have begun to assume" (*AVM*, 27).

I suggest that the *Apprentice's Vade Mecum*, as with Richardson's other non-novelistic writing, then, does not rely on an uncomplicatedly top-down didactic methodology. Leah Price's important study on anthologies and the novel form argued that Richardson's didactic writing addresses "the young, the ignorant, and the idle," seeking to "cra[m]" moral ideas "down their throats, undiluted."[70] I am suggesting precisely the opposite. When read in the context of other apprentice guides, and as part of a broader family of popular didactic material, we can see a more nuanced picture, in which biddable engagement with a set of precepts or body of knowledge is followed by a gaining of agency—a process that replicates the experience of apprenticeship itself.

In reading *The Apprentice's Vade Mecum*, then, we need to be attentive to the specific method of reading the text expects: not a single reading, but repeated reading, sometimes in whole and sometimes in part, and perhaps either annotation or copying out of passages. This is a mode of reading distinct from that normally associated with novel reading, and to appreciate how this and related texts work, we must put to one side conventional ideas about how to read Richardson. Recent considerations of Richardson's relation to literary culture of the period significantly expand previous considerations of his work as a novelist, emphasizing the nuance and contradictions of Richardson's model of authorship, "at once entrepreneurial, combinatory, proprietary, sociable, and creative," as Betty Schellenberg puts it in an important recent collection. Schellenberg explores, for instance, Richardson's "lifelong commitment" to the "scribal form" of letter writing.[71] Among others writing in the same volume as Schellenberg, April London picks out the "tension between inheritance and innovation" inherent in Richardson's practice of novelistic rewriting, and Christopher Flint centralizes "the act of collecting" as important to understand Richardson's relationship to the book, attending to the involvement in eighteenth-century printing of different "hands who functioned as a collective," or "chapel" in the industry jargon.[72] Darryl Domingo's recent probing of Richardson's dramatic quotations represents a significant reconsideration of how silent theatrical allusions and references are woven into the text of his most famous novel.[73] Writing elsewhere, John Dussinger has even more explicitly framed Richardson's authorial practices as derivative. His extensive work on the output of Richardson's press has established Richardson as a writer who frequently "cut-and-pasted" from his own and other people's work when preparing saleable and popular texts.[74] Perhaps, then, we should reconsider not only how we value Richardson's educational writings but also how his better-known texts, too, may encourage other forms of reading.

I suggest finally that in considering Richardson as a *didactic* author, we must jettison an allegiance to "originality" as a criterion of value. Barbara Benedict quotes Shaftesbury, sneering at "*Common-place-Book* Learning," characterized by "cuttings and shreds of learning" and an eschewal of real writerly craft, which involves the independent generation of a distinct, discrete text.[75] Derivativeness is a common characteristic of eighteenth-century didactic writing; genres such as collections of moral sentiments and letter books are highly repetitive. Recognizing the derivative nature of such work, however, often involves a subtle depreciation of its value; even the term "derivative" is laden, in modern critical parlance, with implicit negative judgments about literary importance and value. As Leah Price notes, for example, Richardson's engagement with anthologies (both his own production of anthologies and his quotation from them) opened him up to repeated charges of literary theft.[76] Simply put, the idea that his didactic writing is not "original" can still be framed as a negative. Peter Sabor, a formidably knowledgeable and sensitive reader of Richardson, notes in passing that *The Apprentice's Vade Mecum* "amplifie[s]" a preexisting letter of Richardson's and also "contains material taken from several other authors, most of them unacknowledged," suggesting that this pamphlet "gives little indication of the imaginative powers that Richardson would later display in his fiction."[77] This is undoubtedly true—and yet it arguably imbricates a text such as the *Vade Mecum* in a matrix of value derived from novels. Read instead against the textual tradition of which it is part, where borrowing and repetition are expected, such considerations become less important. *The Apprentice's Vade Mecum* is indeed a highly derivative text, but this is not a reason to dismiss it; instead, it indicates that we should read more closely and attentively the convergences and divergences between Richardson's text and the tradition of which it is part. Equally, although a full discussion of this point is beyond the scope of the present chapter, we might ask also what happens when we turn the tables: instead of reading didactic literature based on our expectations of novels, what happens when we read novels through the reading practices implicit in this early educational writing? Sabor also notes that Richardson, in his novels as well as elsewhere, demands a reader willing to engage in repeated reading and self-application.[78] This demand can be understood, I suggest, only if we return to the roots of Richardson's authorship, his engagement in early didactic writing, with its own set of imperfectly understood and subvisible expectations and traditions.

Only when we interrogate the models of authorship, readership, imagination, and extradiegetic productivity assumed in such early texts will we have a full and rounded understanding of Richardson's practices of authorship more generally.

This chapter has been one small attempt to do just that.

NOTES

1. Samuel Richardson to Benjamin Kennicott, November 26, 1754, in *Correspondence Primarily on Sir Charles Grandison (1750–1754)*, ed. Betty Schellenberg, in *The Cambridge Edition of the Correspondence of Samuel Richardson*, Thomas Keymer and Peter Sabor, gen. eds. (Cambridge: Cambridge University Press, 2015), 278–280, quotation on 279.
2. John A. Dussinger, "Introduction," in *A Collection of the Moral and Instructive Sentiments . . .* (1755), vol. 3 of *Samuel Richardson's Published Commentary on Clarissa, 1745–1765* (London: Pickering and Chatto, 1998), xi.
3. Charles Palmer, *A Collection of Select Aphorisms and Maxims: With Several Historical Observations: Extracted from the Most Eminent Authors* (London: E. Cave, 1748), [A3r]; James Mauclerc, *The Christian's Magazine* (London: S. Richardson, 1750), v; Sir John Fielding, *The Universal Mentor* (London: A. Millar, 1763), iii.
4. It is impossible to give credit to all those responsible for this flourishing of scholarship, but key works include Tom Keymer, *Richardson's "Clarissa" and the Eighteenth-Century Reader* (Cambridge: Cambridge University Press, 1992); Tom Keymer and Peter Sabor, eds., *The Pamela Controversy: Criticisms and Adaptations of Samuel Richardson's "Pamela," 1740–1750*, 6 vols. (Cambridge: Cambridge University Press, 2000); David Blewett, ed., *Passion and Virtue: Essays on the Novels of Samuel Richardson* (Toronto: University of Toronto Press, 2001); Tom Keymer and Peter Sabor, eds., *"Pamela" in the Marketplace: Literary Controversy and Print Culture in Eighteenth-Century Britain and Ireland* (Cambridge: Cambridge University Press, 2005); Kathleen Oliver, *Samuel Richardson, Dress, and Discourse* (London: Palgrave Macmillan, 2008); Lynn Shepherd, *Clarissa's Painter: Portraiture, Illustration, and Representation in the Novels of Samuel Richardson* (Oxford: Oxford University Press, 2009); E. Derek Taylor, *Reason and Religion in "Clarissa": Samuel Richardson and "the Famous Mr. Norris, of Bemerton"* (Aldershot, UK: Ashgate, 2009).
5. See, inter alia, Louise Curran, *Samuel Richardson and the Art of Letter-Writing* (Cambridge: Cambridge University Press, 2016); Louise Curran and Sören Hammerschmidt, eds., "Mediating Richardson," special edition, *Eighteenth-Century Fiction* 29 (2017); Peter Sabor and Betty Schellenberg, eds., *Samuel Richardson in Context* (Cambridge: Cambridge University Press, 2017); Albert Rivero, ed., *The Sentimental Novel in the Eighteenth Century* (Cambridge: Cambridge University Press, 2019).
6. See Alexander Pettit, "General Introduction," in *The Early Works*, ed. Pettit, in Peter Sabor and Tom Keymer, gen. eds., *The Cambridge Edition of the Works of Samuel Richardson* (Cambridge: Cambridge University Press, 2012); John Dussinger, "Samuel Richardson's 'Elegant Disquisitions': Anonymous Writing in the *True Briton* and Other Journals?," *Studies in Bibliography* 53 (2000): 195–226; Dussinger, "'Stealing in the Great Doctrines of Christianity': Samuel Richardson as Journalist," *Eighteenth-Century Fiction* 15 (2003): 451–506; Dussinger, "Fabrications from Samuel Richardson's Press," *Papers of the Bibliographical Society of America* 100 (2006): 259–279. Also indispensable are earlier discussions by Alan D. McKillop ("Samuel Richardson's Advice to an Apprentice," *Journal of English and Germanic Philology* 42 [1943]: 40–54) and the introduction to his facsimile edition of the text (Macon, GA: Garland Press, 1975); Carol Houlihan Flynn, *Samuel Richardson: A Man of Letters* (Princeton, NJ: Princeton University Press, 1982), esp. chap. 1; Stephanie Fysh, "The Apprenticeship of Samuel Richardson: The Significance of *The Apprentice's Vade Mecum*," in *The Work(s) of Samuel Richardson* (Newark: University of Delaware Press, 1997), 27–56.

7. James Smith's *Samuel Richardson and the Theory of Tragedy* (Manchester: Manchester University Press, 2019), 10–14, is a recent instance that engages with the *Vade Mecum* as part of a reinterpretation of the novels.
8. Pettit, "General Introduction," xl–xli.
9. For the "Rules," see Keith Maslen, *Samuel Richardson of London, Printer* (Dunedin: University of Otago Press, 2001), 12.
10. See Dussinger, "'Stealing in the Great Doctrines,'" 459–460, 464–465; Pettit, "General Introduction," xxxix–lii.
11. McKillop, "Advice to an Apprentice," 45.
12. Richardson, *The Apprentice's Vade Mecum* (1733), in Pettit, *The Early Works*, 1–60, quotation on 43 (hereafter cited as *AVM*); Dussinger, "Fabrications from Samuel Richardson's Press," 260–264.
13. McKillop, "Advice to an Apprentice," 41; Fysh, *The Work(s) of Samuel Richardson*, 27.
14. John Rule, "Employment and Authority: Masters and Men in Eighteenth-Century Manufacturing," in *The Experience of Authority in Early Modern England*, ed. Paul Griffiths, Adam Fox, and Steve Hindle (Basingstoke, UK: Palgrave Macmillan, 1996), 286–317, 288, 301.
15. Peter Earle, *The Making of the English Middle Class: Business, Society, and Family Life in London, 1660–1730* (London: Methuen, 1989), 93–96.
16. Ilana Krausman Ben-Amos, *Adolescence and Youth in Early Modern England* (New Haven, CT: Yale University Press, 1994), 84.
17. Patrick Wallis, "Apprenticeship and Training in Premodern England," *Journal of Economic History* 68, no. 3 (2008): 832–861, 832; Patrick Wallis, Cliff Webb, and Chris Minns, "Leaving Home and Entering Service: The Age of Apprenticeship in Early Modern London," *Continuity and Change* 25, no. 3 (2010): 377–404, 379.
18. Ben-Amos, *Adolescence and Youth*, 87–90; cf. Earle, *Making of the English Middle Class*, 93–94.
19. Ben-Amos, *Adolescence and Youth*, 100–101.
20. Richardson to Thomas Verren Richardson, reprint in *The Imperial Review; Or London and Dublin Literary Journal*, August 1804, 609–616, 611.
21. Wallis, "Apprenticeship and Training," 846; cf. Wallis, Webb, and Minns, "Leaving Home and Entering Service," 385–386.
22. Francis Kirkman, *The Unlucky Citizen: Experimentally Described in the Various Misfortunes of an Unlucky Londoner . . .* (London: Anne Johnson, 1673), 35.
23. Wallis, "Apprenticeship and Training," 838. By contrast, Ilana Ben-Amos's study of Bristol's Register of Apprenticeships gives a comparatively low figure of 5 percent of apprenticeships breaking down or being dissolved (*Adolescence and Youth*, 108).
24. Thomas Tryon, *A New Method of Educating Children: Or, Rules and Directions for the Ordering and Governing Them during their Younger Years . . .* (London: J. Salisbury and J. Harris, 1695), 83–84.
25. Earle, *Making of the English Middle Class*, 85. *The Apprentice's Vade Mecum* hints at this when Richardson enjoins observance to journeymen, "who by due Service and Years are become Freemen of the Corporation, or are intitled to be so" (*AVM*, 30).
26. Steven R. Smith, "The London Apprentices as Seventeenth-Century Adolescents," *Past and Present* 61 (1973): 149–161, 151–153.
27. J. A. Sharpe, "Disruption in the Well-Ordered Household: Age, Authority, and Possessed Young People," in Griffiths, Fox, and Hindle, *The Experience of Authority in Early Modern England*, 187–212, 188. See also Ilana Ben-Amos's claim that apprentices were figures for general seventeenth-century Protestant English anxieties over the tendencies of "youth" to "idleness and vanity, thoughtlessness, inconsiderateness, an incapacity to sustain deep feelings, intolerance, indulgence in useless things" (*Adolescence and Youth*, 13–14).
28. Earle, *The Making of the English Middle Classes*, 102.
29. Mihoko Suzuki, "The London Apprentice Riots of the 1590s and the Fiction of Thomas Deloney," *Criticism* 38, no. 2 (1996): 181–217, 182; Anne Wohlcke, "Regulation and

Resistance: Wayward Apprentices and Other 'Evil Disposed Persons' at London's Fairs," in *The Perpetual Fair: Gender, Disorder, and Urban Amusement in Eighteenth-Century London* (Manchester: Manchester University Press, 2014), 78–121, 87–88.

30. Daniel Defoe, *The Complete English Tradesman* (London, 1726), 9.
31. Wallis, "Apprenticeship and Training," 851.
32. Kirkman, *Unlucky Citizen*, 45–46.
33. *The Loyal London Prentice* (London, 1681).
34. R. Campbell, *The London Tradesman: Being a Compendious View of all the Trades, Professions, Arts, Both Liberal and Mechanic . . .* (London: T. Gardner, 1747), 315.
35. Pettit, "General introduction," xlvi.
36. *An Amorous Dialogue between Iohn and his Mistris* (London: P. Brooksby, 1685).
37. Jones DeRitter, "A Cult of Dependence: The Social Context of *The London Merchant*," *Comparative Drama* 21, no. 4 (1987–1988): 374–386, 377.
38. *Gods Justice against Murther, or The Bloudy Apprentice Executed* (London, 1668); *Cruel and Barbarous News from Gheapside* [*sic*] *in London: Being a True and Faithful Relation of an horid* [*sic*] *Fact, acted by an unhuman Mistris upon the body of her Apprentice . . .* (London, 1676).
39. Crouch [pseud. Richard Burton], *The Apprentices Companion, Containing Plain and Useful Directions for Servants, especially Apprentices . . .* (London: Thomas Mercer, 1681), 10–11; Caleb Trenchfield, *A Cap of Gray Hairs for a Green Head: Or, A Fathers Counsel to His Son, an Apprentice in London*, 5th ed. (Glasgow: Robert Sanders, 1692), 29.
40. Crouch, *Apprentices Companion*, 23–26; Trenchfield, *Cap of Gray Hairs*, 28.
41. See Crouch, *Apprentices Companion*, 134–137, 147–156; William Smythies, *Advice to Apprentices, and Other Young Persons, to Beware of Evil Company and Evil Courses: And particularly of THEFT* (London: T. Milbourn, 1687), 5, 19, 21–22; Trenchfield, *Cap of Gray Hairs*, 11, 14, 22–23.
42. *Gods Justice against Murther*, 2–4; see, inter alia, *An excellent Ballad of George Barnwel, an Apprentice of London, who was undone by a strumpet, who having thrice robbed his Master, and murdered his Vncle in Ludlow* (London, 1661).
43. [J. S.], *The Famous History of the Valiant London Prentice* (London: J. Back, 1686), chap. 6.
44. See Paul Griffiths, *Youth and Authority: Formative Experiences in England, 1560–1640* (Oxford: Clarendon, 1996), 161–165.
45. *Apprentice's Faithful Monitor* (London, 1733), 1.
46. Alexander Pettit shows that Richardson had access to *The Apprentice's Faithful Monitor* around October–November 1733, just prior to the publication of the *Vade Mecum*. Noting the resetting of some pages of the *Vade Mecum* to accommodate a mention of the *Monitor*, Pettit suggests convincingly that Richardson "examined a copy of *The Apprentice's Faithful Monitor* before publishing his own manual" (Pettit, "General introduction," xlii–xliii). This is as yet speculative, but on the basis of a similarity of concerns and language (such as the term "Eye-Service"), and the ordering of material, all of which also occur in the letter to Tom Richardson, I wonder if Richardson might have had access to a version of the 1700 *Faithful Monitor* when he was compiling his heads for the initial letter to his nephew in 1732. I am grateful to Dussinger and Pettit for entertaining my speculations on this point.
47. See McKillop, "Richardson's Advice to an Apprentice," 41–43, and Richardson to Thomas Verren Richardson, reprint in *The Imperial Review; Or London and Dublin Literary Journal* (August 1804), 609–616. See also Pettit, "General introduction," xxxix–xl.
48. Crouch, *Apprentices Companion*, 2; Trenchfield, *Cap of Gray Hairs*, 44.
49. DeRitter, "A Cult of Dependence," 383.
50. B. P., *The Prentises Practise in Godlinesse, and His True Freedome* (London: Iohn Bach, 1608), [A3$^{r–v}$].
51. Defoe, *Complete English Tradesman*, 10.
52. Nicholas Zinzano, *The Servants Calling; With Some Advice to the Apprentice* (London, 1725), 67.

53. Kirkman, *Unlucky Citizen*, 34, 37.
54. Trenchfield, *Cap of Gray Hairs*, 98–116; Campbell, *London Tradesman*, 316.
55. Wallis, Webb, and Minns, "Leaving Home and Entering Service," 377–378; Houlihan Flynn, *Man of Letters*, 6.
56. Richardson to Thomas Verren Richardson, 610.
57. McKillop, "Richardson's Advice to an Apprentice," 43. McKillop also notes that Richardson may have made additions to later editions of Defoe's *Complete Tradesman*, puffing his own piece as supplying deficiencies in earlier works (44).
58. "Weekly miscellany," *The Gentleman's Magazine*, December 8, 1733, 639.
59. As Carol Houlihan Flynn puts it, "Beginning with his advice to apprentices and closing with his portrait of the perfect man . . . Richardson investigated the ways in which man can determine his fate" (*Man of Letters*, 3).
60. Smythies, *Advice to Apprentices*, 3.
61. Griffiths, *Youth and Authority*, 161. See also Smith, "The London Apprentices," 157.
62. Cf. Latimer, "Reading for the Sentiment: Richardson's Novels," in Rivero, *The Sentimental Novel in the Eighteenth Century*, 51–68.
63. Barbara Benedict, *Making the Modern Reader: Cultural Mediation in Early Modern Literary Anthologies* (Princeton, NJ: Princeton University Press, 1996), 4.
64. David Allan, *Commonplace Books and Reading in Georgian England* (Cambridge: Cambridge University Press, 2010), 23–25.
65. Richardson to Thomas Verren Richardson, 609, 616.
66. Richardson, *AVM*, 25.
67. Richard Allestree, *The Whole Duty of Man* (London, 1657), [A2v].
68. For more on this idea, and specifically how it underpinned the literacy curriculum widely used in the period, see David Cressy, *Literacy and the Social Order: Reading and Writing in Tudor and Stuart England* (1980; repr., Cambridge: Cambridge University Press, 2006).
69. Jackson, *Pious Prentice*, 33–34.
70. Leah Price, *The Anthology and the Rise of the Novel from Richardson to George Eliot* (Cambridge: Cambridge University Press, 2000), 21–22.
71. Betty A. Schellenberg, "Authorship," in *Samuel Richardson in Context*, ed. Peter Sabor and Betty A. Schellenberg (Cambridge: Cambridge University Press, 2017), 100–107, 100, 104–105.
72. April London, "The Novel," in Sabor and Schellenberg, *Samuel Richardson in Context*, 147–154, 148; Christopher Flint, "The Material Book," in Sabor and Schellenberg, *Samuel Richardson in Context*, 119–127, 119, 121.
73. Darryl Domingo, "Richardson's Unfamiliar Quotations: *Clarissa* and Early-Eighteenth-Century Comedy," *Review of English Studies* 66, no. 277 (2015): 936–953.
74. Dussinger, "Samuel Richardson's 'Elegant Disquisitions,'" 215. See also his "'Stealing in the Great Doctrines,'" 465; "An Overlooked *Æsop* from Samuel Richardson's Press," *Notes and Queries* 56 (2009): 239–243; "Fabrications from Samuel Richardson's Press," 260–262, 274–276; "Another Anonymous Compilation from Samuel Richardson's Press: *A Select Manual of Devotions for Sick Persons* (1733)," *Papers of the Bibliographical Society of America* 102 (2008): 363–385. I am grateful to Professor Dussinger for generously sharing the latter article with me.
75. Benedict, *Making the Modern Reader*, 5; cf. Anthony Ashley Cooper, *Characteristics of Men, Manners, Opinions, Times*, ed. Lawrence E. Klein (Cambridge: Cambridge University Press, 1999), 339–340.
76. Price, *The Anthology and the Rise of the Novel*, 41.
77. Sabor, "Publication History," in Sabor and Schellenberg, *Samuel Richardson in Context*, 18–25, 19.
78. Peter Sabor, "Introduction," in *Letters and Passages Restored from the Original Manuscripts of the History of "Clarissa,"* vol. 2 of *Samuel Richardson's Published Commentary on Clarissa*, 3 vols. (London: Pickering & Chatto, 1998), xiv–xv, xvi, xxxii.

2

QUEER TIME IN *PAMELA*

DECLAN KAVANAGH

> It signifies nothing to ask him: He will have his own Way. There is no putting him out of his Byass. He is a regular Piece of Clockwork, will they joke, and all that: And why, my Dear, should we not be so?
>
> —Samuel Richardson, *Pamela; or Virtue Rewarded*

WHILE WRITING THE EVENTS OF her fourth day of nuptial bliss, Pamela reveals Mr. B's prescribed schedule for their domestic life together. As the epigraph shows, this newfound domestic tempo will seemingly run like clockwork, a fact that Mr. B anticipates will excite bemusement from those acquainted with his former rakishness. Nevertheless, he is keen to reassure that nothing will put him out of his "Byass"; his life will now be characterized by a domesticated order that is shared with, but also, in some crucial sense, achieved through, his marriage to Pamela. In spite of the confidence with which Mr. B outlines this shared daily routine, the question that concludes his speech—"And why, my Dear, should we not be so?"—foreshadows the potential for all scheduling to go awry and, more importantly, for one's bias, that is, inclination or orientation, to suddenly change. As evident from this slight quotation, Mr. B considers fixed orientation and regular time to be mutually informing. As Pamela's account betrays, the temporally ordered space of the home is crucial to the fixity of the rake's newfound orientation toward married life.

This chapter explores how Samuel Richardson both represented and contributed to the emergence of eighteenth-century models of heteronormative, white, and genteel masculinity in his 1740 novel *Pamela; or, Virtue Rewarded*.[1] In particular, it considers how Richardson articulated manliness in relation to the ordered temporality of the domestic space of the home. Critics have long associated Richardson's writing with the production of new cultural and social modes. Michael McKeon argues that the "spectacle of Pamela is a kind of 'glass' in which the gentry see not her 'public' meaning but themselves, the authority of her upward mobility,"[2] while Terry Eagleton claims that "Richardson did not only share in the bourgeois public sphere of eighteenth-century England; he helped to construct it."[3] More recently, critics like Paul Kelleher and Kathleen Lubey have approached *Pamela* from a queer studies perspective with decisive consequences for criticism in the field. Reading the melding of sexuality and sentiment in Richardson, Kelleher has shown how Pamela's attachment to moral goodness "arrests for a time . . . the narrative development of reciprocated heterosexual desire."[4] Meanwhile, placing Richardson in the context of the pornographic, Lubey argues that sex scenes provide "instructive moments that call on readers to imagine sex acts in multiple ways."[5] Adding to these important queer readings, I explore how Richardson's temporal politics in *Pamela* contributed to the emergence of heteronormativity in eighteenth-century Anglophone culture. By heteronormativity I mean to suggest not just heterosexuality but instead "the entire array of polarized taxonomies that organize compulsory heterosexuality and generate its aura of obviousness."[6] As Abby Coykendall and Ana de Freitas Boe identify, "Heteronormativity congeals into a fully fomented hegemony by the end of the eighteenth century, reaching its apex roughly midway through the nineteenth century."[7] Whereas the first volume of *Pamela* demonstrates the importance of a woman's virtue, the second focuses more squarely upon Mr. B's attempts to maintain a new domestic order that arises from conjugality.

Richardson's *Pamela* demonstrates how the companionate marriage is underpinned by an ordering of time that is in the service of a new and regularized heteronormativity. Put differently, B's regimen betrays how structured time is essential to the very ideology of companionate heterosexual marriage formulated by Richardson in his novel. However, ordered time is also always shown to be subject to potential disordering. Such disjointedness occurs suddenly in the novel in material terms with the intrusive presence of Mr. B's rakish friends, but it also, in a more spectral sense, arises at moments in the narrative when the impropriety of Mr. B's libertine past is recalled through the invocation of Miss Sally Godfrey. Richardson's vision of Mr. B's married life with Pamela, his rendering of the companionate marriage, is premised on the rigorous enforcement of a mutually and tacitly understood nonqueer temporality, as much as it is bound to ideas of the supposed natural gendered complementarity of men and women. Queerness in *Pamela*, in part, arises out of the enforcement of temporal order. As I argue in this chapter, Lady Davers operates as a source of internal disorder in the novel through her questioning of the legitimacy of her brother's marriage. Lady Davers's intrusion into Mr. B's bedchamber signals a challenge to the very structuring of the temporality of married hetero-time that Richardson's novel both articulates and promotes. Queer time, in particular, manifests textually as that which threatens to undermine the very daily routine of companionate marriage, as prescribed by Mr. B. This is not to say that those who would disrupt this routine—the rakes and Lady Davers—are queer energies in their own right in the text but rather that the actions of both, in disturbing Mr. B's newfound temporal rhythm with Pamela, unsettle the precarious living time of a marriage that narrativizes new companionate forms of heterosexuality. Although B's professed desire for sobriety as to wine and hours closes down queer possibilities in the text, the possible return of either his rakish friends or his mistress, or Lady Davers's assumption that the marital bedchamber is in fact a sexually irregular space, all affirm the queer potential for the squire to become, once again, like an irregular piece of clockwork.

VIRTUE AND THE MANLY DOMESTIC

> Before Pamela assumes control of the household, its organization resembles nothing so much as a paranoid conspiracy. For Pamela's writing exposes the secrets of life within the aristocratic household, Richardson turns the place into a theatre for sexual intrigue. Household personnel are bound only by the principle of satisfying their master's desire. Time as well as space and human labor are devoted to serving this single end. . . . This principle of order actually creates disorder.[8]

In *Desire and Domestic Fiction* (1987), Nancy Armstrong argues that before Mr. B's marriage to Pamela, the resources of his aristocratic household are mobilized with the sole aim of satisfying the "double tyranny of male desire and aristocratic whim." In Armstrong's reading, Pamela assumes "control" of Mr. B's estate and, in doing so, creates a well-regulated household that is established upon the "moral qualities of the female in charge" and not the erratic desires of a male libertine.[9] While Armstrong notes that the principle of libertine order "actually creates disorder," she does not address how it is that libertine order is rendered disorderly in *Pamela*. I argue that it is through the novel's evolving grammar of heteronormativity that libertinage gets finally reworked as wasteful disorder. If Pamela does, in fact, assume control of the household, she is only ever afforded the power to enforce the domestic schedule that Mr. B has already dictated to her. Mr. B's reformation from rakish squire to companionate husband engenders an economy of male gender performance that is spatially, as well as temporally, construed. The rakish economy of sporadic pleasure is represented as mobile—almost nomadic—while Mr. B's reformation is precariously dependent upon the maintenance of a masculine economy of timed gendered performance that is rooted in *oikos*, that is, in private domesticity. In the final pages of the novel, the word "economy" connects the editor's summation of Mr. B's reformation with the later commentary on Pamela. Pamela's virtue has led to Mr. B's rejection of rakishness. Yet, what is most praised is the oeconomy that Pamela both seemingly promotes and performs. According to the editor, it is: "From the *Oeconomy* she purposes to observe in her Elevation, let even *Ladies of Condition* learn, that there are Family Employments in which they may, and ought to, make themselves useful, and give good Examples to their Inferiors, as well as Equals." In the sentences that follow we are told that through Pamela's example, female readers should glean the recommendation that "Duty to god, Charity to the Poor and Sick, and the different Branches of Household Management, ought to take up the most considerable Portions of their Time."[10]

It is within the domestic space of the household that the practice of prudent oeconomy becomes manifest; as a discourse it regulates the "different Branches of Household Management" and determines how time is passed and what constitutes time spent. By the mid-eighteenth century, readers of *Pamela* would have understood the word "oeconomy" as signifying "the practice of managing the economic and moral resources of the household for the maintenance of good order."[11] Yet the semantics of the word are by no means stable. As Karen Harvey has shown, the meaning of "oeconomy" underwent a semantic shift from the seventeenth century to the early nineteenth century. In tracing this shift in meaning from Aristotle's model of oikos to the many eighteenth-century moral and financial tracts, which advised on domestic prudence, Harvey posits that "It is the discourse of 'oeconomy,' rather than 'domesticity,' 'separate spheres,' or 'political patriarchalism,' that holds the key to understanding men's (and women's) engagements with the domestic in this period."[12]

In the closing summary in *Pamela*, Richardson articulates both male and female relationships to the domestic through this discourse of oeconomy. What is crucial, however, is how Pamela is positioned as the agent of this ordering discourse in the novel. It is important because even the glibbest reading of the novel would reveal that Pamela's agency as an ordering force is entirely constructed by Mr. B. We, as readers, receive a detailed account of the sort of precarious domesticity that Pamela will somehow enable Mr. B to secure. The matrimonial union of Mr. B and Pamela gives rise to the former's lengthy speech about a domestic temporal order that must involve Pamela living according to a strict regimen. Rather harshly, Mr. B begins his speech by warning Pamela that once married she must not let her physical appearance diminish: his "one Rule" for her is that she should "observe in [her] Dress . . . everything that [he] likes or dislike, as it occurs to [him]."[13] It is important that Pamela listens to her implausibly fashion-conscious husband because, as Mr. B warns, "I have often observed in marry'd Folks, that, in a little while, the Lady grows careless in her Dress; which, to me, looks as if she would take no Pains to secure the Affection she had gained . . . I should not forgive it, even in my *Pamela*."[14]

Mr. B's cautionary remarks upon Pamela's sartorial choices drift into a lengthy speech that prescribes his wife's future domestic tempo. According to Mr. B, Pamela should always be "dress'd by Dinner-time."[15] When we as readers think that Mr. B's advice is coming to a (long overdue) close, Pamela pleads with him for "more of [his] sweet Injunctions," and in the extended speech that follows the reader is given a thorough and precise schedule for their daily married life:

> [I] like to go to-bed with my Dearest, by Eleven . . . I ordinarily rise by Six, in Summer. I will allow you to lie half an Hour after me, or so. Then you'll have some time at your own Dispose, till you give me your Company to breakfast; which may be always so, as that we may have done at a little after Nine. Then you will have several Hours again, at your Disposal, till Two o'Clock, when I shall like to sit down at Table.[16]

The proposed schedule is not simply applicable to Pamela but also extends to the inhabitants of the household and to their guests. These "old-fashion'd Rules," as Mr. B relates, will apply to "Visitors . . . [who must] conform to them too."[17] The description of "old-fashion'd" is not coincidental given the aura of historical rootedness that heteronormativity claims as its mask. Although it is not fully articulated, Mr. B is perhaps thinking about the earlier sabotaged visit of his "half mad" rakish friends, when in order to create an elaborate ruse, the squire ordered his chariot to be "got ready" to pretend to be "under an Engagement five Miles off . . . [so as] will set them out of the House, if possible."[18] What is conjured in this passage is the rather ridiculous and contradictory image of Mr. B willfully wasting time and resources driving around in an attempt to "get rid" of the rakes—to keep them out of the house—in order to ensure that the oeconomy of the household—the good order of its economic and moral resources—is maintained. If even the very presence of the rakes threatens to upset domesticity, we might say that the domestic is not just about a definite space but also tied to the compulsory regularity and ordering of certain practices within that space.

OECONOMIES OF LIVING TIME

Since around 2007 there has been something of a temporal turn in queer studies that has seen theorists engage questions of time and timeliness in their work.[19] In *Time Binds* (2010), Elizabeth Freeman asks: "What does it mean to say that domesticity is a particular tempo, a way of living time rather than merely a relationship to the space of the home?" Freeman's question provides a queer lens for tracing the way in which a heteronormative version of living time is promoted in Richardson's *Pamela*. In thinking through the temporalities of female labor, Freeman posits that "domestic manuals such as Catherine Beecher's *A Treatise on Domestic Economy* (1841) stressed the need for order and efficiency in the home, at the same time that women's labor was naturalized into feminine influence through the figure of the angel in the house who magically kept things clean and people fed without seeming to lift a finger."[20] Richardson's *Pamela* pre-empts Beecher's *A Treatise on Domestic Economy* in its insistence on obscuring any trace of Pamela's previous servitude within her new conjugal life with Mr. B. Richardson's rendering of Pamela as an "angel in the house"–like figure naturalizes not only "women's labor" but also the very fact that Pamela's former status was that of a servant and a lady's companion. If Mr. B's insistence that his house be run like clockwork seems too stringent, it is because the seamlessness in the domestic domain that he seeks must, in fact, do the dual work of obscuring not just labor itself but also the former reality of Pamela as a domestic companion who labored, both physically and emotionally.

Time registers in material ways in Richardson's fiction, and the materiality of dress is central to Richardson's temporal politics in *Pamela*.[21] According to Jennie Batchelor, the heroine's progress is often signaled by her changing garb, while her adoption, and subsequent rejection, of her deceased mistress's clothes resonates with debates on the appropriateness of menials dressing above their own station that were current in eighteenth-century Britain.[22] Early in the novel, we encounter Pamela performing her menial status in sartorial choices, which symbolically, if not literally, drag back pastness. Since his mother's death, Mr. B has presented Pamela with clothing that belonged to her, including "half a dozen of her shifts, and six fine handkerchiefs, and three of her cambric aprons, and four Holland ones." When B bestows upon Pamela further items—shoes and "white cotton stockings, three pairs of fine silk ones, and two pair of rich stays"—her response is one of embarrassment.[23] This gifting exposes B's desire to elevate Pamela, at least in terms of her appearance.

Thinking queerly, we might theorize Pamela's sartorial choices, famous in critical readings of the novel, as a kind of menial drag. According to Michael McKeon, Pamela's wearing of her late lady's clothes serves as "a metonymic model of how the little may become great."[24] Yet, if Pamela's elevated costume provides such a model, it is short-lived. Significantly, part of Pamela's strategy for disrupting her master's pleasurable gaze is bound up with temporality, inasmuch as she cleverly opts to reverse time by eschewing the material markers of Mr. B's seduction and opting to wear the "ordinary" dress of her former self. To dress more plainly signifies a material confirmation of station, one that she describes as "descending with ease, innocence, and resignation!"[25] As Batchelor argues, "Pamela claims that in her homespun gown she can now appear to B. as her true self and regain possession of that 'self.'"[26] But if Pamela does wish to possess her true self, then it is worth noting that the self she longs for is a historical one. Her reclaiming of selfhood is enacted through a sartorial display, which involves the rejection of B's gifts of her late mistress's clothes in favor of her own homespun garb that is stylistically an artifact.

In anticipation of her return to her parents, Pamela rejects her late mistress's wardrobe in favor of being, as Mrs. Jervis comments, "metamorphos'd!" in her own handmade garment.[27] Before revealing the outcome of her new sartorial project to the house, Pamela articulates her transformation in the following triumphalist terms:

> And so, when I had din'd, up Stairs I went, and lock'd myself into my little Room. There I trick'd myself up as well as I could in my new Garb, and put on my round-ear'd ordinary Cap; but with a green Knot however, and my homespun Gown and Petticoat, and plain-leather Shoes; but yet they are what they call *Spanish* Leather, and my ordinary Hose, ordinary I mean to what I have been lately used to; tho' I shall think good Yarn may do very well for every Day, when I come home. A plain Muslin Tucker I put on, and my black Silk Necklace, instead of the *French* Necklace my Lady gave me, and put the Ear-rings out of my Ears; and when I was quite 'quip'd, I took my Straw Hat in my Hand, with its two blue Strings, and look'd about me in the Glass, as proud as any thing.—To say Truth, I never lik'd myself so well in my Life.[28]

Pamela's clothing materially gestures toward a time before her employment in the B household and, more pointedly, to a time before her subjection to the desires of Mr. B. Her sartorial choices are calculated to ensure that her lived experience runs counter to the material desires of her master. She disrupts B's claim to her body by refusing to dress as the woman that he wishes to undress. As Chloe Wigston Smith argues, "Richardson's novel . . . demonstrates how women might rewrite the language of gender through practical strategies that attend to material objects."[29] The very materiality of Pamela's articles remains bound to class temporality. The politics of Pamela's menial drag are indeed self-consciously temporal, as she admits to adopting clothing that she has not been "lately used to."[30] Freeman specifies temporal drag as the disruption of the political present by the anachronistic drag of the past in the present: "It may be crucial, then, to complicate the idea of horizontal political generations or waves succeeding each other in progressive time with a notion of 'temporal drag' thought less in the psychic time of the individual than in the movement time of collective political fantasy."[31] The word "drag" is deployed here in all its semantic richness. According to Freeman, drag should be regarded as both a process of gradual movement across time and space and a mode of physical display. Pamela's menial drag is a carefully constituted class protest mounted through the display of coded materials. Yet it also serves a temporal function inasmuch as it *drags* Pamela backward to affirm her laboring past at the very moment that B wishes her to forget it. However, as Batchelor argues, the episode of Pamela's homespun garment "reveals the fallacy that underlies her attempts at self-ownership through costume."[32] Tellingly, Pamela's menial drag fails to thwart B's advances as he simply pretends to mistake Pamela for her sister and pursues her with increased abandon.

Although Pamela might try to sartorially drag time, her agency is later thwarted by B's strict scheduling of their married life (which includes sartorial matters). Although unexpressed, B's exact prescriptions for his wife's daily routine have as much to do with his own self-restraint—with the curbing of libertinism—

as with Pamela's future obedience. Displacing these strictures onto Pamela obscures how such prescriptions defamiliarize the rhythm of companionate domesticity. As Pamela calls for more "sweet injunctions," we as readers can easily lose sight of Mr. B's own rakish past behavior as the boorishness of the rake threatens to upset the household oeconomy he lately champions. As Mr. B cautions, "they [the rakes] are like a Snow-ball, and intend to gather Company as they go, to make a merry Tour of it for some Days together."[33] The snowball momentum of the touring rakes is starkly opposed to the temporal rootedness of Mr. B's companionate married life with Pamela. As discussed below, Charles Churchill in *Night* celebrates the "*narrow circle* of our chosen Friends"—by contrast, Richardson forewarned his readers about homosocial intimacy and its adverse impact upon men. When we consider such sporadic pleasure, within the parameters of a text that premises compulsory heterosexuality on the successful living time of companionate marriage, we can see how these rakes, for their very *untimeliness*, might threaten to queerly disjoint such rhythms.

Richardson's writing out of Pamela's schedule, mouthed by Mr. B, attests to the very fact that routine, however habitual, is still open to revision. The ritual of living time that Mr. B narrates is, to use Freeman's term, a kind of "*chrononormativity*" in the sense that its end goal is to make "people . . . bound to one another, engrouped, made to feel coherently collective, through particular orchestrations of time."[34] Mr. B betrays the ridiculousness of his own exactitude when he concedes that some will joke that he is "a regular Piece of Clockwork," only to then dispel this by reminding Pamela that "Man is as frail a Piece of Machinery, as any Clockwork whatever; and, by Irregularity, is as subject to be disorder'd." The only feasible response to the threat of disorder is for Mr. B is to prescribe order; in time, he suggests, "our Servants too will know, generally, the Times of their Business, and the Hours of their Leisure or Recess; and we, as well as they, shall reap the Benefit of this Regularity. And who knows, my Dear, but we may revive the good old Fashion in our Neighbourhood, by this means?—At least we will be doing our Part towards it." Rather cautiously, Mr. B then concedes that "the worst thing" that might happen will be for the brother rakes "to [break] in upon [them] so unwelcomingly."[35] He downplays this concern by suggesting that the rakes will soon tire of calling when they see how ordered his domestic affairs now are: "If that can ever be, and [the rakes] fall to considering whom they shall go to dine with in their Rambles, they will only say, We must not go to him; for his Dinner-time is over; and so they'll reserve me for another time, when they happen to suit it better; or, perhaps, they will take a Supper and a Bed with me instead of it."[36] For the purpose of dissuading his former rakish friends from bringing their "Rambles" to bear upon the material and moral resources of his household, Mr. B tells Pamela that he must not only reform but also, crucially, perform. The mad rakes are bound to the queer economy of B's former libertinism. Libertine rambling is itself premised on the pleasures of an amorphous temporality. Not curtailed by any enforced schedule, their chaotic pleasure seeking is also queerly timed as the rakes actually delay the consummation of Mr. B and Pamela's marriage since the wedding ceremony was performed on the morning of their intrusion. To regulate his living time, B must enter into a schedule with Pamela that is rooted in the daily regimen of a house that runs its affairs like clockwork. A visit from Mr. B's rakish friends could unsettle the manly domestic being described at this point. Such a rupture might unravel the cross-sex intimacies of Pamela and Mr. B that Richardson is keen to endorse. While B is content that his friends will eventually learn to follow the rhythms of his newfound living time by opting for supper and bed as opposed to "a merry Tour," this passage, ultimately, does more to illuminate the precariousness of living time than to affirm it in any way.

GODFREY VERSUS "GOOD HOURS"

In "The Return of Anachronism" (2001), Srinivas Aravamudan discusses Jacques Derrida's theorizing of spectrality across the various texts of William Shakespeare and Karl Marx. Building upon Derrida, Aravamudan clarifies that "The phenomenon of spectrality testifies to the overlapping, disadjusted, and noncontemporaneous nature of time, to its whirls and eddies, as understood within the brackets of a contemporaneity that carries along various things even as it is not fully cognizant of itself." For Aravamudan, spectrality haunts the historiographical record, and in doing so, it frustrates the historiographer's desire for narrative closure. More precisely, the spectral, according to Aravamudan, "infects contemporaneity, as does the historical era, or the event one is looking at, with the condition of unfinalizability."[37] If spectrality haunts the historiographical record, then we might also say, following Aravamudan, that the spectral also haunts the novelistic record. Pamela's companionate marriage to Mr. B is itself haunted, in Aravamudan's terms, by the figure of Mr. B's former mistress, Sally Godfrey and by his rakish brothers. As Albert J. Rivero shows, the "secret" of Godfrey becomes a "narrative obsession, both for Pamela and . . . Richardson" inasmuch as "the novel cannot end until Sally Godfrey has been disposed of."[38] Richardson fails to fully "dispose" of Godfrey in narrative terms. Godfrey's own spectrality—as an unrealized and therefore unfinalizable character—infects Richardson's narrative in two ways. First, as an aristocratic woman who has succumbed to the ruinous sexual advances of a libertine, Godfrey closely resembles the heroines of amatory fiction, many of whom experienced death or exile as a result of their own libertine seduction and betrayal. Richardson's loose inclusion of Godfrey has the potential to infect form. Godfrey's ambiguous place within *Pamela*, a conduct book masquerading as a novel, threatens to generically destabilize the work's intended elevated status. When Pamela reflects upon Godfrey and remarks "I have had the Grace to escape the like Unhappiness with this poor Gentlewoman," Richardson, on another level, is also emphatically reminding his reader that Pamela's own story is not an amatory one.[39] Godfrey is an amatory heroine-like figure who offers Pamela, and the readers of her letters, a cautionary tale, which bristles against the novel's invested articulation of the companionate marriage. Second, Miss Godfrey also haunts the epistolary record of Pamela's married life. As such, Godfrey is Mr. B's past mistress but is also a current mistress to the living time of his companionate marriage.

Godfrey's anachronism does not simply arise from her potential to return; her pastness is always questionable as a figure Pamela thinks may be deceased, but who is, in fact, exiled in Jamaica. The emergence of Miss Goodwin, who Pamela later learns is the illegitimate child of Mr. B and Godfrey, demonstrates that Godfrey has, in a spectral sense, never really entered, nor exited, the novelistic stage; she is an anachronism, in the way that Aravamudan describes: a figure who hauntingly frustrates narrative closure by being never fully contemporary nor fully past. The introduction of Miss Goodwin troubles the teleology of the companionate marriage ideology, which Richardson's *Pamela* deals in. Yet, the resolution of Miss Goodwin's case—her admittance into the reformed B household—also provides Richardson with an opportunity to close down the queer temporality haunting his text. Such an effort in closure also comes in the final pages of *Pamela*, when the supposed editor of Pamela's letters asks if "the Reader will indulge . . . in a few brief Observations, which naturally result from [this little History]; and which will serve as so many Applications, of its most material Incidents, to the Minds of the Youth of both Sexes."[40] After this brief prefatory statement, the editor surveys a range of characters, with some receiving admonishment and others praise. Mr. B's sister, Lady Davers, is described as being too "Proud and . . . High-born [to] see the Deformity of unreasonable Passion," while rather unkindly, Godfrey—a nonpresence in the text—is aligned with the female sex worker, whom Richardson describes as the "poor deluded Female, who, . . . at first inadvertently drawn, hurries herself into filthy Diseases, and an untimely Death."[41] Although Lady Davers and Miss Godfrey signify vastly different types of woman, they are both criticized for lapses in their respective judgments, which mark them out in the editor's closing appraisal as being poorly self-disciplined. They are both, in a sense, untimely characters: Lady Davers's presence is often intrusive, whereas Miss Godfrey's actions lead her to exile. More precisely, Lady Davers's untimeliness is connected to plot as she belatedly attempts to discipline her brother's passions in relation to Pamela. In Sally Godfrey's case, untimeliness registers as beyond the time of the plot as she never enters into the temporality of the novel itself but, instead, narratively haunts its epistolic boundaries through Pamela's clipped retelling of her fate.

In sharp contrast to these ill-equipped managers, readers are confronted with characters who have learned to become better self-regulators, such as Mr. B, or who, in the case of Pamela, have exhibited "*Oeconomy*" from the outset. According to Nancy Armstrong, Richardson invests Pamela with the "power to restore order by inverting the patterns established by the idleness and amusement of the aristocratic woman."[42] As Pamela's ability to counter aristocratic wastefulness with prudent economy is well established, Mr. B receives the most sustained comments from the editor, who narrates the squire's transformation from rake to husband:

> Yet as he betimes sees his Errors, and reforms in the Bloom of Youth, an edifying Lesson may be drawn from it, for the Use of such as are born to large Fortunes; and who may be taught, by his Example, the inexpressible Difference between the Hazards and Remorse which attend a profligate Course of Life; and the Pleasures which flow from virtuous Love, and virtuous Actions. The Generosity of his Mind; his Sobriety, as to *Wine* and *Hours*; his prudent Oeconomy and Hospitality.[43]

In this, the editor's summation, we are told that Mr. B's "profligate Course of Life" has been reformed; a "prudent Oeconomy" has replaced his formerly thriftless behavior. Richardson was familiar with the work of his friend, the physician George Cheyne, with whom he regularly corresponded. Cheyne's *An Essay on Health and Long Life* (1724) advised, among other things, on keeping good hours and taking regular exercise, which "should always be gone about with an *empty Stomach*."[44] Moreover, the lauding of Mr. B's "Sobriety, as to *Wine* and *Hours*" resonates with, but also importantly predates, the Scottish pornographer and physician John Armstrong's didactic poem, *The Art of Preserving Health* (1744). Armstrong, following Richardson, presented his readers with a manly health regime of keeping "good hours," which meant, in part, the refusal of late nights and a rejection of unfettered pleasure seeking. Armstrong's *The Art of Preserving Health* recalls Richardson's praise of Mr. B's commitment to keeping "good hours" with an extended caveat against the influence of "the night's unwholesome breath" on the body, which "exhausted and unstrung, / Weakly resists" the night's "mirth and wine."[45]

The libertine-poet Charles Churchill would later satirize Armstrong's treatise and, by extension, Richardson's Mr. B in his 1761 poem *Night*. Railing against Richardson's and Armstrong's manly health regime of keeping "good hours," Churchill recounts his late-night drinking meetings with his friend and fellow poet, Robert Lloyd:

> THUS have we liv'd, and whilst the fates afford
> Plain Plenty to supply the frugal board,
> Whilst MIRTH, with DECENY his lovely bride,
> And Wine's gay GOD, with TEMP'RANCE by his side,
> Their welcome visit pay; whilst HEALTH attends
> The *narrow circle* of our chosen Friends,

> Whilst frank GOOD-Humour consecrates the treat,
> And—makes society complete . . . [46]

Whereas John Armstrong cautions against a man's nighttime exposure to inclemency, Churchill mocks this anxiety by anthropomorphizing the "damps and vapours" that "sap the walls of health" as if by stealth.[47] John Armstrong is later depicted as one of those physicians who engender an effeminate culture of malaise through their diagnoses of imagined symptoms.[48] Rather than lament a depressing isolation, *Night* buoyantly defends a libertinage diametrically opposed to "Those Hackney Strumpets, PRUDENCE and the WORLD."[49] If keeping "good hours," as Richardson and Armstrong advise, keeps men manly, Churchill's poem *Night* unapologetically offers a celebration of an alternative masculinist agenda, which rejects Richardson's and Armstrong's measured diurnal world by embracing the unpredictable and hedonistic rhythms of the nocturnal. The line "THUS have we liv'd, and whilst the fates afford" places agency over one's health with "the fates" and not within the confines of a manly self-governance. More pointedly, the debauchery of libertine late-night meetings is time limited for Churchill's speaker in *Night* as the phrase: "Whilst Health attends" raises the conditional nature of such pleasure seeking. Whether Richardson and Armstrong ever persuaded male readers to keep "good hours," or men were later seduced by Churchill's "GOOD-humour," it is clear that during the midcentury, the discursive parameters for the performance of manliness hinged on timing, both inside and outside of one's home. For this unlikely triumvirate of male authors, masculinity and its embodiment involved the maintenance of timed economies of regulation and excess.

INTRUSIVE DISORDER

While the brother rakes from the outside threaten to scatter household resources, visitors from within the house itself also put Mr. B's domestic bliss under pressure. So far in this chapter, I have examined how the rakish outsiders, marginal to the conjugal union of Pamela and Mr. B, act as an anachronism that threatens to drag the temporal order of the house backward. Yet, as I will show, guests are also agents of disorder. Lady Davers, Mr. B's sister, routinely threatens to unhinge the temporal order of the house. For one thing, her very presence initiates a kind of temporal drag in the sense that she not only reminds Pamela of her late mistress but also serves to drag the house back under matriarchal rule. Lady Davers is an intrusive and untimely figure, appearing as she does at inopportune moments. The household oeconomy that she disrupts the most is that of privacy. Historical work on masculinity has shown how gender formation in any period is tied to questions of publicity and privacy. Michel Foucault's account of the mid-eighteenth-century bourgeois construction of a "'class' body with its health, hygiene, descent, and race" instances another manifestation of how desire was embodied in order to affirm cultural and class differences.[50] More recently, Thomas A. King has built upon Foucault's account of this historical discontinuity between a "*deployment of alliance*" and the "*deployment of sexuality*" to specify how this transfer shifted away from relations of pederasty (which signal the erotic enactment of early modern subjection) toward a modern economy of heterosexual, homosexual, and bisexual subjectivities.[51] Arguing against Randolph Trumbach's historical view of a shift from universal bisexuality to a modern regime of hetero- and homosexual identities, King instead posits a transition from *ars erotica* sutured to patriarchy, in which women, servants, and many men were property (erotic and otherwise) of other men and some women, to an erotic economy announced by ideals of egalitarianism, domesticity, and companionship.[52]

Even the most cursory reading of Richardson's novel *Pamela* reveals how it endorses the transition from *ars erotica* (sutured to patriarchy) to a modern erotic economy built upon the ideals of domestic bliss and companionate marriage. Pamela's own trajectory from erotic property to companionate wife rehearses the transition that King identifies. Yet, *Pamela*, in an almost self-conscious way, does more to copper fasten this development. Importantly, according to King, this shift is located not in the individual embodiment or subjectivities of men or women but in the new private social practices and agencies that produced it. As King argues, "The male subject of desire would locate his freedom in the pleasurable and subjective experience of his own sensations. This erasure of positioning, mobility, and mimesis constitutes the myth of modern male phallic equivalency. . . . Increasingly, an innate masculinity vested the natural group of men as private subjects with common rights, obligations, and interests linked to their alleged equivalency within the public domain." The harmonious temporal oeconomy of the house allows Mr. B, as King puts it, to "locate his freedom in the pleasurable and subjective experience of his own sensations."[53] Toward the end of the novel, Lady Davers challenges Mr. B's very manliness when she embarks upon "a whimsical Scheme in her Head, to try to find whether" her brother is in bed with Pamela.[54] The passage, although so often overlooked in criticism on the novel, is quite an important one as unlike the boorish rakes, Lady Davers actually succeeds in interrupting Mr. B by knocking unannounced on the door of the room where he is sleeping with Pamela. In doing so, she threatens to undermine her brother's public claim to phallic equivalence from within the privacy of his own domestic closet.

In insisting that the door opens, Mr. B's sister disrupts the temporal order by breaching the privacy of the newly wedded couple. Her intrusion unmans Mr. B as it directly interferes with his male entitlement to privacy, while it also disrupts the temporal flow that his regimen ensures:

> My Master was wak'd at the Noise, and asked who was there? Open the Door, said she; open it this Minute! I said, clinging about his Neck, Dear, dear Sir, pray, pray don't!—O save me, save me! Don't fear, *Pamela*, said he. The Woman's mad, I believe. But he call'd out, Who are you? What do you want?— . . . So he slipt out of Bed, and putting on some of his Cloaths, and Gown, and Slippers, he said, What bold body dares disturb my Repose thus?[55]

Lady Davers breaches the closet thinking that Mr. B and Pamela "are not marry'd, and are afraid to be found a-bed together." In disturbing their "Repose," Lady Davers, accompanied by her maid and kinsman, attempts to "bear Witness" to the scene of her brother's assignation. In doing so, she threatens to make public a private man's "pleasurable and subjective experience of his own sensations." While Pamela's reaction is to "cover . . . [herself] over Head and Ears," Mr. B objects to the publishing of his pleasure by demanding that the intruders leave his room. Notably, he takes particular umbrage at his sister's kinsman, who stands "at the Feet of the Bed." The rakish Jackey, when admitted into the conjugal apartment, threatens, by his very presence, to queerly reverse the order of the couple's living time. Mr. B dismisses him by calling out, "How now, Sir? What's your Business in this Apartment! Begone this Moment!—And he went away directly." This declamatory outburst, "What's your Business in this Apartment!," may seem rhetorical, and yet, in a disordered house, the rake's presence in Mr. B's apartment may not have been questioned. The scene ends, tellingly, with Mr. B carrying Lady Davers out of the room: "At that he took her in his Arms, as if she had been nothing, and carrying her out of the Room, she cry'd out."[56] The passage relates, in quite a literal way, the extent to which the white, heterosexual male subject's entitlement to privacy now refuses conjugality as a public scene.

Lady Davers's expulsion from her brother's apartment rehearses the conceptualization of manliness as autonomy from subjection within space, be it public or private. The concept of marriage, as defined by Mr. B, abolishes any sense of privacy for Pamela, along with any sense that she has "free time," which is independent of him. As a servant, Pamela could defend the idea that she had earned herself some privacy and leisure time. As Mr. B's wife, she no longer has grounds for any distinction of time; once married, all time is scheduled by Mr. B. Yet the colonization of temporality by heteronormativity in the form of the companionate marriage is shown to literally take its time in *Pamela*. There is always the potential for schedules to run awry, for dinner to be late, for intrusions to recur. Mr. B's libertinage continues to anachronistically haunt the text in the form of Miss Sally Godfrey. However, Pamela's acceptance of Miss Goodwin into her family serves to domesticate the living record of B's libertine transgressions. By attending in this chapter to the temporal politics within Richardson's presentation of marriage in *Pamela*, this queer reading has shown how the reformed Mr. B's obsession with schedule positions rakish living as a queer "irregularity" or anachronism that always, like the exiled Godfrey, has the potential to return and, in doing so, to disjoint the living time of the companionate marriage.

NOTES

Epigraph: Samuel Richardson, *Pamela; or, Virtue Rewarded*, ed. Thomas Keymer and Alice Wakely (Oxford: Oxford University Press, 2001), 369.

1. My argument in this chapter could be fruitfully extended into a reading of *Pamela in Her Exalted Condition* (1742), not least because the sequel deals with Mr. B's apparent desire to return to a more disruptive premarital temporality; however, for the purposes of this chapter my focus is squarely on *Pamela* (1740).
2. Michael McKeon, *The Secret History of Domesticity: Public, Private and the Division of Knowledge* (Baltimore: Johns Hopkins University Press, 2005), 648.
3. Terry Eagleton, *The Rape of Clarissa: Writing, Sexuality and Class Struggle in Samuel Richardson* (Oxford: Blackwell, 1982), 7.
4. Paul Kelleher, *Making Love: Sentiment and Sexuality in Eighteenth-Century British Literature* (Lewisburg, PA: Bucknell University Press, 2015), 133.
5. Kathleen Lubey, *Excitable Imaginations: Eroticism and Reading in Britain, 1660–1760* (Lewisburg, PA: Bucknell University Press, 2012), 110.
6. Ana de Freitas Boe and Abby Coykendall, "Introduction," in *Heteronormativity in Eighteenth-Century Literature and Culture*, ed. Ana de Freitas Boe and Abby Coykendall (Farnham, UK: Ashgate, 2014), 7.
7. Boe and Coykendall, "Introduction," 14.
8. Nancy Armstrong, *Desire and Domestic Fiction: A Political History of the Novel* (New York: Oxford University Press, 1987), 125.
9. Armstrong, *Desire and Domestic Fiction*, 125.
10. Richardson, *Pamela*, 502.
11. Karen Harvey, *The Little Republic: Masculinity and Domestic Authority in Eighteenth-Century Britain* (Oxford: Oxford University Press, 2012), 24.
12. Harvey, *The Little Republic*, 24.
13. Richardson, *Pamela*, 367.
14. Richardson, *Pamela*, 368.
15. Richardson, *Pamela*, 369.
16. Richardson, *Pamela*, 369.
17. Richardson, *Pamela*, 369.
18. Richardson, *Pamela*, 348.
19. See Carolyn Dinshaw, Lee Edelman, Roderick A. Ferguson, Carla Freccero, Elizabeth Freeman, Judith (Jack) Halberstam, Annamarie Jagose, Christopher Nealon, and Nguyen Tan Hoang, "Theorizing Queer Temporalities: A Roundtable Discussion," *GLQ: A Journal of Lesbian and Gay Studies* 13, no. 2–3 (2007): 177–195.
20. Elizabeth Freeman, *Time Binds: Queer Temporalities, Queer Histories* (Durham, NC: Duke University Press, 2010), 39.
21. Jennie Batchelor, *Dress, Distress and Desire: Clothing and the Female Body in Eighteenth-Century Literature* (Houndmills, UK: Palgrave Macmillan, 2005), 19–20.
22. For a rich discussion of Richardson's *Pamela* and the wider debates on servant dress, see Batchelor, *Dress, Distress and Desire*, 22–31.
23. Richardson, *Pamela*, 7.
24. McKeon, *The Secret History of Domesticity*, 648.
25. Richardson, *Pamela*, 42.
26. Batchelor, *Dress, Distress and Desire*, 32.

27. Richardson, *Pamela*, 55.
28. Richardson, *Pamela*, 55.
29. Chloe Wigston Smith, *Women, Work, and Clothes in the Eighteenth-Century Novel* (Cambridge: Cambridge University Press, 2013), 14.
30. Richardson, *Pamela*, 55.
31. Freeman, *Time Binds*, 65.
32. Batchelor, *Dress, Distress and Desire*, 37.
33. Richardson, *Pamela*, 348.
34. Freeman, *Time Binds*, 3.
35. Richardson, *Pamela*, 369.
36. Richardson, *Pamela*, 370.
37. Srinivas Aravamudan, "The Return of Anachronism," *Modern Language Quarterly* 62, no. 4 (December 2001): 347.
38. Albert J. Rivero, "The Place of Sally Godfrey in Richardson's *Pamela*," *Eighteenth-Century Fiction* 6, no. 1 (October 1993): 30.
39. Richardson, *Pamela*, 479.
40. Richardson, *Pamela*, 500.
41. Richardson, *Pamela*, 500–501.
42. Armstrong, *Desire and Domestic Fiction*, 126.
43. Richardson, *Pamela*, 500.
44. George Cheyne, *An Essay of Health and Long Life* (London: George Strahan, 1724), 108.
45. John Armstrong, *The Art of Preserving Health*, vol. 3 (Dublin: James Rudd, 1756), 421–433.
46. Charles Churchill, *Night*, in *The Poetical Works of Charles Churchill*, ed. Douglas Grant (Oxford: Clarendon Press, 1956), 51–62, 58, ll. 286–293.
47. Churchill, *Night*, 52, ll. 61–62.
48. Churchill, *Night*, 53, ll. 71–72.
49. Churchill, *Night*, 58, ll. 296.
50. Michel Foucault, *The Will to Knowledge*, vol. 1: *The History of Sexuality*, trans. Robert Hurley (London: Penguin, 1998), 126–127.
51. Foucault, *The Will to Knowledge*, 106.
52. Randolph Trumbach, *Sex and the Gender Revolution*, vol. 1: *Heterosexuality and the Third Gender in Enlightenment London* (Chicago: University of Chicago Press, 1998).
53. King notes that the "establishment of an oppositional public sphere in England in the seventeenth century did not just privilege men or equate them with the position of public speaker. Among the educated and propertied, it *made men*." See Thomas A. King, *The Gendering of Men, 1660–1750*, vol. 1: *The English Phallus* (Madison: University of Wisconsin Press, 2004), 117.
54. Richardson, *Pamela*, 416.
55. Richardson, *Pamela*, 416.
56. Richardson, *Pamela*, 416.

3

"HAPPY, HAPPY, HAPPY, THRICE HAPPY PAMELA"?

Gendered Happiness and the Happiness Gap in *Pamela* and *Pamela II*

HEATHER LADD

SAMUEL RICHARDSON'S PAMELA IS NOT just "happy" but "thrice happy," a refrain that appears multiple times in both *Pamela* (1740) and Richardson's authorized continuation, *Pamela in Her Exalted Condition* (1742), hereafter referred to as *Pamela II*. Although the phrase has religious resonances, "thrice happy" is used thrice in John Milton's *Paradise Lost* (1667), it also might echo the secular epithalamium "Thrice Happy Lovers" from Henry Purcell's *The Fairy-Queen* (1692). This song, set to a text by Elkanah Settle, appears in Act 5 of the Restoration semi-opera and serves as a wedding blessing:

> Thrice happy Lovers, may you be
> For ever, ever free,
> From that tormenting Devil, Jealousie.
> From all that anxious Care and Strife,
> That attends a married Life.[1]

Close to an event of great happiness, the specter of unhappiness looms, as it does throughout the Pamela novels: even when the eponymous heroine is not unhappy, her felicity is still fraught, a dependent, self-conscious, and precarious thing antithetical to Mr. B's self-oriented happiness. Happiness as a function of both gender and class, and thus defined and achieved differently by Richardson's characters, is at the center of both *Pamela* and *Pamela II*; these narratives illuminate the plurality of eighteenth-century happiness and fictionalize the happiness gap, "differences in happiness by gender,"[2] a contemporary concept in the field of happiness studies that can be usefully applied to these eighteenth-century works. This chapter investigates how the Pamela novels clarify tensions between competing notions of happiness and differences in the degree and kind of happiness experienced by men and women, and by members of different social classes. I propose that the heroine herself experiences a persistent and revealing "happiness gap," which has implications for how we read the gendering of happiness in the eighteenth-century novel more widely.

In keeping with the eighteenth century's well-established preoccupation with individual temporal happiness, what Roy Porter memorably identifies as the Enlightenment's "validation of pleasure,"[3] Richardson's Pamela novels fixate on their character's feelings and fortunes. The words "happy" and "happiness" are ubiquitous in both *Pamela* and *Pamela II*. Pamela herself frequently declares herself happy and marvels at her own happiness, with other characters, such as Miss Polly Darnford (who exchanges letters with Mrs. B in Richardson's sequel), also chiming in. Vivasvan Soni remarks on "the uncontrollable multiplication of references to 'happy' and 'happiness'" in the second half of *Pamela*, and notes Richardson's "hollow repetition of the word 'happy.'"[4] Richardson's heroine is the "good Pamela," but more often the "happy" or "unhappy Pamela," depending on her immediate circumstances and emotional state. Samuel Johnson's second definition of "happy" as "lucky; successful; fortunate" applies to many of this word's occurrences in both novels.[5] For Pamela, her happiness is a blessing, a gift that becomes central to her identity as an engaged and married woman; the occasion of her wedding is termed by Richardson "this happy Day," her matrimonial union "the happy Knot."[6] Pamela's letters to her parents as Mrs. B are regularly signed with overt reminders of her happiness, her first missive in *Pamela II* closing with "*Your dutiful and happy daughter.*"[7] The repetition of the term "happiness" is less "hollow," I contend, than increasingly freighted with significance.

Pamela certainly believes herself fortunate, but Johnson's first definition of happy—"felicity; state in which the desires are satisfied"—is problematic as it applies to Richardson's fiction and the period's prevailing gendering of happiness.[8] For the heroines of many an eighteenth-century novel, Richardson's included, happiness is less a matter of entitlement than unexpected boon on earth created by a confluence of virtue and luck. The period's authors conceived of happiness differently for their male and female characters, gendering the very concept: male happiness, an inalienable right to be actively pursued, contrasts with female happiness, less individualistic and more passively granted, even within feminocentric narratives like *Pamela* and *Pamela II*. While Mr. B's felicity involves acquiring what he wants and satiating his desires, Pamela's happiness stands on not having her innocence taken from her; his happiness is positive, while hers is a "negative happiness" to use Adam Barkman's phrase, which "sees true happiness as simply *the absence of suffering*."[9] The plight of Richardson's heroine is a novelized argument for a woman's right not to be *made* unhappy, but not necessarily her right to seek temporal happiness as it is unconnected to the betterment of the community.

Consequently, unhappiness, particularly female unhappiness, is also a central and recurring individual and social problem within the extended narrative comprised by *Pamela* and *Pamela II*. Pamela spills much putative ink on the conditions that undermine her well-being as well as erode her master's class supremacy. Despite her countervailing protestations of happiness and joy in every volume of her story, by almost every measure, the heroine is objectively less happy than Mr. B.[10] The question of whether this disjunct corresponds to a pervasive happiness gap between male and female characters in the eighteenth-century novel is beyond the scope of this chapter but can be reasonably posited. As Elizabeth Kraft reminds us, "Eighteenth-century discussions of happiness were, of course, primarily discussions of the happiness available to men."[11] Enlightenment happiness is implicitly male and is not simply a goal but a given. Mr. B, the novel's persecutor-turned-husband, also attains a different kind of happiness in *Pamela* than his wife, belying David Hume's claim, paraphrased by James Boswell in *The Life of Samuel Johnson* (1791), that "all who are happy, are equally happy."[12] *Pamela* reproduces the period's lack of sociocultural investment in female happiness; fictive women are depicted with fewer avenues to human flourishing than their male counterparts, their texts therefore featuring more negative portraits of their psychological and social functioning. Then as now, sexist treatment impacts on personal happiness and the autonomous pursuit of happiness is unequally accessible, women experiencing different barriers to personal felicity than their male counterparts.

Despite Richardson's apparent focus on the happy individual, the novelist's ideal happiness—like that of Enlightenment moralists like Francis Hutcheson—is social, ethical, and instrumental, tending toward communal good rather than simply the satisfaction of personal wants.[13] Scholars, notably Betty A. Schellenberg and Rebecca Anne Barr, have explored the anti-individualist dimensions of Richardson's fictive moral societies, and I would concur that happiness in *Pamela* and *Pamela II* is socially oriented.[14] Although Mr. B's masculine, self-serving happiness appears ascendant throughout the Pamela novels, Richardson at least attempts to convince readers that Pamela's happiness is superior, wrought of more durable materials and productive of more lasting good than his, despite the unhappiness she experiences en route to the continuation's happy ending.

PAMELA'S UNHAPPINESS: *PAMELA*

Richardson's *Pamela*, as scholars have long discussed, can be divided into two ideologically distinct parts: first, Pamela's unhappy ordeal as a servant and, second, her happy marriage, her virtue's earthly reward. In *Mourning Happiness*, Vivasvan Soni terms this "the bipartite structure of the novel—trial followed by happiness," which he analyzes and complicates.[15] In Richardson's *Clarissa* (1748), this basic structure is reversed, with again a man engendering the affective shift from happiness to unhappiness. This later heroine is described as preternaturally happy before her encounters with Lovelace. In Anna Howe's words, she "was immensely happy, above the happiness of a mortal creature."[16] Jocelyn Harris links Clarissa to a prelapsarian Eve.[17] Like Eve, Clarissa will "fall" from this state of happiness, suffer, and finally achieve redemption, a more perfect happiness promised by resurrection in heaven. Richardson's heroine conceives of death as "the beginning of a life of immortal happiness."[18]

In *Pamela*, the heroine's happiness is brought about by marriage, and in *Pamela II*, Lady Davers, observing her wedded brother and sister-in-law, confesses that she now comprehends "the Happiness of the first Pair before the Fall" (*II*, 225). B's interest in the Countess causes Pamela "to fall from so much Happiness," but this domestic paradise is eventually regained (*II*, 404). As Mr. B's unwanted advances begin very early in *Pamela*, Richardson's readers receive only a general sense of Pamela's life before the action of the novel begins. Pamela's background speaks of moderate happiness, coming as she does from a close-knit, harmonious family without means: "tho' poor," Pamela's parents "are a very happy Pair" (*I*, 326). The prospect of reuniting with them gives Pamela hope of escaping unhappiness, but just returning with her innocence, piety, and filial love intact is no complete formula for a happy life. Richardson recognizes Pamela's need for mental stimulation as well as a sense of purpose through labor. She writes of her future happiness at home in conditional terms: "If I can but get Work, with a little Time for reading, I hope we shall be very happy, over our Peat Fires" (*I*, 77). In *Pamela* and *Clarissa*, Richardson makes female happiness dependent on chastity but does not wholly correlate sexual innocence with happiness; he develops heroines whose subjective happiness is built on their emotional and intellectual associations and activities: friendship, familial love, conversation, and writing.

Although Pamela's life before her persecution is not established as an Eden of happiness, the stark contrast between the past and present is a source of distress; subjected to Mr. B's insults and horrified to realize she is her master's intended sexual conquest, Pamela exclaims, "How happy was I a-while ago! How miserable now!" (*I*, 27). After Mr. B kidnaps and imprisons her, she relieves some of her stress by journaling her harrowing experiences. Pamela begins one entry with the typical header: "*I am now come to MONDAY, the 5th Day of my Bondage and Misery*" (*I*, 119). During the awful period of Pamela's harassment, Richardson's heroine is not simply unhappy, but an "unhappy creature," dehumanized, denied her natural human right not to be made unhappy. Conversing with Mrs. Jewkes as they fish, Pamela draws an elaborate analogy between herself and the prey animal, which the heroine throws back in: "I was thinking this poor Carp was the unhappy *Pamela*," she muses and explains her empathetic action (*I*, 131). She recognizes that they both desire "Liberty," and sees in the fish a fellow "hooked and deceived" creature. Vainly, she attempts to rouse Mrs. Jewkes's imaginative sympathy by drawing her attention to the animal's response—"And did you not see the Joy with which the happy Carp flounced from us!"—and draws the parallel again to herself (*I*, 131). Unlike her male literary counterparts, Pamela is not on a quest for happiness but rather is forced into discursive and physical schemes and missions to avert an unhappy fate.

Isolation compounding her psychological distress, Pamela's lowest emotional point occurs when she contemplates suicide by the side of the pond during her failed escape attempt. Even shortly before this spiritual crisis, she prayed God would preserve her innocence while also expressing a willingness to die: "happy shall I be to lay down my worthless Life, and see an End to all my Troubles and Anxieties" (*I*, 158). Grappling alone with her despair, she nonetheless succeeds in regaining the peace of mind requisite to contentment. She never returns to these affective depths in the succeeding volumes of her narrative, having done this necessary spiritual work, recorded in lengthy passages of internal argumentation. Rather than crediting herself, however, she ascribes her salvation to God's grace, in which she rejoices for pulling her back from the brink of "the lowest last Abyss of Misery and Perdition" (*I*, 170).

Lacking autonomy at every turn, Pamela is unhappier than Mr. B, whose unhappiness is the peevish ill humor of thwarted desire to his victim's acute psychic anguish. Mr. B's steward, Mr. Longman, remarks on his employer's unhappiness once he begins preying on Pamela: "I never saw such an Alteration in any Man in my Life! He is pleas'd with nobody" (*I*, 50). Mr. B gives himself free rein to his own negative emotions, a function of both his gender and his class. Conversely, disadvantaged on both fronts and therefore subject to greater social scrutiny, Pamela suffers under the pressure to stifle her feelings. She is harshly judged for outbursts of feeling and Mr. B punishes her for baring the very unhappiness he has caused. Early in Mr. B's reign of terror over Pamela, the heroine recounts an unsettling encounter with her master, whose intimidating looks alarm her; while she later recounts that she "sobb'd and cry'd most sadly," Mr. B dismissively terms this response "blubbering" in his demand for its cessation (*I*, 23, 24). Such marks of her unhappiness, reminders of his culpability, incite his anger rather than his sympathy. Discomfiture with female emotion, particularly female tears, has a disturbing underside: mental and bodily control. Mr. B wants not only power over his servant's sexuality but mastery over her feelings—both her expressed feelings and those in her inner life. Prefacing his attempt to force his kisses on Pamela, he tries manipulating her mood with "Why so serious, my pretty *Pamela* . . . why so grave" (*I*, 69). Even when Mr. B's harassment ends, the heroine waits anxiously on the border between happiness and unhappiness. Confused by her master's newfound kindness, Pamela writes that she is "either nearer my Happiness or Misery than ever I was," her remark underscoring her disorientation and the uncertainty of her hopes (*I*, 211); at the very least, her unhappiness no longer seems certain. In contrast, Mr. B's happiness is always in his own power, the question being how he chooses to define it, as either pleasure or virtue, or some admixture of the two.

COMPETING CONCEPTIONS OF HAPPINESS IN *PAMELA*

The meaning of words matters deeply in *Pamela*, a claim corroborated by generations of Richardson scholars. "The novel's central struggle," Patricia Meyer Spacks avers, "focuses on the manipulation of language" and makes the claim that "if Pamela can win her pursuers over to her version of what key terms mean, she will win her battle for self-preservation and self-advancement."[19] Jennie Batchelor assesses competing ideologies within the novel, namely "aristocratic licence and a moral integrity that transcends class hierarchies," and observes that "this battle is waged on a linguistic level."[20] Indeed, "happiness" is a much-contested term in *Pamela*. By turns, happiness is synonymous with salvation, virtue, pleasure, and money. Pamela's parents have a religiously conservative understanding of happiness that stresses chastity. Virginity, the pious Andrews impress on their unmarried daughter, is a vital passport to her soul's "future Happiness" (*I*, 14). Richardson agrees, relentlessly associating the extramarital loss of female sexual innocence with spiritual unhappiness. An outlook of Christian resignation informs the heroine's stoical acceptance of the prospect of virtuous poverty. When Pamela is apparently allowed to return home, the heroine considers herself happy in avoiding sexual ruin and resisting the temptation of riches, declaring in her "VERSES on my going away":

> *But what makes out true Happiness*
> *But Innocence, and inward Peace?*
> *And that, thank God, I do possess*
> *O happy, happy* Pamela! (*I*, 90)

Her blessing to those she leaves behind, "*Thrice happy may you ever be, / Each one in his and her Degree*" (*I*, 91), reflects her parents' laboring-class brand of modest, contented felicity. As Kristina Booker maintains in her exploration of the novel's "servant problem," Richardson promotes "the idea that true happiness is a result of performing one's God-given role."[21]

A scene of verbal misunderstanding in Lincolnshire demonstrates exactly how social position shapes characters' ideas of happiness. Pamela's father and Mr. B speak at cross purposes when the former visits his recently imperiled daughter. Mr. B blithely informs Goodman Andrews, "your Daughter is in the way to be happy!" (*I*, 291). Goodman Andrews is "alarm'd" by this news and responds, "What! then she is dying? And trembled he could scarce stand" (*I*, 291). The older man jumps to this conclusion, believing that happiness, especially for a penniless servant, is found in the next world; he automatically associates happiness with the afterlife, temporal bliss being a privilege of the well-off. In Mr. B's discourse, "happy" means rich, as Pamela will be marrying up socially and financially. This awkward, faintly comical episode in the text points to the ontological gulf between Mr. B's happiness and that of Pamela's parents whose poverty goes hand in hand with the consolation of religion. In *Pamela II*, the heroine's parents continue to highlight how happiness is a function of class, being for the lowly an emotional state indivisible from gratitude. Although Pamela's parents are "happy Creatures" (*II*, 201), their social status limits their performance of happiness as individualistic pleasure. As dependents, reliant on B for their financial and emotional wellbeing, they pay for their happiness by being thankful and useful. Gratitude and happiness are fruitfully as well as oppressively entwined in Richardson's sequel. Pamela, anticipatory of a mutualistic happiness between the Andrews, including herself, and Mr. B, declares to her parents, "And thus will our Gratitude be the inspirer of Joy to our common Benefactor; and his Joy will heighten our Gratitude; and so we shall proceed, as Cause and Effect to each other's Happiness" (*II*, 13). Happiness—no zero-sum game in Pamela's philosophy—will naturally multiply, yet crucially without Mr. B's felicity being unseated as paramount. Likewise, even after her social elevation by marriage, Pamela shows the ways happiness, as both a woman and a former servant, is something earned, often by herself bestowing happiness upon the worthy. With a tidy sum of £40, she is able to "make Mrs. *Jervis* happy at home," and, in reporting this act of charity to her spouse, proves her own merit: "I have made the good Woman quite happy, and if I have your Approbation, I shall be as much so myself in this Instance, as I am in all others" (*II*, 68). Frequently, she serves as B's proxy—her charitable giving modeling an economy of happiness that is both personally and socially advantageous. She reflects on her own privilege in this capacity, exclaiming "how many Opportunities have the beneficent *Rich* to make themselves, as well as their *Fellow-creatures* happy" (*II*, 69). In this proposed redistribution of wealth/happiness, the distinctions between those who give and those who receive remain; for many, happiness is still a gift rather than a universal right, happiness bestowing a luxury to be enjoyed (i.e., a moral pleasure for the giver). Particularly as it involves women and the lower classes, happiness in the Pamela novels is transactional, reflecting the period's investment in hierarchies that are leveled only in theory by happiness.

In opposition to the Andrewses' notions of happiness are those of their son-in-law, Mr. B. His view of happiness is worldly, closely tied to bodily pleasure, material comfort, and the emotional ease enabled by others' mandatory "Chearfulness" (*II*, 317). He incorrectly anticipates that Pamela can be swayed to abandon her ethics by his promise to "make all [her] Family happy," happy here being synonymous with comfortably off (*I*, 83). His letter to Mr. Williams promising him a living confirms Mr. B's conflation of money and happiness; he uses "happy" or "happiness" five times in this missive to his dependent, which begins with the sentiment that he has "long wanted to make [Mr. Williams] happy" (*I*, 146).

Pamela, however, is adamant in refusing her master's materially oriented happiness; as a servant soon to return to her poor family, she professes, "I am as happy as a Princess. I am quite as rich as I wish to be!" (*I*, 81). Conversely, like Mr. B, Mrs. Jewkes also equates wealth and happiness. Commenting on Pamela's opportunity to become Mr. B's mistress, Mrs. Jewkes asserts, "Why, ne'er a Lady in the Land may live happier than you, if you will, or be more honourably used" (*I*, 137). Pamela objects to her keeper's specious use of the word "honour," and likewise rejects Jewkes's equally perverse understanding of "happiness" by announcing, "'Tis is out of his Power . . . to make me happy, great and rich as he is!" (*I*, 123). The only way it *is* in his power is by sparing her virtue and permitting her return home. One thing Jewkes and Pamela agree on, however, is the idea of female happiness as a passive state, a by-product even of male happiness, or a state enabled or disabled by male prerogative.

THE MARRIAGE: *PAMELA*

Richardson plots marriage as the major "happy Change" for his principal characters, both of whom appreciate their improved life circumstances (*I*, 271). Their happiness gains are different, however, Mr. B's felicity being self-concordant, or autonomously pursued, rather than granted. He becomes the "happy, happy Mr. *B*," his union with Pamela being the ratification of his moral reform and foundation of his happiness (*I*, 491). Ironically, Pamela's account of her unhappiness catalyzes the moral change that will advance her tormentor's own happiness. Nonetheless, he puts greater emphasis on himself as a reader than on Pamela as a writer. Labeled "a conversion narrative" by Christopher Flint, *Pamela* is arguably more concerned with Mr. B's happiness than with Pamela's.[22] He has access to the Enlightenment ideals identified by Roy Porter: "individualism, the right to self-improvement—and to *happiness*."[23] He pursues happiness, albeit initially with a wrongheaded conception of happiness as private gratification; yet even after his ethical makeover, Mr. B's references to marital happiness are never free of the selfishness that characterized his earlier attitude as a would-be rapist. Waiting for Pamela to settle on a wedding date, Mr. B reminds his bride-to-be that "of a *Thursday* it was, you nam'd to me that Fourteen Days from that, you would confirm my Happiness," and he had previously ordered her to "fix on one, to *make me happy*" (*I*, 326, emphasis added; 298). His imperatives underline their economy of happiness in the novel: he is the primary beneficiary of the happiness engendered by their union. He is likelier than Pamela to use the possessive when speaking of his happiness, laying claim to his own felicity, even as he attributes it to others. Although he recognizes the role of Pamela's parents in his happiness, he phrases his thanks in a way that keeps the focus on himself. With a strange combination of gratitude and selfishness, he pronounces, "God bless you both, for being the happy Means of procuring for me so great a Blessing" (*I*, 292). As Pamela's husband, he enjoys his neighbors' esteem, evidencing the connection between happiness and external approval articulated by Locke and his classical predecessors.[24] Mr. B is more likely than his spouse to publicize his emotional gains and show off his marital felicity; he displays Pamela, the living emblem of his happiness, to the local gentry, gloating to his wife, "I will now defy the sawcy, busy Censurers of the World, and bid them know your Excellence and, and my Happiness" (*I*, 265). His happiness is both individualistic and ego-driven, as Mr. B obviously craves outside affirmation, even the envy of onlookers. Lady Towers (the person who terms him the "happy, happy Mr. *B*!") exclaims, "what Reputation have you not brought upon your Judgment!" (*I*, 491). The self-satisfied Mr. B agrees, viewing himself as a key agent in his own happiness's making after hearing his chosen being praised.

Richardson's heroine, however, is no happiness seeker, but a recipient of happiness, Vivasvan Soni explaining that "Pamela's ability to sacrifice all thought of happiness for her virtue is what allows her to earn the reward of happiness."[25] Michael McKeon likewise recognizes this negative conduct as her "essential power," although I view interpretations of Pamela's supposed autonomy through passivity with greater cynicism.[26] She sees her master's transformation from rake to husband as a divine gift and her new position as his wife as a blessing from "that gracious God, who has thus chang'd [her] Distress to Happiness" (*I*, 275). In celebrating this event as divinely wrought, she undersells her own role in these changes. In Pamela's estimation, she is the spouse made happy, referring to Mr. B as "the generous Author of [her] happiness" (*I*, 353) when she herself is the cause, being the literal author of the moving narrative that initiates Mr. B's change of heart.[27] Still, she refers to her writing with self-effacing detachment as the "Means to promote my Happiness" (*I*, 309). Being a woman, Pamela possesses happiness as a state conferred on her rather than one sought after and self-attained.

Pamela considers being married to Mr. B as synonymous with being happy, the words "happiness" and "marriage" becoming interchangeable in her writing.[28] She begins a "Journal of all that passes in these first Stages of [her] Happiness" and numbers the days of marriage as the days of her happiness (*I*, 448). Occurring midway through *Pamela*, marriage is not so much a happy ending but an event that recasts the events that came before it, a happy rebeginning. *Pamela*, like Laurence Sterne's *Tristram Shandy* (1759–1767), as described by Brian Michael Norton, "never relinquishes the idea that misfortune can be transmuted through the alchemy of representation."[29] Pamela herself performs this labor of reframing her unhappiness as a precursor to her happiness, as her persecution by her master is later discursively softened into a courtship. I agree with Alicia L. Kerfoot, who perceptively re-evaluates Pamela's ostensive social elevation: "It is less that Pamela rises, than she returns to a reconfigured servant-mistress/master relationship."[30] Early in *Pamela II*, Richardson's heroine figures her husband as a godlike creator, deistically terming him "the first Mover and Cause of all his own Happiness, of my Happiness, and that of my dear, my ever dear Parents" (*II*, 7). In *Pamela*, the heroine is delighted to use her own happiness as a means of venerating Mr. B, claiming that "it will be a Pleasure to me to shew every one, that, with respect to my Happiness in this Life, I am intirely the Work of your Bounty" (*I*, 272). Even her happiness, publicly displayed rather than simply privately enjoyed, serves her husband-master.

Particularly in Richardson's original novel, Pamela's happiness is ironically also a significant generator of unhappiness. After her marriage, she is self-conscious about her social background and afflicted with feelings of inadequacy, feeling undeserving of her newfound felicity. Dwelling on her supposed unworthiness, Pamela expresses the wish that she was born "a Duchess," and sighs she "must labour under the Weight of an Obligation, even had this Happiness befallen me, that would have press'd me to Death" (*I*, 248). In one sentence, she can acknowledge being "in such an enviable Prospect of Happiness" while also confessing to her parents that she has "something very awful upon my Mind" (*I*, 288). She obsessively refers to herself as happy in its sense of being favored by fortune rather than feeling good. Belief in her supposed inferiority colors her every interaction with her former master; even as his wife, she falls on her knees to thank him. Clearly, hers is an attenuated happiness, if not in fact another unhappy state, lesser in degree than the distress she experienced as a prisoner, but painful nonetheless. Carol Houlihan Flynn observes that "Pamela never stops proving her right to happiness: she is always on trial."[31] Flynn is only partly right, however, as Pamela really insists only on her right not to be made unhappy.

Given the evidence of Pamela's continuing unhappiness, the idea of the couple's mutual happiness is a pleasing fiction for Mr. B, who enjoys both his own felicity and the lordly pleasure of conferring happiness on his wife. Mr. B sporadically tries to obviate Pamela's intense sense of "Obligation" and insists, "let us talk of nothing henceforth but Equality" (*I*, 350). Yet even in this conversation, he speaks of their shared future as contingent; they "have a Prospect of perpetuating each other's Happiness," but only after she has been "confirm'd and improv'd by [Mr. B]" (*I*, 351). More often, he confirms her sense of entwined financial and emotional dependence. In another irony, their happy marriage demands her submission, her "chearful" acquiescence on points small and large (*II*, 317), even when her own happiness is at stake. Although he promises to contribute to her happiness and listen to her concerns, he attaches conditions that undermine his supposed kindness and magnanimity, including "as long as your Merit lasts" and "so far as is agreeable to me" (*I*, 357). In *Pamela II*, Mr. B is referred to as both a "*British* Monarch" and "a Tyrant" (*II*, 74). The impermanence of female happiness, subject to the (potentially) autocratic rule of the husband, is underscored in both novels. Indeed, in the sequel, Pamela admits that her own happiness is dependent on the permanence of B's reform into a virtuous man. Once B recommits to virtue after his lapse with the Countess, Pamela imagines an even happier existence, which would "complete all the Happiness I wish'd for in this Life" (*II*, 549). Specifically, she hopes for B's conversion into a "*Religious* Gentleman" (*II*, 549), so she can pray with her husband and not half-hide her own piety.

Pamela's happiness is not only provisional but also a matter of much emotion work. Jennie Batchelor astutely remarks on the mixed blessing of the heroine's fate in *Pamela*: "Pamela's rewards, as the novel's title suggests, have been great, but they demand considerable labor and self-restraint to maintain."[32] While Pamela must earn her continuing happiness, B always believes himself entitled to the present and long-term happiness he now happens to deserve more as a husband than he did as a rake. Absolute in his desires and demands, he expects perfect happiness facilitated by Pamela's perfection, as he announces that he "could not have been contented to have been *but moderately happy* in a Wife" (*I*, 447). Pamela largely complies, performing cheerfulness, and from their engagement onward plans to "devote herself to preserving her husband's love through self-effacing behavior."[33] Alongside her decreased autonomy, Pamela's individuality is diluted after she weds her master and unlike Mr. B, who has access to the happiness predicated on personal growth, she does not develop as a person. As Christopher Flint summarizes, "She is altered very little, but the conditions about her change significantly according to how she is situated."[34] Richardson establishes Pamela in this first novel as a facilitator of others' happiness, but not essentially a maker of her own. That said, Miss Darnford, one of Pamela's chief correspondents in Richardson's sequel, observes the dynamics of the B marriage. In *Pamela II*, she remarks that Pamela "must make the best of it . . . [and] make your own Will his. This . . . any Lady must do, be her Quality ever so great, who would be happy with Mr. *B*" (*II*, 288). In other words, Pamela is strategically subservient, relinquishing her will to happiness in a tacit bid to happiness, albeit on her husband's terms.

PAMELA'S HAPPINESS AND UNHAPPINESS IN *PAMELA II*

Richardson's sequel maintains the original novel's interest in socially beneficial marital happiness, but also shares with *Pamela* representations of female unhappiness and a gendered happiness gap. The first year of their marriage, a honeymoon period, is happy for Pamela, and for a time Mr. B checks some of his crueler tendencies. Her marital happiness is so complete, so empirically verifiable that she cannot delineate all that makes her happy, there being "so many Specimens of my Felicity" (*II*, 303). The language of plenitude characterizes her talk of happiness. Even when she spies future unhappiness on the horizon, she exclaims, "But what Pleasures, what Happiness have I not crouded [*sic*] into this last, and this first happy, thrice happy Year" (*II*, 375). Pamela's parents are likewise echoers of Pamela's happiness, almost an anxiety detectable in their need to proclaim Pamela's ever-expanding felicity: "Come, my dear Child, you are happy, very happy to be sure you are, and, if it *can* be, may you be yet happier and happier!" (*II*, 104). The repetition serves as an intensifier, seemingly leaving little room for doubting the heroine's happiness, but often inviting it from the reader. John and Elizabeth Andrews—like the lady—doth protest too much, methinks.

Yet as much as Pamela self-identifies as "a happy, happy Creature" (*II*, 393), masculine felicity is still central within the emotional economy represented in *Pamela II*, however central the heroine's consciousness is to the narrative. Accepting and internalizing the heteropatriarchy's privileging of male happiness, Pamela gushes to her husband, "I have only therefore to acknowledge, with the deepest Sense of your Goodness to me, and with the most Heart-affecting Gratitude, that from the happy, the thrice-happy Hour, that you generously made me yours, til this Moment, you have not left me one Thing, on my own Part, to wish for, but the Continuance and Increase of your Felicity, and that I might be worthier and worthier of the unexpected Goodness, Tenderness, and Condescension, wherewith you have always treated me" (*II*, 373). As this passage evidences, gratitude is still central to Pamela's credo and still weighs on the personal happiness she is convinced has been undeservingly conferred on her; nonetheless, despite these supposedly "*unreturnable* Obligations," she frets less than in *Pamela* about her unworthiness (*II*, 393). Other characters repeatedly validate the justness of the heroine's temporal rewards; Mrs. Wrightston (formerly, Miss Sally Godfrey), for example, begins a typical letter to Pamela with the greeting, "*Happy, deservedly happy, dear lady*" (*II*, 482).

Pamela's happiness is only temporary, however, and the heroine's trials again become the novelist's narrative focus; her writing reverts to accounts of her distress, her emotional wellbeing being so determined (but not entirely so) by her husband-master's treatment of her. As in *Pamela*, the heroine's unhappiness is grounded in fear; instead of fearing the loss of her virtue, she now fears losing her husband and child. She philosophizes on the obstacles to human happiness, namely future-oriented worry, what she terms "Apprehensiveness" (*II*, 83). Near the very beginning of *Pamela II*, Pamela considers herself at the summit of happiness, believing "more bless'd, and more happy, in my own Mind, surely I cannot be" (*II*, 6). When she is happy, she says that she cannot imagine being happier, yet when she is unhappy, she can easily imagine becoming far unhappier. Yet this negativity bias is understandable in light of her limitations as a happiness-seeking subject. Again, in the face of male selfishness, Pamela's lack of personal agency—a function of her gender—imperils her long-term happiness. Praying for the couple's felicity, but understanding Mr. B's character failings, Lady Davers predicts her brother's conjugal sabotage. Indeed, he threatens the heroine's peace of mind and domestic equanimity, most seriously in his pursuit of the Countess, whom he meets at a masquerade. Mr. B's emotional infidelity stirs Pamela's jealousy and renews her feelings of inadequacy. Pamela exclaims, "O my happy Rivaless" and later the "too happy Rivaless" when she contemplates the Countess, her apparent usurper as the woman who can make Mr. B happy, and in turn be made happy by him (*II*, 404, 419). Pamela's immediate happiness is severely compromised as she waits for the outcome of Mr. B's romantic interest in the Countess. At one point she cries, "I cannot bear this cruel Suspense!" (*II*, 416). Mr. B does not understand her pain and accuses her of overreacting, to the point that he questions her sanity in infantilizing language: "Surely your Head, Child, is a little affected" (*II*, 417). She requests that he begin the "Trial" that would decide her fate, but he considers that her "Mind has taken much too solemn a Turn, to enter now into such a Subject" (*II*, 417). Controlling when and how they will talk, he prolongs her distress, and repeatedly disciplines her for showing emotion. Although this is his last night with her before leaving for London, he stonewalls her, denying her the relief of communicating her feelings. She is pained but hides her agony: "I weep in the Night, when he is asleep; and in the Day, when he is absent: And I am happy, when I can, un'observ'd, steal this poor Relief" (*II*, 404). In obliging Pamela to conceal the negative emotions incited by his own misbehavior, Mr. B is an enforcer of the social pressure on women to appear happy regardless of their internal state. Pamela, charged by her husband to "resume your former Chearfulness" (*II*, 433), is made unhappier by such injunctions not to express her emotions freely. Indeed, at several points in *Pamela II* Pamela must resort to "Chearfulness," an enforced, performative happiness put on for the benefit of men who are under no such obligation to elide their emotions.

Motherhood adds to Pamela's happiness, but also renders her vulnerable to new kinds of unhappiness and new scenes in which she must be falsely cheerful. Happy is a word repeated multiple times by Richardson's characters when Pamela gives birth to a son, Billy, an heir to Mr. B's estate. Yet the heroine suffers when Mr. B exercises his authority over her mothering in ways that conflict with her own personal values and desires. He will not allow her to breastfeed her infants and, when Billy is gravely ill with the smallpox, bars her from the sickroom. Selfishly, he wants her to preserve her slim figure and lovely, unmarked face, her superficial but crucial attractions as a wife; Pamela obeys, "for fear of forfeiting the protection and love of a husband."[35] As in *Pamela*, fear—the happiness corrosive of "virtue in distress"—periodically dominates her mental landscape in Richardson's sequel. She fears replacement in the household by the Countess and fears being parted from her firstborn child, tormented by jealousy as she watches this woman hold Billy. As a woman, Pamela has no legal right to child custody, English law maintaining the father's (almost) exclusive guardianship.[36] Imagining Mr. B leaving her for the Countess and taking Billy with him, Pamela declares, "he will at once burst asunder the Strings of my Heart" (*II*, 404). Again, Pamela's unhappiness is both a personal and social problem, as its cause, her husband's inconstancy, poses a threat to the community of people who surround Mr. and Mrs. B. In an imagined future in which she is exiled to Kent with Billy, she can still enjoy "a two-fold Happiness" by doing her "Duty" to her child and parents (*II*, 404), but without her current scope for enacting charity and living as an exemplum of virtuous wifeliness.

SOCIAL HAPPINESS IN *PAMELA* AND *PAMELA II*

In both *Pamela* and *Pamela II*, the making of happiness *by* the happy couple is periodically foregrounded; individual happiness, female or male, is arguably less valuable in Richardson's fiction than the net social benefit a happy individual can facilitate. Barr's observations on *Sir Charles Grandison* (1753), which "elevates those who prefer another's happiness to their own," can be applied to *Pamela* and *Pamela II*, novels that also promote a communal conception of felicity.[37] The private happiness yielded by the union between Pamela and Mr. B radiates outward into the community, and many minor characters are rendered happier and better by the protagonists. During their brief engagement, Mr. B's neighbors anticipate the bridegroom's increased involvement in their social life. Pamela reports that they say to her, "We hope, when the happy Knot is ty'd, you will induce the Squire to reside more among us" (*I*, 298). Pamela, like her husband, welcomes the publicity of her happy union, as she documents how others come to view them as a template for marital felicity. One such observer, Lady Jones, judges Mr. and Mrs. B to be a model happy couple. "The Company and Behaviour of you two happy Ones to each other," she declares to them at Sir Simon's afternoon tea, "are the most edifying I ever knew. I am always improv'd when I see you. How happy would every good Lady be with such a Gentleman, and every good Gentleman with such a Lady!" (*I*, 408). Pamela's appreciation of these compliments lies in her social conception of happiness; she is less concerned about her own personal felicity than about how it can translate into greater social harmony. This collectivist, interdependent happiness is gendered female in Richardson's novel, and Pamela's own happiness is intensified by the prospect that she will contribute on her husband's behalf to others' happiness, as she declares to her mother, "What a happy Creature, my dear Mother, is your *Pamela*!—O may my thankful Heart, and the good Use I may be enabled to make of the Blessings before me, be a Means to continue this delightful Prospect to a long Date, for the sake of the dear good Gentleman, who thus becomes the happy Instrument, in the Hands of Providence, to bless all he smiles upon!" (*I*, 308–309). Similarly, in this novel's sequel, Pamela expresses her delight in serving others, and mentions her expanding family and the attendant increase in "domestic Duties, which are increased upon me" (*II*, 543). These responsibilities include the education of her eldest son, the care of Mr. B's illegitimate daughter Sally Goodwin, and the mentorship of four young women near the novel's end. She accepts the task to improve them, declaring that if she succeeds, "it will be an Addition to my Happiness" (*II*, 568). Pamela's happiness is entrenched in a gendered moral economy, an ethical, socially responsible system whereby female happiness must irradiate outward and simultaneously reflect backward on its masculine sources, temporal and divine. Schellenberg makes the following observation, applicable to both *Pamela* and *Pamela II*: "Pamela's destiny as wife is figured not in terms of progress towards a defined, if unattainable happiness, but in terms of an ever-increasing atemporality and typology as the centre of a stabilized circle."[38] As a paragon to model correct upper-class morality for an aristocracy in economic and moral decline, Richardson's heroine is in a sense beyond individual happiness. For Pamela, her felicity is burdened with a duty to "diffuse the Blessings" she herself has received, as she exclaims, "What is my *single* Happiness, if I suffer it, Niggard-like to extend no further than myself?—But then, *indeed*, do God Almighty's Creatures act worthy of the Blessings they receive, when they make, or endeavor to make, the whole Creation, so far as is in the Circle of their Power, happy!" (*I*, 363). However uncomfortable Richardson seems with the prospect of his heroine's "*single* Happiness," he concludes his first Pamela novel by conservatively underlining the happiness accrued by his main male character. In this book's conclusion, the narrator appends to Pamela's narrative the assurance that the heroine "made her beloved Spouse happy in a numerous and hopeful Progeny" (*I*, 499). The putative editor enumerates the other positive outcomes of Pamela's influence and stresses her "Social Virtues" (*I*, 503). He also highlights the pious purpose or "happy Issue which the Troubles and Trials of PAMELA met with": to praise God and illustrate "the Power of Providence" (*I*, 501). *Pamela*'s happiness gap seems to narrow with this happy ending without being really eliminated; temporal female happiness is still secondary to both male happiness and social happiness, and liable to be eclipsed by its divine source.

The heroine's felicity in *Pamela II* is even more insistently communal and outwardly facing than in Richardson's original novel. Pamela's happiness continually emanates beyond her immediate family and serves her wider circle of friends, acquaintances, and dependents. Miss Darnford regularly celebrates Pamela's contributions to others' happiness. "What an excellent Lady are you," she gushes, "And, how happy, how good you make every one who knows you" (*II*, 228). Pamela's virtuous happiness is contagious. In his sequel, Richardson is more explicit still in establishing his heroine as a model of feminine morality on both an intradiegetic and extradiegetic level. The final episode of *Pamela II* confirms the novel's investment in female happiness as a nonindividualistic affair, despite the emphasis on individual emotion inherent to the epistolary form. Pamela tells the four young ladies an allegorical and instructional tale about Coquetillia, Prudiana, Profusiana (*II*, 593), and "the Happy, & the Happy-Making Prudentia" (*II*, 599).

Unsurprisingly, the only virtuous lady is the only happy one, as Prudentia (Pamela's fictive version of herself) learns by example and "endeavours to appropriate to herself the domestic Virtues, which shall one day make her the Crown of some worthy Gentleman's earthly Happiness . . . and secure and heighten her own" (*II*, 599). Here, as elsewhere in the novel, she teaches a basic formula for happiness and unhappiness, despite her own narrative showing the complexities of securing a happy existence, especially for women who are responsible for the feelings of others as well as for masking their own.

CONCLUSION: RENEWED HAPPINESS IN *PAMELA II*

Richardson assures us of Pamela's future happiness in *Pamela II* by transferring more of the authorship of the heroine's happiness to Pamela herself. Although her imagination has often been a source of unhappiness through the volumes of her story, it becomes a tool for looking forward with equanimity rather than fear, and for fostering the self-love, which Hutcheson defines as the "desire of private interest,"[39] so often connected to male eighteenth-century happiness. When the danger of Mr. B's infidelity passes, Pamela optimistically asserts to Lady Davers, "I am happy, and shall be happier than I ever was; and that I thought, so did every body, was impossible" (*II*, 424). While she anticipates with Mr. B's second reform "a happy Futurity" (*II*, 552), her renewed happiness is not solely dependent on her spouse. His threatening order for his wife to "be easy and happy, while it was *yet* in [her] own Power" (*II*, 417) is emotional blackmail, but also foreshadows Pamela's reclamation of her own happiness *before* he recommits to their marriage. She finds consolation in her virtue, taking comfort in the prediction that she will be happier than the erring adulterers, not just in the next world but in this one as well. The interest of *Pamela II* lies in the novel's multifaceted representation of Pamela's happiness as domestic and social, but individual as well. She works through her feelings in her letter writing and resigns herself to the prospect of losing Mr. B, as well as the social capital of being his wife; Pamela imagines her stoic acceptance of this future, assuring her correspondent, "After a while, I shall be no unhappy Person," in part because she values "a high Estate less than other people" (*II*, 620). Pamela's subjective life satisfaction will recover, resting as it does on a more solid foundation than Mr. B's. Moreover, Pamela's philosophical reading equips her with the tools of enlightened happiness. "To moderate Desires," observes Pamela, quoting John Locke, is "the ready way to make a contented Man" (*II*, 535). Indeed, her desires exceed her expectations when Mr. B renounces the Countess, thus augmenting Pamela's felicity by creating a powerful contrast between "this dreadful Affair" (*II*, 436) and what comes afterward.

Marital disagreements resolved, *Pamela II* ends happily with Mr. B reintegrated into the home, the mechanism for propagating the social happiness so celebrated in Richardson's fiction. By the final quarter of the novel, Pamela can pronounce with confidence, "We are a happy Family, united by the best and most solid Motives!" (*II*, 555). As a domestic unit, familial happiness is produced by its members knowing and practicing their duties, essentially, by modeling Pamela and by converting others to the creed of virtuous happiness. The Bs' future promises a continuance of that happy domesticity founded on unchanging morality and the household routines that enact the ethical happiness upon which the heroine's identity has always been founded. Schellenberg describes this happy state as "a felicity figured as rapturous stasis."[40] The happiness of *Pamela II* then looks forward to the communal felicity represented within *Sir Charles Grandison*, a novel that complicates the gendering of happiness through a selfless male protagonist deeply invested in others' happiness; Grandison may be read as a paternalistic guardian of female happiness, a precursor to Jane Austen's Mr. Darcy, but also represents a significant improvement on Mr. B's brand of masculinity in his rejection of self-interested pleasure seeking and his ingrained recognition of a universal right to freedom from unhappiness.[41] *Pamela* and *Pamela II* are not, like Austen's novels, championing the female pursuit of happiness as "the business of life," but they do represent women's internal and external obstacles to felicity and show a socially created happiness gap between male and female characters.[42] Although the eighteenth century saw the evolution and secularization of ideas of happiness, *Pamela* and *Pamela II* illuminate the attendant gendering of temporal happiness in the cultural imagination. Mr. B attains happiness, ostensibly through his moral conversion, but first by way of a self-involvement largely—although not wholly—unavailable to Pamela in her gratitude, submission, and mandatory cheerfulness.

NOTES

1. "The Fairy-Queen Libretto," Operas Arias Composers Singers, https://www.opera-arias.com/purcell/the-fairy-queen/libretto/.
2. María Laura Arrosa and Néstor Gandelman, "Happiness Decomposition: Female Optimism," *Journal of Happiness Studies* 17 (2016): 731.
3. Roy Porter, *Enlightenment: Britain and the Creation of the Modern World* (London: Penguin, 2001), 258.
4. Vivasvan Soni, *Mourning Happiness: Narrative and the Politics of* Modernity (Ithaca, NY: Cornell University Press, 2010), 238.
5. Samuel Johnson, *A Dictionary of the English Language* (1755), s.v. "Happy," https://johnsonsdictionaryonline.com/happy/.
6. Samuel Richardson, *Pamela; or, Virtue Rewarded*, ed. Thomas Keymer and Alice Wakely (Oxford: Oxford University Press, 2001), 326, 298. All subsequent citations appear in the text.
7. Samuel Richardson, *Pamela in Her Exalted Condition*, ed. Albert J. Rivero (Cambridge: Cambridge University Press, 2012), 7. All subsequent citations appear in the text.
8. Johnson, *A Dictionary of the English Language*, s.v. "Happy."
9. Adam Barkman, "Negative Happiness," *Kritike: An Online Journal of Philosophy* 3, no. 1 (2009): 72–77, 72.

10. In distinguishing happiness and joy, Adam Potkay defines the former as "a mental disposition or an ethical evaluation" and notes that "happiness typically admits degrees (i.e., one's happiness whether understood subjectively or objectively, can be perfect or lesser or greater)." Adam Potkay, *The Story of Joy: From the Bible to Late Romanticism* (Cambridge: Cambridge University Press, 2011), 2.
11. Elizabeth Kraft, "'Happy the Man': The Eighteenth-Century Novel and the Pursuit of Happiness," *The Eighteenth Century* 57, no. 11 (2016): 151–155, 153.
12. James Boswell, *The Life of Samuel Johnson, LL.D.*, ed. John Wilson Croker, 2 vols (New York: Harper and Brothers, 1846), 1:227.
13. In *An Inquiry into the Origin of Our Ideas of Beauty and Virtue*, Francis Hutcheson pronounces "*that Action is best*, which procures the *greatest Happiness* for the *greatest Numbers;* and *that, worst,* which in *like manner* occasions *Misery*" (London: J. Darby, 1726), 177–178.
14. See Betty A. Schellenberg, *The Conversational Circle: Re-reading the English Novel, 1740–1775* (Lexington: University Press of Kentucky, 1996), and Rebecca Anne Barr, "Richardson's *Sir Charles Grandison* and the Symptoms of Subjectivity," *The Eighteenth Century* 51, no. 4 (Winter 2010): 391–411.
15. Soni, *Mourning Happiness*, 190.
16. Samuel Richardson, *Clarissa*, ed. Angus Ross (London: Penguin, 2004), 578.
17. Jocelyn Harris, *Samuel Richardson* (Cambridge: Cambridge University Press, 1987), 56.
18. Richardson, *Clarissa*, 1117.
19. Patricia Meyer Spacks, *Imagining a Self: Autobiography and Novel in Eighteenth-Century England* (Cambridge, MA: Harvard University Press, 1976), 210.
20. Jennie Batchelor, *Dress, Distress and Desire: Clothing and the Female Body in Eighteenth-Century Literature* (Houndmills, UK: Palgrave Macmillan, 2005), 20.
21. Kristina Booker, "Richardson's Pamela, Defoe's Roxana, and Emulation Anxiety in Eighteenth-Century Britain," *Journal for Early Modern Cultural Studies* 14, no. 2 (2014): 51.
22. Christopher Flint, "The Anxiety of Affluence: Family and Class (Dis)order in *Pamela: Or, Virtue Rewarded,*" *Studies in English Literature 1500–1900* 29, no. 3 (Summer 1989): 501, 496.
23. Porter, *Enlightenment*, 512.
24. Tim Stuart-Buttle, *From Moral Theology to Moral Philosophy: Cicero and Visions of Humanity from Locke to Hume* (Oxford: Oxford University Press, 2019), 62.
25. Soni, *Mourning Happiness*, 15.
26. Michael McKeon, *Origins of the English Novel* (Baltimore: Johns Hopkins University Press, 1987), 364.
27. It is noteworthy that Mr. B was previously the "Author of all [her] Miseries" (*I*, 118).
28. Richardson's conflation of marriage and happiness in *Pamela* is by no means universal in his fiction. In *Clarissa*, Anna Howe views marriage as an expedient solution, a means by which women can achieve comfort and security. Nonetheless, Anna does not pretend that a legal union between the titular heroine and Lovelace will deliver on the emotional front, observing as she does that of "happiness, there is no saying" (1087).
29. Brian Michael Norton, *Fiction and the Philosophy of Happiness: Ethical Inquiries in the Age of Enlightenment* (Lewisburg, PA: Bucknell University Press, 2012), 40.
30. Alicia L. Kerfoot, "Virtuous Footwear: Pamela's Shoe Heel and Cinderilla's 'Little Glass Slipper,'" *Eighteenth-Century Fiction* 31, no. 2 (2019): 347.
31. Carol Houlihan Flynn, *Samuel Richardson: A Man of Letters* (Princeton, NJ: Princeton University Press, 1982), 167.
32. Batchelor, *Dress, Distress and Desire*, 511.
33. Raymond F. Hilliard, "*Pamela*: Autonomy, Subordination, and the 'State of Childhood,'" *Studies in Philology* 83, no. 2 (Spring 1986): 214.
34. Flint, "The Anxiety of Affluence," 506.

35. Rebecca S. Davies notes Mr. B's surveillance and control, delineating Pamela's untenable situation in which her body serves "as a site of conflict between the roles of wife and mother." Rebecca S. Davies, "The Maternal Contradiction: Representing the Fictional Mother in Richardson's *Pamela II* (1741)," *Journal for Eighteenth-Century Studies* 33, no. 3 (September 2010): 391.
36. See Sarah Abramowicz, "English Child Custody Law, 1660–1839: The Origins of Judicial Intervention in Paternal Custody," *Columbia Law Review* 99, no. 5 (June 1999): 1344–1392.
37. Barr, "Richardson's *Sir Charles Grandison*," 407.
38. Schellenberg, *The Conversational Circle*, 78.
39. Hutcheson, *An Inquiry into the Origin of Our Ideas of Beauty and Virtue*, 138.
40. Schellenberg, *The Conversational Circle*, 83.
41. See Claudia L. Johnson, *Jane Austen: Women, Politics and the Novel* (Chicago: University of Chicago Press, 1990), esp. chap. 4, "*Pride and Prejudice* and the Pursuit of Happiness."
42. Johnson, *Jane Austen*, 80.

4

CONCEPTUAL RICHARDSON

Amelia Dale

It is a common—perhaps tired—trope in literature classrooms to compare the burgeoning print culture of the eighteenth century with the contemporary digital moment. Scholars in eighteenth-century studies look at the past through the lens of the post-digital present, an age that casts anew a reader's relation to print and page. In our time among screens, a book no longer is just a body of paper and text but has a digital, coded materiality. Contemporary criticism and its treatment of the book, such as Christina Lupton's account of the spatiality and directionality of the codex in *Reading and the Making of Time in the Eighteenth Century* (2018), is informed by a moment when e-readers are ordinary rather than fresh, when the workings of the codex book machine have become more apparent now that it is no longer the default technology through which readers read text.[1]

A similar motivation drives this chapter's examination of two contemporary, conceptually minded reworkings of Richardson: Nicholas D. Nace's *catch-words* (2017) and Trisha Low's *The Compleat Purge* (2013). I read them not as interesting examples of *Clarissa* and *Pamela*'s afterlives (though they are that too) but as a means of thinking through the implications of bringing two different moments in media history together. Specifically, what does it mean to look at a moment of post-print in a post-digital age? The term "post-digital," to quote the media theorist Florian Cramer, is "a term that sucks but is useful."[2] "Post-digital," for Kim Cascone, refers to a state in which the disruption brought upon by digital information technology has already occurred, in other words a postrevolutionary period of the digital information age, or as Cramer puts it, "the state of affairs after the initial upheaval caused by the computerization and global digital networking of communication."[3] "Digital" here is used as it is colloquially understood, a reference to the screens, technology, networks that are now globally pervasive. We are exhausted with these technologies, but we cannot escape them. They are familiar. Cramer states that "the term 'post-digital' can be used to describe either a contemporary disenchantment with digital information systems and media gadgets, or a period in which our fascination with these systems and gadgets has become historical."[4] So, like "postcolonialism," post-digital does not suggest that the "digital" is over, but rather indicates a continuation of digital culture that is also beyond or past a first point of disruption.

POST-PRINT

I offer the term "post-print" as an analogous term to "post-digital." "Post-print" attempts to describe a period of post-print revolution, where the familiarity with printed objects and the culture of handing them, buying, lending and reading them that comes with print culture is familiar but no longer fresh; the presence of print is not only ubiquitous but mundane in its familiarity. I use, then, the term not to describe a transformation in print technology, as N. Katherine Hayles does, but rather to identify, through the "post," a disenchantment and familiarity with print media.[5] When Sarah Fielding and Jane Collier say in *The Cry: A New Dramatic Fable* (1754), "Yet stories and novels have flowed in such abundance for these last ten years, that we would wish, if possible, to strike a little out of a road already so much beaten," they take the proliferation of printed prose as a given before venturing into experimentation with familiar forms.[6]

Samuel Richardson's work as a printer, as well as a novelist, is steeped in a congruent exhaustion. Keith Maslen's painstaking tracking of Richardson's use of printer's ornaments notes that though they became less fashionable as the century progressed, Richardson was reluctant to give up using them.[7] As a result, the book objects Richardson prints look back to an earlier age of print culture still in living memory, appropriate for the books he printed like volume 1 of Charlotte Lennox's *The Female Quixote* (1752), featuring a heroine with an anachronistic relation to literary fashion, or a novel like *Clarissa*, which, as Thomas Keymer asserts, seems to mark an "exhaustion" of the epistolary form.[8] All this suggests a need to historicize an exhaustion of media. It is not unusual to feel a sense of nostalgia for a slightly earlier moment in media history. As Justin Clemens puts it, "It is very common for people to think that they live in times of dissolution and decay."[9] However, I posit that there are specific parallels that we can draw between post-digital and post-print media exhaustion.

"Poetry is dead, print is dead, long live both," writes Brian Reed in his account of twenty-first-century "Avant-Garde" poetics.[10] Recent movements in contemporary poetry respond to print's death and afterlife in a time of familiarity and disillusionment with screens and digital texts. Conceptual writing, appropriately for a post-digital movement, is self-consciously belated, using the technique of the Duchampian readymade a hundred years after it was already ready made: subordinating the material object to the idea of its reuse and re-presentation.

Presentation is stressed, rather than representation; the content of conceptual writing becomes subordinated to the concept and the material form of the object that contains it. Kenneth Goldsmith, one of conceptual writing's most prominent proponents, repurposed conceptual artist Sol LeWitt's words—replacing "art" with "writing"—to state, "In conceptual writing the idea or concept is the most important aspect of the work. When an author uses a conceptual form of writing, it means that all of the planning and decisions are made beforehand and the execution is a perfunctory affair. The idea becomes a machine that makes the text."[11]

While Nace and Low's remediations of Richardson occur within printed book objects, they approach the printed book with a sense of it as a historical object that has, for a while now, been shadowed by the screen. Conceptual writing repurposes material sourced from elsewhere within the self-consciously obsolescent object of the printed book of poetry. As Goldsmith puts it, "Faced with an unprecedented amount of available digital text, writing needs to redefine itself to adapt to the new environment of textual abundance."[12] Conceptualist citational writing responds directly to the saturation of text via digital media. Writing as textual recycling is a direct answer to the age of the online archive and the copy-and-paste tool.

Versions of this kind of writing, what Marjorie Perloff terms the "poetics of 'unoriginality,'" have a long history, extending beyond, if now notorious through, Goldsmith's claims for unoriginal writing, and the necessarily smaller, and more geographically, temporally, and culturally specific grouping of conceptual writers that have been associated with him.[13] They can be identified in mid-eighteenth-century post-print. Vanessa Place and Robert Fitterman's manifesto *Notes on Conceptualisms* (2009) and Craig Dworkin and Goldsmith's anthology *Against Expression* (2011) both take examples from literary history in their formulation of "unoriginal" writing.[14] Place and Fitterman cite the passage from *Tristram Shandy* (1759–1767) that proclaims:

> Tell me, ye learned, shall we for ever be adding so much to the bulk—so little to the *stock*?
>
> Shall we for ever make new books, as apothecaries make new mixtures, by pouring only out of one vessel into another?
>
> Are we for ever to be twisting, and untwisting the same rope? for ever in the same track–for ever at the same pace?
>
> Shall we be destined to the days of eternity, on holy-days, as well as working-days, to be shewing the *relicks of learning*, as monks do the relicks of their saints—without working one—one single miracle with them?[15]

This impassioned pronouncement against plagiarism takes the proliferation of books and their unoriginality as a given. Textual recycling is a staple of eighteenth-century and early modern texts. Here, recycling is used to make a point about recycling, this paragraph itself repurposing Robert Burton's *Anatomy of Melancholy.*[16] Yet the "joke" is visible only to those in the know, who can identify Burton in Sterne. What is interesting for conceptual writers is not simply that textual recycling occurs but the way it is framed, how the reworked text might subordinate the words themselves to ideas surrounding originality and plagiarism.

Certainly, Sterne is the eighteenth-century author with the most obvious connections to conceptual writing. Exhibitions and projects by the Laurence Sterne Trust have incorporated work by North American poets who have been associated with conceptualism, such as Dworkin, Christian Bök, Kim Rosenfield, Jen Bervin, and Derek Beaulieu.[17] Dworkin's *Chapter XXIV—The Missing Chapter* (2013) takes a conceptual experiment by Sterne—the omission of a chapter—as a starting point for a chapbook.[18] However, Sterne is not the only eighteenth-century European source material for citational poetics: take Susan Howe's "writing through" of Jonathan Swift's *A Journal to Stella* in *The Liberties* (1980), M. NourbeSe Philip's *Zong!* (2008), an epic response to the documents surrounding the Zong massacre, or Bella Li's collagistic repurposing of the journals of Jean-François de Galaup, comte de Lapérouse in *Argosy* (2017).[19] This chapter explores what contemporary citational poetry does with Richardsonian epistolarity in order to examine how digital exhaustion uses and reuses an eighteenth-century exhaustion with print.

CATCH-WORDS

Nicholas D. Nace's book *catch-words* (2017) was published with the English small press, information as material. The very name of the publisher evokes the concerns of conceptual writing, while its website pronounces it as a publisher of writers "who use extant material—selecting it and reframing it to generate new meanings—and who, in doing so, disrupt the existing order of things."[20] Nace's book reprints, lineated as if poetry, all the catchwords of *Clarissa*. A catchword is a feature of eighteenth-century print: a word printed at the bottom of the page and then repeated as the first word in the next. It aided binders in assembling gatherings in the correct order, and printers in their imposition of forme, and in their anticipation of subsequent pages.[21] A section from volume 6 of *catch-words* reads,

> by
> My
> of
> Living
> helpless.
> Say,
> LETTER
> to

till
of
with
quest
coach
have
Mrs.[22]

This is a bare-bones rendition of *Clarissa*'s voluminous narrative that starkly gestures, in its minimalism, toward the proportions of the novel. Its procedure captures the concerns of the plot: confinement, epistolarity, sexual paranoia, and exertions of power. The collection and transcription of catchwords produces resonant combinations of different images, "quest / coach," accidental rhymes, "by / my," and poignant collocations like "Living / helpless" and "LETTER / to / till."[23]

Nace, himself a scholar of eighteenth-century literature working in Hampden-Sydney College in Virginia, has written on intersections between the eighteenth-century novel and conceptual writing.[24] Book history, descriptive bibliography, and novel criticism collide in *catch-words*. Helen Williams, Peter de Voogd, and Christopher Fanning have argued for closely reading Sterne's catchwords in *Tristram Shandy*, with Williams questioning the widespread assumption "that the catchword is a paratext without semantic potential."[25] Nace demands in *catch-words* that we pay similar attention to Richardson's; forcing the reader to read them as poetry.

The preoccupation with the machinery of print in *catch-words* is evident in its own objecthood. It is a product of a small press, rather a mass-produced item, which brings it closer to the hand-press production and smaller print run of mid-eighteenth-century novels. Nace's book is not the only production of information as material to make this connection. Dworkin, Simon Morris, and Nick Thurston's polemical essay on do-it-yourself publishing, *Do or DIY* (2012), cites Sterne as a reference point in radical small-press publishing, with Sterne himself featuring prominently on the cover of the booklet.[26] As for *catch-words*, the typeface evokes eighteenth-century print, something underscored in the copyright page, which announces with unexpected discursivity that the production of *catch-words* is consciously steeped in book history: "The text of this book is set in Caslon, an old-style typeface modeled on seventeenth-century Dutch baroque types and named after the English printer William Caslon (1692–1766), who cut the original Caslon type in 1725. This contemporary digital version was designed by Carol Twombly for Adobe in 1989."[27] A digitally printed but small-press book-object comments on the media and design history that shapes its own construction. It is simultaneously steeped in the post-digital procedures of both conceptualism and contemporary book production and in earlier modes of print.

In its final pages, *catch-words* subordinates itself to the physical procedures of its own composition, turning its procedure in on itself, until all content is exhausted. It itself has catchwords, and the "[Second Voice]" sequence lineates all the catchwords (so far) contained within *catch-words* itself.[28] The "[Third Voice]" then takes up the catchwords from the "[Second Voice]" section, its content shaped by how the structure and pagination of *catch-words* separates out different volumes of *Clarissa*:

VOL-
VOL-
VOL-
VOL-
VOL-
VOL-
[ ][29]

The empty square brackets mark the absence of a catchword on this, the last page of the poem. The book ends with what appears to be, on one hand, a radically abbreviated contents page, or, on the other, a minimalist poem. Here *catch-words* looks to the poem/musical analogy, as expressed in the book's blurb: "The process repeats in the manner of a musical catch until, finally, all 883,716 of Richardson's words are gone." Like many long experimental poems, a musical analogy serves a structuring function.[30] Nace draws on multiple connotations of "catch" to produce a work for, or of, three voices. This musical turn itself evokes Richardson, who interpolated a musical score in the text of *Clarissa*.[31] Janine Barchas argues that this inclusion of a score is an allusion to "the materiality of bookmaking."[32] For the first three editions of *Clarissa*, the musical score unfolds to larger than twice the size of any other of the novel's pages, disrupting "established textual boundaries, physically extending the textual space of the novel outward past the established margins of the text."[33] In *catch-words*, the presence of musical forms does the opposite, producing instead erasure and a paring back that points toward and eventually involves the deletion of all words, even as it introduces multiple voices.

For Barchas, not only is Richardson's score an "experiment" in graphic design, it also anticipates Sterne's writing through how it violates "a novel-reader's expectations by incorporating a familiar cultural artifact into the novel."[34] In this respect *catch-words* also mirrors *Clarissa*. Whereas *Clarissa* incorporates a score into a novel, *catch-words* brings into a book of poetry words on the eighteenth-century novel page that appears to exist for the manufacture of the book rather than for the novel reader's pleasure. A work of conceptual writing, *catch-words* incorporates into the printed book of poetry textual content that is unexpected but also familiar.

A potential counterpart to *Clarissa*'s fold-out score is a pamphlet enclosed within *catch-words*, "DIRECTIONS FOR READING" (figure 4.1). It offers, like

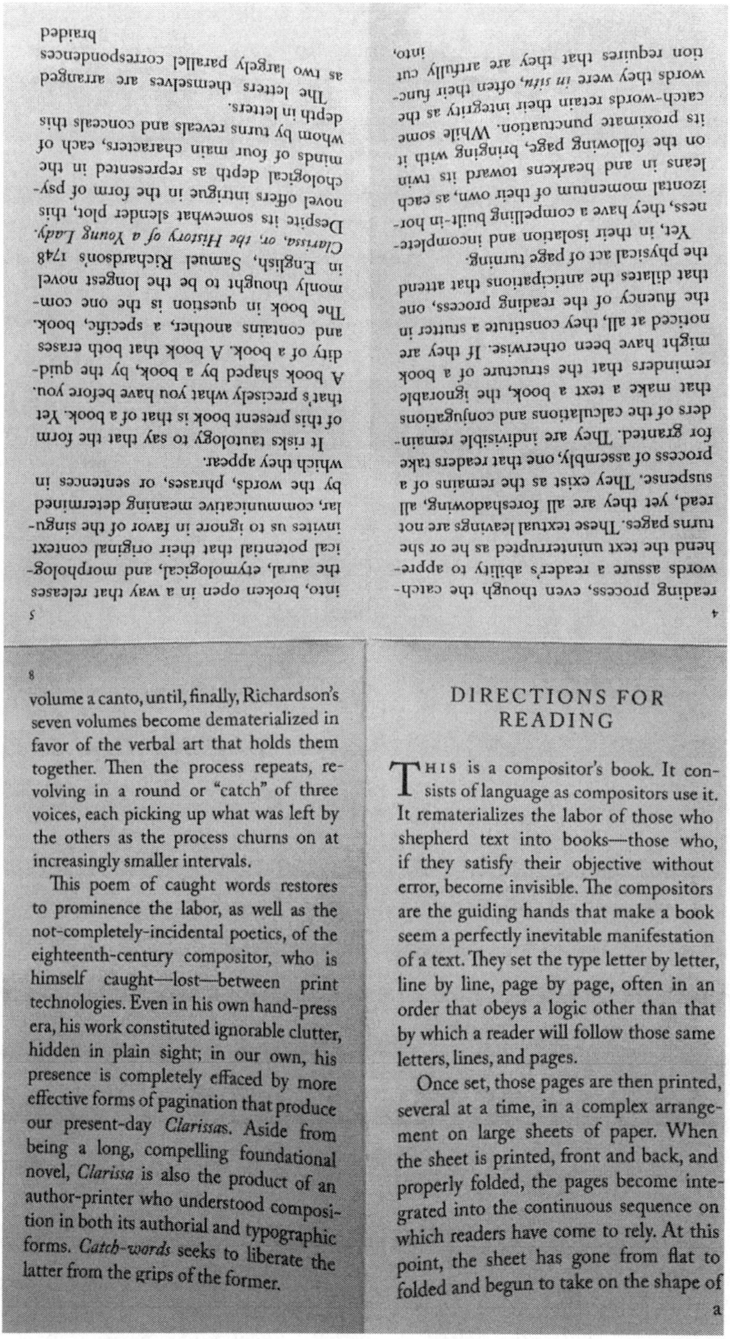

DIRECTIONS FOR READING

THIS is a compositor's book. It consists of language as compositors use it. It rematerializes the labor of those who shepherd text into books—those who, if they satisfy their objective without error, become invisible. The compositors are the guiding hands that make a book seem a perfectly inevitable manifestation of a text. They set the type letter by letter, line by line, page by page, often in an order that obeys a logic other than that by which a reader will follow those same letters, lines, and pages.

Once set, those pages are then printed, several at a time, in a complex arrangement on large sheets of paper. When the sheet is printed, front and back, and properly folded, the pages become integrated into the continuous sequence on which readers have come to rely. At this point, the sheet has gone from flat to folded and begun to take on the shape of

a

4

reading process, even though the catch-words assure a reader's ability to apprehend the text uninterrupted as he or she turns pages. These textual leavings are not read, yet they are all foreshadowing, all suspense. They exist as the remains of a process of assembly, one that readers take for granted. They are indivisible remainders of the calculations and conjugations that make a text a book, the ignorable reminders that the structure of a book might have been otherwise. If they are noticed at all, they constitute a stutter in the fluency of the reading process, one that dilates the anticipations that attend the physical act of page turning.

Yet, in their isolation and incompleteness, they have a compelling built-in horizontal momentum of their own, as each leans in and hearkens toward its twin on the following page, bringing with it its proximate punctuation. While some catch-words retain their integrity as the words they were *in situ*, often their function requires that they are artfully cut

into,

5

into, broken open in a way that releases the aural, etymological, and morphological potential that their original context invites us to ignore in favor of the singular, communicative meaning determined by the words, phrases, or sentences in which they appear.

It risks tautology to say that the form of this present book is that of a book. Yet that's precisely what you have before you. A book shaped by a book, by the quiddity of a book. A book that both erases and contains another, a specific, book. The book in question is the one commonly thought to be the longest novel in English, Samuel Richardson's 1748 *Clarissa, or, the History of a Young Lady*. Despite its somewhat slender plot, this novel offers intrigue in the form of psychological depth as represented in the minds of four main characters, each of whom by turns reveals and conceals this depth in letters.

The letters themselves are arranged as two largely parallel correspondences

braided

8

volume a canto, until, finally, Richardson's seven volumes become dematerialized in favor of the verbal art that holds them together. Then the process repeats, revolving in a round or "catch" of three voices, each picking up what was left by the others as the process churns on at increasingly smaller intervals.

This poem of caught words restores to prominence the labor, as well as the not-completely-incidental poetics, of the eighteenth-century compositor, who is himself caught—lost—between print technologies. Even in his own hand-press era, his work constituted ignorable clutter, hidden in plain sight; in our own, his presence is completely effaced by more effective forms of pagination that produce our present-day *Clarissas*. Aside from being a long, compelling foundational novel, *Clarissa* is also the product of an author-printer who understood composition in both its authorial and typographic forms. *Catch-words* seeks to liberate the latter from the grips of the former.

Figure 4.1. Nicolas Nace, "DIRECTIONS FOR READING," in *catch-words* (York, UK: information as material, 2018).

Richardson's footnotes to *Clarissa*'s second edition, authorial directions for the reader's interpretation. Here, Nace claims *catch-words* to be a work about printing as much as it is about *Clarissa*'s narrative. The material form of this pamphlet, in a typical conceptual maneuver, enacts its content. It forces the reader of the pamphlet to engage in the same process as an eighteenth-century compositor, working out which page follows what. Within the pamphlet, Nace pronounces, "The poem of caught words restores to prominence the labor, as well as the not-completely-incidental poetics, of the eighteenth-century compositor, who is himself caught—lost—between print technologies. . . . *Clarissa* is also the product of an author-printer who understood composition in both its authorial and typographic forms. *catch-words* seeks to liberate the latter from the grips of the former."[35] Nace's book is a creative echo of a strain of Richardsonian criticism that reassesses the importance of Richardson's work as a printer to his authorial practice, how Richardson's deep familiarity with the processes behind the construction of the printed book-object shapes his experiments with print in his novels.[36] At the same time *catch-words* could be characterized as a paradigmatic work of conceptual writing: a single procedure, a single source text, a book object that is about its own objecthood. Echoing Goldsmith (via LeWitt), Nace's role as an author of *catch-words* is that of someone who has come up with an idea that, machinelike, produces a book. Compared to conventional literary authorship Nace's role might appear administrative and even mechanical: the (catch)words are already written, Nace reframes them within a printed book. The phrase "liberation of typography from authorship" points to how in *catch-words* Nace, as much as Richardson, might be a printer-author rather than author-printer.

THE COMPLEAT PURGE

A completely different reinterpretation of Richardsonian authorship is offered by Trisha Low in *The Compleat Purge* (2013). Echoing the prefatory material of an epistolary novel, it claims itself to be, in its "DISCLAIMER" a "transcription of personal ephemera." *The Compleat Purge* collates an intensely, deliberately discomforting personal archive—wills, confessions, printouts of online chats—which merge uncannily with fragments from *Pamela*, Eliza Haywood's novel *Fantomina: or, Love in a Maze* (1725), and John Cleland's *Memoirs of a Woman of Pleasure* (1748–1749), among other sources.[37] *The Compleat Purge* is a work of self-avowedly post-conceptual writing. Low makes this clear in the afterword to *The Compleat Purge*, "4 REAL," and Low's self-identification as a post-conceptual writer is reiterated in Low's preface to Felix Bernstein's *Notes on Post-Conceptual Poetry* (2015).[38] Since the term "post-conceptual" is central to *The Compleat Purge*'s framing of its approach to confession and citation, it is necessary to attend to it. I would suggest post-conceptualism as most productively understood as a submovement within conceptualism: a particular generational community within conceptual writing at a particular place and time, rather than a global, asynchronous, and diffuse process that a term like post-digital evokes.[39] Hazel Smith characterizes both Low and Bernstein as reacting to experimental poetry's prior "turn against the personal."[40] Specifically, Low stresses the way conceptual procedures do not have to result in the subordination of authorial subjectivity that Nace potentially proffers in *catch-words*. Post-conceptualism draws on conceptual procedures and irony but ultimately works within a complexly confessional mode. Bernstein states, "Post-conceptual poets can assert authorship by deferring to the confessional/affective/lyrical (traditional, Romantic poetics) or the mechanical/conceptual or, better yet, they can mix both together (as a conceptual strategy or as a heartfelt impulse or some hybrid of both)."[41]

Low's work is saturated with an awareness of the long history of poetic splicings of the "confessional/affective" and the "mechanical/conceptual" and takes the eighteenth-century novel, and specifically Richardson, as a reference point for a mode of confessionalism that is simultaneously raw and violently self-aware. "I'm about to get really nerdy for a second, but I guess when I think about confessional writing, I think back to the eighteenth century," comments Low in a panel discussion published in *Guernica* (2013), and then cites *Pamela* directly.[42] Low's work combines confessionalism with conceptual practices via Richardsonian epistolarity. Christopher Flint tracks in *Pamela* the "gradual shift in Pamela's discourse from the personal, instinctive confessions to the self-conscious rhetoric of public address."[43] Even from the start Pamela's letters are, by virtue of being letters, written to be read. Given that Pamela's correspondence is simultaneously raw and textually knowing, it makes sense that experimental writers like Low, invested in a mode of confessionalism that is, on one hand, confrontational in its messy intimacy and, on the other, self-aware of its construction and mediation, return to Richardson's epistolary novels, where the writing and written "I" is ostentatiously inextricable from the material stuff of language.

The promotional blurb for *The Compleat Purge* on the Kenning Editions website is worth quoting in full:

> Trisha Low is just another feminist, confessional writer trying to find a good way to deal with all her literary dads. She siphons the remix culture of social media into the binge and purge cycle of an engrossing read, with the emphasis on gross. She reads the diaries of teenage girls, their blog comments and love letters; she dresses like one in performance then throws up fake blood on herself. She once surveyed the reactions of Catholic fathers to scripted confessionals she made regarding rough sex with men, secretly recorded the conversations, and transcribed the tapes. The results were anthologized by a major university press. Her first book, THE COMPLEAT PURGE, consists of the last will and testament of one Trisha

> Low, who seems to commit suicide annually; the legal documents accumulate into a coming of age story. It goes on to chronicle the sexual fantasies of indie rock fangirls, who may or may not be exorcising the effects of abuse through their blithe avatars (the guy from The Strokes, etc.). Then Trisha Low finds herself trapped in an 18th century romance novel in the most punishing way, but for whom—we're not really sure. "How is Poetry complicit in the urge to falsely 'heal' societal wounds into the silent fixity of It Gets Better? What better place to look than the teen girl, whose cut wrist is an abject fuck-you; whose cute Band-Aid and its artificial 'healing' is really just your sentimental fantasy."[44]

These "literary dads" could be Goldsmith and Charles Bernstein, Low's teachers at the University of Pennsylvania: Felix Bernstein (the son of Charles), with self-conscious oedipality, explicitly positions them as such in *Notes on Post-Conceptual Poetry.*[45] However, another "literary dad" is Samuel Richardson. "Dads" here is also colored by its placement near "Catholic fathers." Low read Catholic priests scripted confessionals about rough sex and published the transcripts as "Confessions" in Goldsmith and Dworkin's anthology *Against Expression* and as part of a pdf chapbook *Confessions [of a Variety]* (2010), which also contains enumerations of a body's scarification: insect bites, pimple scars, cigarette burns, working up to scars on cut wrists from knives.[46] The blurb's reference to Low's "Confessions" project therefore positions *The Compleat Purge* as part of Low's ongoing preoccupation with the complex, libidinal history of confession.

The spelling of "Compleat" in the title is both "styled after archaic amatory fiction" and redolent of the deliberate misspellings that populate online cultures, the "eat" in "Compleat" also evoking the obverse to the excretion of "Purge."[47] As with *Pamela*, a shifting, complex "I" is aligned with a collection of documents, documents that, the title implies, are themselves an abject, bodily emission, reminiscent of Low's performance practice of throwing up fake blood. To present these texts is potentially an act of self-harm, analogous to the purge of the disordered eater. Low's more recent book, *Socialist Realism* (2019), at one point seems to reflect, in the third person, on Low's earlier work, and the personal cost of authoring the visceral confessions of texts like *Confessions [of a Variety]* or *The Compleat Purge*, as well as what they demand of their audience: "No matter what anyone believes, only she knows that Art cannot save a whale but can ruin someone's personal life. She writes a poem that will ruin someone's personal life—her own. She knows what matters most is Art's deep and unparalleled ability to torture its audience. She wants to drag every reader's heart through the mud and hand their dissected guilt to them on a platter. She wants to push appropriate behavior to its edge."[48] Like *Confessions [of a Variety]*, *The Compleat Purge* can be read as a performance script, tied to the body, a score for the author's humiliation, to be performed by herself.

Low offers in *The Compleat Purge* a contemporary equivalent of *Pamela*'s account of a teenage girl's private life. In an interview with *Bookslut*, Low comments how its three-volume structure evokes Richardson's three major novels.[49] The first volume is an epistolary novel that takes the form of a collection of wills, each written by "Trisha Low" at 6, 13, 15, 17, 19, 20, 21, 23, and 24, and each will containing multiple letters addressed to her family and her friends, to significant people in "Trisha's" life at the time: "Dear Mom, Dad and Marsha, / I think it's quite a nice feeling to know that in a couple of hours I'll be gone."[50] Within the formal frameworks of the will, the suicide note, and the letter, Low writes an eviscerating bildungsroman and dies again and again. In the second volume, which I will discuss further below, eighteenth-century conduct book injunctions merge into scenes of rough and tender sex between male punk rock avatars. In the third volume, "DO YOU FEEL BETTER YET?," the narration switches to third person and the prose appears on the page as more novelistic. "TRISHA LOW" is a novel heroine who undergoes various rituals in order to forward a reconciliation with "CHIP E. MACGUFFIN." The text in this volume borrows material from Charles Edward Montague's collection of essays *Disenchantment* (1922), miscellaneous LiveJournal postings, and other sources, while the stylization of the names invokes eighteenth-century typography. Each volume involves scarred and sexual bodies repetitively colliding and collapsing within established textual forms.

PAMELA ON LIVEJOURNAL

Volume 2 is titled *The Sexual Assault of Trisha Low as Circulated by Love in a Maze, or, Virtue Rewarded*, a titular conflation of *Pamela* and Haywood's *Fantomina*, though *Fanny Hill* is also sampled throughout. The bulk of volume 2 is transcriptions of online conversations by "Trisha Low" and "Delly," as they chat on an online message board as male avatars named after punk rock musicians. They play out various sexual scenarios, punctuated by the metadata of each posting. The posting below, for instance, is headed by the metadata "anthony rossomando—The Dirty Pretty Things: January 16 2005, 19:15:03 UTC"; "anthony rossomando" or "Stan" is Trisha's avatar, "fabrizio moretti" or "Fab" is Delly's.[51] Two celebrities, Anthony Rossomando, of the band Dirty Pretty Things, and Fabrizio Moretti, from the Strokes, repeatedly and repetitively have sex, as well as negotiate their relationship and desire for each other.[52]

[[I'm going to have to go soon cause I'm on restricted internet time, so I don't know if I'm going to be able to finish this thread ☹]]
(watches you, smiling coyly as you bite finger)
(twists a curl around finger)
(moans as you pull zipper down)

(licks lips, watching you)
(closes eyes as you touch)
Mmph. Nice.[53]

This posting is a typical one of this volume, where above the role play, in square brackets, are conversations between Trisha and Delly as Trisha and Delly, a knowing transmutation of Richardsonian writing to the moment, adapted to a new—or what theories of "post-digital" reminds us is newly not-new—online space of their writing.

Mediation is central to Low's formulation of authorship; she asserts that "authorship is not pure and blank and dead like Kenny [Kenneth Goldsmith] and Vanessa [Place] have proposed—rather, it's ugly and useless, always mutated by whatever platform it chooses. Every platform, contains a struggle."[54] Tellingly, when Low talks about *Pamela*, she talks about it in terms of sex, space, and media. Low states that *Pamela* "is based on the idea of this servant girl going into this small space and writing this confessional story of what happened to her."[55] In an interview with *Bookslut*, Low explicitly connects the eroticization of the space where Pamela writes to that of Trisha and Delly's message board conversations: "The place where novels like *Pamela* were fantasizing about a woman's private life, and representing it as 'authentic' or 'true' take place, leading neither to the eroticization not of the woman, nor the fulfillment of any kind of voyeuristic desire, but the eroticization of the space itself, the space of the closet, much like the genre of the confessional, or maybe a virtual space like LiveJournal."[56] LiveJournal, a site sutured in the post-digital imaginary to the early days of the internet and feminized writing, becomes, for Low, analogous to the eighteenth-century closet.[57] LiveJournal in *The Compleat Purge* and Pamela's closet in *Pamela* both offer spaces for feminine, fraught confessions that are ultimately packaged within printed book-objects that refer insistently back to the differently mediated origins of their content, and make it clear that the agonized writing "I" is constituted by the space, materials, and textual forms that the same "I" uses to write.

The Compleat Purge emphatically presents the sex scenes between Stan and Fab as pieces of writing. As with the quote above, each physical act of Stan or Fab is bestowed a line. In Trisha-as-Stan's postings, each act is marked by parentheses, in Delly-as-Fab's, by asterisks. The scenes between the two avatars are framed by discussions in square brackets between Delly and Trisha, where they greet each other, inquire about each other's well-being, or wish each other goodnight. These conversations inhabit a different temporality to Stan and Fab's interactions. Though Stan and Fab's relationship is subject to some narrative development and jealous tension, there is also a pornographic stasis to their exchange of actions and acts, with their groans, moans, whispers, thrusts, and hard kisses repeated within and across multiple postings; Delly-as-Fab, for instance, again and again "*rolls hips*."[58]

Low's work can be connected to long-standing interpretations of Richardson that identify a pornographic aspect, or even core to *Pamela* and *Clarissa*.[59] John Frow positions Marquis de Sade and Pierre Choderlos de Laclos, as "rewriter[s] of Richardson's eroticized spectacle of virtue in distress."[60] While the title of the second volume of *The Compleat Purge*, *The Sexual Assault of Trisha Low as Circulated by Love in a Maze, or, Virtue Rewarded*, likewise suggests a narrative of eroticized distress, pornography here is preoccupied with a different subject, or rather object. Low rewrites Richardson via Haywood's *Fantomina*, and Haywood's description of sexual activity that is both impelled by female desire and episodically and fantastically embodied by multiple avatars.

To put this another way, *The Compleat Purge* is interested in post-Richardson pornography beyond that which centers on violations of virtue. The sexual assault of Trisha (and Delly) is demoted to their bracketed conversations, brief notes subordinated to what constitutes bulk of the material of volume 2, the sexual and romantic interactions of Stan and Fab: "[[the roofie thing—I mean, I don't think what happened to me is anywhere near as bad as some of the stories on here but it doesn't mean it didn't happen, right?]]."[61] If the narratives of *Pamela* and *Clarissa* gain their energy through vectors of sexual violence, and involve the presentation of—on some level—eroticized female distress, *The Compleat Purge* directs its libidinal gaze elsewhere. It contains the private writings of a young woman distressed, but she does not choose to write about the violence directed at her own body. Instead, Trisha and Delly write slash fiction (fan fiction focusing on a same-sex relationship).[62]

Since slash fan fiction is formulated around, for the most part, an erotic exchange between women, it exists within, Kristina Busse observes, as a "queer" space (as well as the narratives being usually about men having sex with men, or sometimes women with women).[63] The way the "slashing" of "Anthony Rossomando" and "Fabrizio Moretti" acts as a form of erotic exchange between the two women is something Trisha underlines, saying to Delly in their bracketed conversations, "You perv. I'm barely sixteen," and "you're only saying that because I'm kinda sorta having sex with you on the internet."[64] Delly replies, "i'm not having sex with you! we're just watching some other people we know really well have sex."[65] Ultimately, what takes place both encompasses and exceeds both these descriptions, with the developing—and occasionally rocky—relationship between Stan and Fab both mirroring Trisha and Delly's, and constituting and shaping the bulk of their interactions with each other. For instance when Delly-as-Fab refuses Trisha-as-Stan's proposition, "Well if you want to punish me . . . you want me on my knees, Master?," the awkwardness that results extends beyond the interactions between Fab and Stan to the bracketed conversation between Trisha and Delly, "[[owtch, girl, rejection much?]]," a hurt that Delly later apologizes for, "I'm sorry about that last time. Fab was just really not feeling it you know?"[66] The structure of this apology underlines the complex tangle of identity and desire that takes place in these libidinal exchanges: Delly apologizes but references Fab's "feeling," rather than her own. This volume's titular reference to Haywood's *Fantomina* suggests congruities between Trisha and Delly's slash writing practice and the sexual role-play of the nameless heroine of *Fantomina*, who meets her love interest in the guise of a sex worker, country maid, widow, and finally masked "Incognita." Low's reference to Haywood also situates slash fan fiction within the larger category and longer history of women's writing. Upsetting gendered distinctions between high art and fan fiction, *The Compleat Purge* presents m/m erotica written between women within a book of poetry.

Trisha and Delly's slash writing becomes a form of sexual therapy, the online message board a safe, or at least safer, space, "this is a girls only zone, apart from our boys anyway. no men. Safe space," states Delly, punctuating a postcoital moment between Fab and Stan.[67] However, like Pamela in *Pamela*, Trisha's space and opportunities for her writing are limited, surreptitious, dangerous, restricted, reflected in writing-to-the-moment interpolations, "[[fuck, delly, i gotta run, i think they're gonna cut me off in a minute, sorry sorry sorry]]."[68] She needs a private space, she needs a room, she writes in the school computer lab, or "sneaking round my dad's computer" wondering what her father would say if he read her writing, an instance that self-reflexively comments on *The Compleat Purge*'s own public printedness, and Low's own public commentary on her parents'—particularly her father's—issues around her "reckless confessionalism."[69]

CONCLUSION

Nace and Low's conceptually inflected rewritings of Richardson both respond to Richardson's relationship with print and the book object, while attending to different aspects of his authorial practice. Nace looks to the margins of the printed book-object to make the reader read *Clarissa* as it was read during the process of its manufacture and, through so doing, stresses Richardson's work as a printer. Low's rewriting grapples with sexual trauma, subjectivity, and epistolarity. *The Compleat Purge* is a post-digital reworking of the epistolary novel. Its intensely private communications from a teenage girl, with their early 2000s timestamp, look back to an earlier moment in online culture, while their appearance within what is ostensibly a book of (post-)conceptual poetry, reframes and remediates pornographic and (ostensibly) private teenage writing within a printed, literary object. Low's work elaborates upon Richardson's preoccupation with mediation, materiality, privacy, and confession and probes his use of eroticism. Richardson's novel-objects innovated with the printed page in part through looking backward to earlier moments in print and partly through looking forward to ongoing experiments with the limits of what can be incorporated in a literary printed object. Post-print meets post-digital. Together, *The Compleat Purge* and *catch-words* demonstrate Richardson's complex legacy in contemporary literary experiment and render *Pamela* and *Clarissa* newly strange.

NOTES

1. Christina Lupton, *Reading and the Making of Time in the Eighteenth Century* (Baltimore: Johns Hopkins University Press, 2018).
2. Florian Cramer, "What Is 'Post-Digital'?," *APRJA* 3, no. 1 (2014), 10–24: 3.
3. Kim Cascone, "The Aesthetics of Failure: 'Post-Digital' Tendencies in Contemporary Computer Music," *Computer Music Journal* 24, no. 4 (2000): 12–18; Cramer, "What Is 'Post-Digital'?," 5.
4. Cramer, "What Is 'Post-Digital'?," 3.
5. N. Katherine Hayles uses "postprint" to designate the post-2000s period after computational technology transformed the book printing industry. *Postprint: Books and Becoming Computational* (New York: Columbia University Press, 2021), 1–2.
6. Sarah Fielding and Jane Collier, *The Cry: A New Dramatic Fable*, ed. Carolyn Woodward (1754; Lexington: University Press of Kentucky, 2018), 39.
7. Keith Maslen, *Samuel Richardson of London, Printer: A Study of His Printing Based on Ornament Use and Business Accounts* (Christchurch, NZ: University of Otago, 2001), 47.
8. Thomas Keymer, "Epistolary Writing in the Long Eighteenth Century," in *A Companion to British Literature*, ed. Robert DeMaria Jr., Heesok Chang, and Samantha Zacher (Chichester, UK: John Wiley, 2014), 171.
9. Justin Clemens, "After After Finitude: An Afterword," in *Aesthetics After Finitude*, ed. Baylee Brits, Prudence Gibson, and Amy Ireland (Melbourne: re.press, 2016), 229.
10. Brian Reed, *Nobody's Business: Twenty-First Century Avant Garde Poetics* (Ithaca, NY: Cornell University Press, 2013), 3.
11. Kenneth Goldsmith, "Paragraphs on Conceptual Writing" (Poetry Foundation, May 10, 2007), https://www.poetryfoundation.org/harriet-books/2007/05/paragraphs-on-conceptual-writing/. Sol LeWitt's original text reads: "In conceptual art the idea of concept is the most important aspect of the work. When an artist uses a conceptual form of art, it means that all of the planning and decisions are made beforehand and the execution is a perfunctory affair. The idea becomes a machine that makes the art." "Paragraphs on Conceptual Art" (1967), in *Conceptual Art: A Critical Anthology*, ed. Alexander Alberro and Blake Stimson (Cambridge, MA: MIT Press, 1999), 12.
12. Kenneth Goldsmith, "Why Conceptual Writing? Why Now?," in *Against Expression: An Anthology of Conceptual Writing*, ed. Craig Dworkin and Kenneth Goldsmith (Evanston, IL: Northwestern University Press, 2011), xvii. Goldsmith's own work responds directly to this problem, for instance, in the installation *Printing Out the Internet* (2013).
13. Marjorie Perloff, *Unoriginal Genius: Poetry by Other Means in the New Century* (Chicago: University of Chicago Press, 2010), 12. It is beyond the remit of this chapter to review the long and global history of citational practices in poetry and text art and the various political ends they have been used for. For a sense of its pertinence beyond the North American context, see, for instance, the essay by Philippine writer and activist Angelo V. Suárez, "Appropriative Resistance," *Jacket2*, February 5, 2016, http://jacket2.org/article/appropriative-resistance/; the poetic and political use of document in Gomeroi author Alison Whittaker's collection *Blakwork* (Broome, Australia: Magabala Books, 2018); Narungga writer Natalie Harkin's *Dirty Words* (Melbourne: Cordite Books, 2015); and A. J. Carruthers, "Sound, Visual, Digital and Conceptual Poetries in Australia," in *The Cambridge Companion to Australian Poetry*, ed. Anne Vickery (Cambridge: Cambridge University Press, 2024), 348–349.
14. Dworkin and Goldsmith, *Against Expression*; Vanessa Place and Robert Fitterman, *Notes on Conceptualisms* (Brooklyn, NY: Ugly Duckling Presse, 2009).

15. Laurence Sterne, *Tristram Shandy: The Text*, ed. Melvyn New and Joan New (Gainesville: University Press of Florida, 1978), 1:408; Place and Fitterman, *Notes on Conceptualisms*, 46. Dworkin and Goldsmith cite Denis Diderot's citational reworking of *Tristram Shandy* in *Jacques le fataliste et son maître*. Dworkin and Goldsmith, *Against Expression*, 186.
16. This was pointed out by John Ferriar, *Illustrations of Sterne: With Other Essays and Verses*, 2nd ed., 2 vols. (London: T. Cadell and W. Davies, 1812), 1:94–95; see Melvyn New, "Introduction," in *The Life and Opinions of Tristram Shandy, Gentleman: The Notes*, by Melvyn New with Richard A. Davies and W. G. Day (Gainesville: University Press of Florida, 1984), 12–24; Robert Burton, *The Anatomy of Melancholy*, vol. 1, *Text*, ed. Thomas C. Faulkner, Nicolas K. Kiessling, and Rhonda L. Blair (Oxford: Clarendon Press, 1989), 10.
17. "Emblem of My Work," http://emblemofmywork169.blogspot.co.uk/, accessed November 9, 2019; "The Black Page," http://blackpage73.blogspot.com/, accessed November 9, 2019; "Paint Her to Your Own Mind," https://blankpage147.wordpress.com/, accessed November 9, 2019. I discuss some of these conceptually oriented reworkings of *Tristram Shandy*'s black pages in Amelia Dale, "Black Page: *Tristram Shandy* after Conceptualism," *The Shandean* 33 (2022): 101–131. See also Nicholas D. Nace, "Unprinted Matter: Conceptual Writing and *Tristram Shandy*'s 'Chasm of Ten Pages,'" *The Shandean* 24 (2013): 31–58; Amelia Dale, "Contemporary Art and the Eighteenth-Century Novel," in *The Edinburgh Companion to the Eighteenth-Century British Novel and the Arts*, ed. Jakub Lipski and M-C. Newbould (Edinburgh: Edinburgh University Press, 2024), 488–491.
18. Craig Dworkin, *Chapter XXIV—The Missing Chapter* (Salt Lake City, UT: Red Butte Press, 2013); Nace, "Unprinted Matter," 31–58.
19. Susan Howe, *The Liberties* (Guilford, CT: Loon Books, 1980); M. NourbeSe Philip, *Zong!* (Middletown, CT: Wesleyan University Press, 2008); Bella Li, *Argosy* (Sydney: Vagabond Press, 2017). Conceptually minded repurposing of eighteenth-century text is everywhere. Within art, Michael Cook reframes quotations from James Cook, William Dampier, and Lachlan Macquarie, among others, in the series *Civilised* (2012). In terms of performance, Sophie Seita takes it-narratives and works by Margaret Cavendish, Denis Diderot, and Bernard Le Bovier de Fontanelle as prompts for performance in *Les Bijoux Indiscrets, or, Paper Tigers* (first performed December 17, 2016, published by gauss pdf, 2017), and Felix Bernstein and Gabe Rubin likewise repurpose work of Marquis de Sade in their installation and performance *Folie à Deux* (2018). See also Dale, "Contemporary Art and the Eighteenth-Century Novel," 485–502.
20. Information as material, www.informationasmaterial.org/about/, accessed October 18, 2024.
21. "Catchwords," in *The Oxford Companion to the Book*, ed. Michael F. Suarez, S.J., and H. R. Woudhuysen (Oxford: Oxford University Press, 2010), 1:593.
22. Nicholas D. Nace, *catch-words* (York, UK: information as material, 2018), 90.
23. Nace, *catch-words*, 90.
24. Nace, "Unprinted Matter," 31–58. Nace has published on both contemporary poetry and poetics, and on the eighteenth-century novel. See for example, Charles Altieri and Nicholas D. Nace, eds., *The Fate of Difficulty in the Poetry of Our Time* (Evaston, IL: Northwestern University Press, 2018); Clorinda Donato and Nicholas D. Nace, eds., "*Fanny Hill* Now: Papers Occasioned by the 50th Anniversary of the 1966 Supreme Court Decision Allowing Publication of *Fanny Hill*," Special issue, *Eighteenth-Century Life* 43, no. 2 (2019).
25. Helen Williams, *Laurence Sterne and the Eighteenth-Century Book* (Cambridge: Cambridge University Press, 2021), 141; Peter de Voogd, "*Tristram Shandy* as Aesthetic Object," *Word and Image: A Journal of Verbal/Visual Enquiry* 4, no. 1 (1988): 383–392; Christopher Fanning, "'On Sterne's Page': Spatial Layout, Spatial Form, and Social Spaces in *Tristram Shandy*," *Eighteenth-Century Fiction* 10, no. 4 (1998): 444–445.
26. Craig Dworkin, Simon Morris, and Nick Thurston, *Do or DIY* (York, UK: information as material, 2012).
27. Nace, *catch-words*, 144.

28. Nace, *catch-words*, 127–141.
29. Nace, *catch-words*, 143.
30. For a description of contemporary experimental poetry looking to the musical analogy as a structuring device, see A. J. Carruthers, *Notational Experiments in North American Long Poems, 1961–2011: Stave Sightings* (Cham, Switzerland: Palgrave Macmillan, 2017), xxv–xxvi.
31. Samuel Richardson, *Clarissa, or the History of a Young Lady: Comprehending the Most Important Concerns of Private Life*, 9 vols. (London: Printed for S. Richardson, 1748), 2:50.
32. Janine Barchas, *Graphic Design, Print Culture, and the Eighteenth-Century Novel* (Cambridge: Cambridge University Press, 2003), 96.
33. Barchas, *Graphic Design*, 99.
34. Barchas, *Graphic Design*, 94.
35. Nicholas D. Nace, "Directions for Reading," in *catch-words*, 8.
36. For work on Richardson as printer and author, see, for instance, Christopher Flint, "The Material Book," in *Samuel Richardson in Context*, ed. Peter Sabor and Betty A. Schellenberg (Cambridge: Cambridge University Press, 2017), 119–127; Betty A. Schellenberg, "Authorship," in Sabor and Schellenberg, *Samuel Richardson in Context*, 102–104.
37. Trisha Low, *The Compleat Purge* (Chicago: Kenning Editions, 2013), 230.
38. Low, *The Compleat Purge*, 7; Trisha Low, "You Guys, We Need to Talk about Felix," in *Notes on Post-Conceptual Poetry*, by Felix Bernstein (Los Angeles: Insert Blanc Press, 2015), 9–13. *Notes on Post-Conceptual Poetry* can be read as a response to, and a reworking of, Place and Fitterman's *Notes on Conceptualisms*.
39. In this regard, the North American specificity of both Bernstein's list of post-conceptual writers and his "Brief Timeline" of post-conceptual writing is telling. Bernstein, *Notes on Post-Conceptual Poetry*, 22, 99–104.
40. Hazel Smith, "Experimental Confessionalism: The Personal Turn in American Post-Conceptual Poetry," *Cordite Poetry Review* 87 (2018): 1. For another account of Low's confessionalism, see Elina Siltanen, "Conceptual Confession: Asymmetrical Emotion in Writer-Reader Relations in Trisha Low's the *Compleat Purge*," *Journal of Modern Literature* 43, no. 4 (2020): 108–126.
41. Bernstein, *Notes on Post-Conceptual Poetry*, 25.
42. Trisha Low, Benjamin Anastas, and Agata Tuszynska, "Better Off Said," interview by Rachel Riederer, *Guernica*, June 3, 2013, https://www.guernicamag.com/better-off-said/.
43. Christopher Flint, "The Anxiety of Affluence: Family and Class (Dis)Order in *Pamela: Or, Virtue Rewarded*," *Studies in English Literature 1500–1900* 29, no. 3 (1989): 509.
44. Kenning Editions, https://www.kenningeditions.com/shop/the-compleat-purge/, accessed October 2, 2019.
45. "Have I, does this, align totally with the museum, with my father's name, with Kenny Goldsmith's name?" Bernstein, *Notes on Post-Conceptual Poetry*, 78. In an interview with *Bookslut*, Low calls Sigmund Freud "the original literary dad." Danielle Sherrod, "An Interview with Trisha Low," *Bookslut*, December 2013, http://www.bookslut.com/features/2013_12_020428.php/.
46. Trisha Low, "Confessions," in Dworkin and Goldsmith, *Against Expression*, 352–358; Trisha Low, *Confessions [of a Variety]* (Oakland: gauss pdf, 2010).
47. Sherrod, "An Interview with Trisha Low."
48. Trisha Low, *Socialist Realism* (Minneapolis: Coffee House Press, 2019), 11.
49. Sherrod, "An Interview with Trisha Low."
50. Low, *The Compleat Purge*, 19.
51. Low, *The Compleat Purge*, 145.
52. Low states, "I feel so bad for Anthony because everybody knows who Fab Moretti is and nobody knows who he is, and he was the one who I really had a crush on back in those days. I just saw him walking down the street the other day and it was one of those things where I thought, *I need to consciously veer away from you because I spent years writing pornography*

as you and it's really obvious and awkward to me right now." Sarah Gerard, "Trisha Low," *Bomb Magazine*, June 3, 2014, https://bombmagazine.org/articles/trisha-low/.

53. Low, *The Compleat Purge*, 145.
54. Trisha Low, "On Being-Hated: Conceptualism, the Mongrel Coalition, the House That Built Me," Open Space, May 20, 2015, https://openspace.sfmoma.org/2015/05/on-being-hated-conceptualism-the-mongrel-coalition-the-house-that-built-me/.
55. Low, Anastas, and Tuszynska, "Better Off Said."
56. Sherrod, "An Interview with Trisha Low."
57. For examples of the nostalgia through which the contemporary Anglophone internet regards LiveJournal, see Jack Morse, "Was LiveJournal Ever Actually Any Good? A Nostalgia-Tinged Investigation," Mashable, May 13, 2018, https://mashable.com/2018/05/13/was-livejournal-ever-good/; Lindsey Gates-Markel, "In Celebration of Old-School LiveJournal," The Toast, April 1, 2015, https://the-toast.net/2015/04/01/in-celebration-old-school-livejournal/.
58. Low, *The Compleat Purge*, 112, 113, 144, 171.
59. Kathleen Lubey both examines how eighteenth-century readers responded to *Pamela* as erotic writing and situates *Pamela* alongside contemporaneous erotic writing in *Excitable Imaginations: Eroticism and Reading in Britain, 1660–1760* (Lewisburg, PA: Bucknell University Press, 2012), 109–160. See also Lubey's account of "reading *Clarissa* pornographically": "Sexual Remembrance in *Clarissa*," *Eighteenth Century Fiction* 29, no. 2 (2016–2017): 175; John Frow, *Character and Person* (Oxford: Oxford University Press, 2014), 70.
60. Frow, *Character and Person*, 66–67.
61. Low, *The Compleat Purge*, 151.
62. Their writing could be further categorized as Real Person Fanfiction (RPF), Real Person Slash (RPS), and Band Slash, a subset of RPS involving members of a band. For further discussion see Kristina Busse, *Framing Fan Fiction: Literary and Social Practices in Fan Fiction Communities* (Iowa City: University of Iowa Press, 2017), 41–56.
63. Busse, *Framing Fan Fiction*, 13.
64. Low, *The Compleat Purge*, 163, 168.
65. Low, *The Compleat Purge*, 169.
66. Low, *The Compleat Purge*, 132–133, 160.
67. Low, *The Compleat Purge*, 179.
68. Low, *The Compleat Purge*, 148.
69. Low, *The Compleat Purge*, 178; Low, "On Being-Hated."

5

CLARISSA WITH SADE

Persecution and Plot after Richardson

Samuel Rowe

WAS SAMUEL RICHARDSON A SADIST? Such is the uncomfortable question posed by Mario Praz in his 1930 classic *The Romantic Agony*, which in its chapter on "the shadow of the divine Marquis" plots a course from Richardson to the Marquis de Sade and beyond to the decadent writers of the nineteenth century. For Praz, "the unctuous pietism of Richardson's novels succeeds in covering only in appearance their sensual, turbid background." Praz's Richardson is a perverse manipulator, subjecting readers to "the slow Calvary of pious Clarissa" ostensibly as a way of glorifying virtue, but actually in order to enjoy the show. An emblem of Puritan sexual hypocrisy, Richardson claims to delight in seeing virtue rewarded, but devotes much of his considerable talent to depicting virtuous women captured, humiliated, and injured. In his continental admirers, and particularly in Sade, this pretense falls away: "His moralizing reveals itself fully for what it was—namely, little more than a veneer—in his French imitators, who sought in the subject of the persecuted woman chiefly an excuse for situations of heightened sensuality."[1] Praz's account of Richardson, read almost a century later, is crude, and its sense of historical context shallow. It nevertheless raises questions that Richardson studies still confronts.

Much commentary on Richardson's fiction turns on the fact that the novels are devoted overwhelmingly to scenes of persecution and to questions about how to reconcile this fact with Richardson's place in the history of the novel and his controversial status as a protofeminist. And though recent scholarship on Richardson tends to view his influence as running primarily through the late eighteenth-century culture of sensibility, Praz is also correct to identify a "dark" Richardsonian lineage, running through 1790s gothic to Sade and beyond.[2] Richardson can almost be said to have two reception histories: sentimental and gothic, Austenian and Sadean. Praz failed to record, in fact, that Sade—the most notoriously violent libertine novelist of the eighteenth century—was a professed admirer of Richardson's narrative art. Here, I suggest that this strange affinity of

Sade and sadists for Richardson can be understood in narratological terms, as an effect of Richardson's innovations in the actantial structure of narrative. In Richardson's most influential fiction, the desire and activity that propel narrative are lodged not in the protagonist but in the libertine villain. The experiment of putting Richardson alongside Sade, among other things, contributes in a small way to Margaret Cohen and Carolyn Dever's call to attend to the "literary channel" between France and Britain and to develop a binational account of the rise of the novel.[3]

This chapter has two aims. First, it records an odd episode in Richardson's reception history: the Marquis de Sade's championing of Richardson, and especially *Clarissa*, as a model for fiction. Second, it suggests that Sade's comments about Richardson contain a deep insight into the latter's narrative technique. Building on James Fowler's account of the affinities between Richardson and the continental *roman libertin*, I document Sade's consistent references to Richardson as he developed, refined, and defended his thought on the novel.[4] With Richardson for support, Sade championed a persecutory theory of fiction, advocating for the subjection of virtue to vice as a fundamental narrative principle. Sade's perverse and opportunistic use of the great British moralist hits a bit too close for comfort, not because it is entirely correct, but because it grasps something profound about Richardson's innovations in novelistic form. If Richardson was no sadist, his explosive success and broad influence can be understood in relation to his discovery of the generative capacity of villainy and villain characters in narrative. The resulting narrative pattern, which I call the "persecutory plot," takes the desires of persecutors rather than protagonists as its impetus. It is therefore subject to a fundamental ethical ambiguity that could not escape a reader like Sade.

I

The main statement of Sade's theory of fiction is "Idées sur le roman," an essay published as a preface to *Les crimes de l'amour* in 1800. This collection of novellas was Sade's ill-fated attempt to establish a respectable literary reputation after the decade in which *Justine* had scandalized the French scene. Sade had worked on the opening essay, however, through the late 1780s and 1790s, as attested by an early draft from 1788. It can therefore be taken as a document of the theory of fiction in the background of some of his notorious productions during the revolutionary decade: *Justine*, *Juliette*, *La Philosophie dans la boudoir*, and *Aline et Valcour*.

One of the central themes in Sade's theory of the novel is that vice must be allowed to triumph over virtue. In attempting to justify this narrative principle, he tacks between mimetic, didactic, and affective approaches. Among his arguments are that the triumph of virtue is not inevitable in life, and therefore should not be so in fiction; that representing vicious crimes is instructive in that it throws virtue into glorious contrast and encourages contemplation of providence; and that the sufferings of the virtuous are necessary to solicit sustained emotional involvement from the reader. Returning to the topic repeatedly over the course of his most productive period (between 1788 and 1800), Sade always finds his way back to the paramount importance of a central scenario: virtue laid low by indomitable forces of persecution. Certainly, Sade's theory of the novel can be viewed as an ingenious attempt at an intellectual alibi for his predilections. As Simone de Beauvoir put it, Sade's pontificating amounts to an attempt "to make of his psycho-physical destiny [that is, sadism] an ethical choice."[5] Read carefully, however, Sade's commentary also offers a set of startlingly acute insights into the architecture of eighteenth-century fiction. Stranger still, Sade understands the persecutory model of fiction he champions to be an English innovation—an innovation associated especially with Samuel Richardson, and very especially with *Clarissa*.

As early as the 1788 draft of his essay on the novel, Sade gives a prominent place to Richardson in the genealogy of his own fiction. In Sade's account, the Abbé Prévost—Richardson's most important French translator—is the great modernizer of the French novel precisely because he "opened up the French language to the masterpieces of the English novel." This English influence, to which Sade traces Prévost's mastery of plot and narrative tension, consists in abandoning the triumph of virtue as narrative's *summum bonum*: "Schooled by Fielding and Richardson, we learned from them that it is not always with virtue that we catch the reader's interest." In fact, striving for virtue's ascendance over vice produces at least two detrimental effects on narrative. First, it elevates morality over nature, since virtue's triumph, though certainly to be wished for, is "not a law of nature, merely a law by which we would like all men to abide." Second, it interferes with the reader's emotional absorption, since "when virtue triumphs, things being as they of necessity are, my tears dry up by themselves. But if, on the contrary, virtue, after being most sorely tested, finally succumbs to the repeated assaults of vice, then our hearts will not fail to be torn and, having brought us to the ultimate pitch of involvement, the author cannot fail to succeed."[6] Persecution, Sade seems to assume, procures more readerly "involvement" than its relief, and a plot in which vice gains the upper hand will therefore tend to be aesthetically stronger.

Sade's 1788 draft, then, sketches a multinational history of the eighteenth-century novel in which English novelists, via Prévost, introduce "the true form of the novel" by letting the forces of vice and persecution carry the day (*CL*, 305). Readers of mid-eighteenth-century British fiction may be taken aback by this account, since the predominant tendency of plot in Richardson and Fielding is, as with *Pamela*, to see "virtue rewarded." (The subtitle of Sade's *Justine*, in fact, is possibly a deliberate inversion of the Richardsonian motto: "good conduct well chastised.") The example foremost in Sade's mind, however, is not *Pamela* or *Tom Jones* but *Clarissa*: "if Richardson, after fifteen volumes, had brought matters to a chaste conclusion by converting Lovelace and allowing him to marry Clarissa quietly, then it might well be asked if readers . . . would have shed the precious tears which we could not prevent the author extracting from us" (*CL*, 306). Sade weighs the precise denouement for which Lady Bradshaigh, forty years earlier, had supplicated Richardson, and finds it wanting. The extraordinary affective charge of Richardson's novel, he holds, stems precisely from the fact that its plot does not attempt to save morality from nature. Implicitly, it seems, Sade views the truly "English" novel as tragedy and not comedy, *Clarissa* and not *Pamela*.

In the final, 1800 version of "Idées sur le roman," Sade retains this account of an English tradition of persecutory novels, with a new sense of the narrative role of persecutory characters:

> And then English novels, the vigorous works of Richardson and Fielding, appeared and taught the French that it is not by describing the tedious languors of love, or by reporting the dull conversation of cliques and coteries, that success is achieved in this genre, but by creating strong, manly characters who, as the playthings and victims of that effervescence of the heart otherwise known as love, show both the dangers and miseries it generates. It is the only way to achieve the progression of plot and the workings of passion which are so well depicted in English novels. (*CL*, 11)

This account—which, once again, seems far more apt for Richardson than for Fielding—identifies a certain kind of turbulent, destructive character as the central contribution of the English novel. Figures like Mr. B and Lovelace dominate the novels they inhabit while themselves dominated by—"jouets" or "playthings" of—their own desire. Accustomed as we are to reading Richardson as a proselyte of emergent bourgeois femininity and of the domestic sphere, identifying such figures as his central contribution to the novel is bound to sound strange. Sade might share, for example, Dr. Johnson's reported designation of *Clarissa* as "the first book in the world for the knowledge it displays of the human heart."[7] But in Sade's perverse reading, such knowledge is attained only at the cost of persecution, and only through the elevation of villain characters.

In a way that Sade does not fully explain, crucially, the "progression of plot" ("développements") characteristic of Richardson's fiction depends on such violent figures. In a closely following passage, he hints at what he might have in mind by describing Prévost's importance as a disseminator of Richardson's narrative innovations. Prévost, the "French Richardson," "possessed the art of devising intricate plots which keep the reader's interest over many volumes, by never allowing the main business to flag though it divides and diversifies." As Sade further explains, Prévost "handled . . . episodes so skillfully that the main plot always gained rather than lost by their number and complexity" (*CL*, 12).[8] A good plot, it seems, is constructed according to the principle of unity in diversity, with narrative complexity and digression permissible only insofar as they strengthen the "main plot" or "intrigue principale." All of this corresponds well with, for example, Anna Laetitia Barbauld's description of the plot of *Clarissa*: "we see her fate from afar, as it were through a long avenue, the gradual approach to which, without ever losing sight of the object, has more of simplicity and grandeur than the most cunning labyrinth that can be contrived by art."[9] For Barbauld, and perhaps for Sade, the strength and consistency of narrative tension in a novel like *Clarissa* is such that its immense length only adds to its power. Sade's troubling contribution is to attribute such narrative force to the novel's interest in domination and suffering, its willingness to give a Lovelace nearly unlimited power over a Clarissa.

When it became necessary to defend "Idées sur le roman," Sade further developed his account of persecution and readerly absorption. The essay's persecutory theory of the novel was immediately noticed by at least one moralistically inclined critic, Alexandre-Louis de Villeterque. In his review of *The Crimes of Love*, Villeterque expresses outrage at Sade's claim that seeing "virtue crushed by vice" heightens the pathetic power of fiction. Villeterque shrewdly conjectures that this maxim is "an attempt to give intellectual respectability to the infamous book which the author has disowned," namely *Justine* (*CL*, 311).

Sade quickly published an acid-tongued response to Villeterque that—in addition to strenuously and falsely denying authorship of *Justine*—defends his persecutory theory of fiction in terms of readerly absorption. The crushing of virtue by vice, Sade insists, is the most effective way of drawing the reader into narrative. Richardson, once again, is the exemplary novelist in this regard: when the vulgar critic "gets home and picks up his Richardson he will see to what extent the famous English novelist holds our attention by showing virtue under siege." Sade attributes Richardson's famed power to spellbind his readers, so often understood through the lens of the culture of sentiment, to his willingness to make his heroines suffer. More generally, "I claim that for a book to involve and hold the reader, vice must sometimes be shown to hold virtue hostage." The virtuous heroine, in Sade's account, remains the center of readerly identification: "Indeed, if virtue were not so fine a thing, would anyone weep for the misfortunes that befall it?" Yet the most effective way to glorify virtue, in Sade's perverse argument, is to besiege it (*CL*, 315–316). Roger Chartier has argued, in a reading of Denis Diderot's "Éloge de Richardson," that the eighteenth-century novel, and in particular Richardson's novels, inspired new readerly experiences of sustained, deep affective investment.[10] For Sade, the narrative technique best suited to producing such emotional absorption is the persecutory plot.

The Crimes of Love, in fact, contains a novella modeled directly on "English" persecutory fiction à la Richardson. "Miss Henriette Stralson, ou les effets du désespoir" opens the second volume of Sade's collection, under the heading "nouvelle anglaise." "Henriette Stralson" follows the pursuit of the eponymous heroine by the sinister libertine Lord Granwel ("the most debauched, wicked, cruel man in all England and unfortunately one of the richest" *CL*, 21). After an initial sighting in Ranelagh gardens, that classic scene of rakish predation, Granwel engages in an elaborate game of seduction, deception, and confinement, only to be thwarted by the steely resolve of the woman under his power. The novella reaches an inevitable tragic denouement with Henriette's confinement on Granwel's manorial estate, followed by the violent death of both persecuted and persecutor. In other words, "Henriette Stralson" is a Sadean rewriting of *Clarissa*. In his reply to Villeterque, Sade made the comparison quite explicit: "As in *Clarissa*, virtue succumbs, I concede, in 'Henrietta Stralson'" (*CL*, 317).

To encounter Sade's novella as a reader of Richardson is an unsettling experience: the themes and lines of narrative development are quite familiar, but the identification with the rakish persecutor is a bit too strong, and the shades of Gothicism a bit too dark. Granwel, at the outset of the tale, appears to explicitly echo Lovelace's rake's creed, which dismisses the aim of seduction in favor of the pleasures of pursuit: "For me, having a woman is satisfying only by reason of the trouble I am put to on the way. . . . The only way of avoiding the monotony of insipid triumphs is to achieve them by using only subterfuge" (*CL*, 22). Though Sade may be inspired by other sources in the libertine novel here, Lovelace repeatedly makes similar claims throughout *Clarissa*. The most unnerving correspondence with Richardson's novel, however, may come in the scenes in which Henriette supplicates her captor for mercy: "As she said these words she was on her knees at his Lordship's feet, with her arms raised to heaven. . . . Down her delicate cheeks coursed tears which, prompted by fear and desperation, fell on to her bare breasts which were many times whiter than alabaster" (*CL*, 34). It's as if Sade had taken the infamous "fire scene" in *Clarissa*—or any of the novel's other scenes of unavailing supplication—and rewritten it with a subtle shift of identification from victim to persecutor. As everywhere in Sade, cruelty is not far below the surface in this passage as it lingers on the fleshly manifestations of Henriette's suffering and powerlessness. But the truly disquieting element of such moments in Sade is how much they resemble scenes that recur continuously in Richardson, and among his imitators in the sentimental tradition. The tissue separating Richardsonian pathos from sadism, one worries at such moments, may be thin.

There is evidence, then, that Sade viewed Richardson as an important influence on his own fiction, and at moments even consciously emulated him. Specifically, Sade saw in Richardson a fellow traveler in his own project of building narratives around the persecution of virtue, and elevating persecutors to a central narrative status. The troubling irony here becomes acute if one turns from Sade's "lumière" writing to his "sombre," anonymous canon, and specifically to the preface to *Justine*, in which Sade offers an apologia for the narrative to follow. "The ascendency of Virtue over Vice, good rewarded and evil punished," for Sade, are tiresome and played-out narrative devices. Seeing virtue succumb to vice, in contrast, will help the reader develop a sense of providential resignation to the fate of the virtuous in a fallen world, and is therefore an ingenious way of glorifying virtue. As his imagined reader exclaims, "Oh, how these portraits of crime make me proud to love Virtue! How sublime she is when she weeps! How beautiful she is in misfortune!"[11] Here, as in his commentary on Richardson, Sade insists on the importance of persecution as a fundamental principle of narrative. The theory of fiction he uses to justify his ultraviolent libertine novel is hard to distinguish from that which he uses to praise *Clarissa*.

II

Sade's reading of Richardson, to be sure, is deeply distorted, and would certainly be unrecognizable to Richardson himself. Yet his fundamental claims are not easy to dispute. Richardson does indeed linger at infamous length over scenes of virtue in distress. As Sade claims, much of the emotional investment solicited by the novels does indeed result from seeing virtue crushed by vice, or close to it. The most famous example of such readerly response is, of course, Lady Bradshaigh's titanic epistolary efforts to secure a reprieve for Clarissa. And most crucially for my purposes, Sade is correct that Richardson's novels rely for their narrative "dévelopements" on what he calls their "strong, manly figures." As he suggests, it is Mr. B and Lovelace who, with their primordial threat of sexual danger and inexhaustible energy, set the stories of Pamela and Clarissa in motion. The centrality of persecution and persecutors to Richardson's signature emotional timbre and to his narrative technique has been important to multiple tendencies in the criticism. There is an ambivalent strain in feminist Richardson studies which, while acknowledging his unusual investment in women's experience, sees in his courtship plots subtle—if not quite Sadean—assertions of male power. Such assertions have led Paula Backscheider to question the degree to which Richardson was, as some accounts would have it, a "Friend to Women."[12] Rebecca Anne Barr, in her contribution to this volume, argues that even *Sir Charles Grandison*, that most protofeminist of Richardson's works, has hard limits on its attempt to imagine more equitable gender relations. In Grandison's professed virginity—a remarkable experiment in extending a characteristically female virtue to the other half of humanity—Barr sees a sly rearticulation of patriarchy. Vivasvan Soni, meanwhile, has developed a narratology of the "trial narrative" that takes *Pamela* as its central case. In the trial narrative, according to Soni, virtue must be proved in the fire of persecution in order to achieve happiness.[13] Reconsidering the novels through Sade's comments on them provides further support for this tradition of critical ambivalence. Sade's reading of Richardson, due to the accident of his perverse identification with the persecutors rather than the heroines, contains a deep insight in the narrative structure of the novels.

In each of Richardson's four novels, there is quite simply no plot without persecution. Mr. B and Lovelace, of course, are the central persecutory figures in the Richardson canon. Yet throughout each of the novels, we find minor persecutory figures introduced precisely where narrative begins to lose momentum. Since the first half of *Pamela* is dominated by Mr. B's lecherous machinations, his neutralization via marriage presents a problem for the second half of the novel. Thus the introduction of his sister Lady Davers, whose fierce anti-Pamelism sustains the persecutory drama after the marriage. If the notorious bedroom scenes are the traumatic peaks of the action in the novel's first half, the climax of the second half is a long, agonizing sequence in which Lady Davers confines Pamela in her own dining room. It is only with Lady Davers's gradual acceptance of Pamela as a sister-in-law that the novel's dramatic tension is fully resolved. When Mr. B discloses his affair with Sally Godfrey and recites the story of her seduction, furthermore, his status as a persecutory figure is reactivated, albeit at a second remove. In this way, the novel's famously extraneous (or apparently so) second volume, following the resolution of the marriage plot, in fact maintains the essential narrative dynamics of the first.

The persecutory function is weakest in *Pamela in her Exalted Condition*, the novel in which, as Pamela puts it, "my Persecutor [has] become my Protector."[14] It is perhaps for this reason that critics have tended to deride it, in Margaret Doody's phrase, as "the sequel that failed."[15] Yet even here the ghosts of persecutory figures reappear, and tend to do so just at the points at which the novel's baggy narrative is in danger of collapsing. In volume 3, Mr. B and Lady Davers periodically subject Pamela to a kind of raillery that seems to echo their former persecutory functions. Sir Simon Darnford and Sir Jacob Swynford, an aging rake and an oafish peer, transpose the persecutory energies formerly focused in Mr. B and Lady Davers into a satirical register, as if the sexual predation and class hostility of the first installment still lingered on after their comic neutralization. And in volume 4, which threatens to stagnate into a compilation of Pamela's theatrical reviews and pedagogical musings, the introduction of a new persecutory figure rouses narrative and provides the novel with its dramatic climax, insofar as it has one. Mr. B encounters a widowed countess at a masquerade and contemplates, without consummating, an affair; a young barrister named Mr. Turner (a rival for the Countess's affections) represents the situation to Pamela as blacker than it in fact is. Turner, a peripheral figure, is introduced only to supply the persecutory function in its pure form, as if a supplement were needed to assist the semi-reformed Mr. B in his former demonic office. Even in the most lugubrious of Richardson's fictions, persecutors periodically make an appearance, perturbing the quiescence of virtuous married life, and thus permitting narrative to occur. The very fact that these characters are minor, and introduced only episodically, points to their function as an engine of the persecutory plot.

Sir Charles Grandison famously replaces the central male persecutory figure with a paragon. The novel sets itself what E. Derek Taylor, in his contribution to this volume, calls the "Superman problem" by adopting a protagonist who is neither morally complex nor, unlike Richardson's heroines, physically or socially vulnerable. The Superman problem is not just a problem of characterization but also, clearly, presents challenges for the narrative pattern Richardson had established in *Pamela* and *Clarissa*. Richardson responds to the absence of a central persecutor with a proliferation of minor persecutory figures: Sir Hargrave Pollexfen and Greville, the two aggressive rakes who compete for the heroine Harriet Byron's attentions; Sir Thomas Grandison, Sir Charles's dissipated father who wastes the family fortune and refuses to allow the Grandison sisters to marry; Mrs. Jervois, the unstable mother of Sir Charles's ward Emily, Lady Olivia, a kind of female rake who aggressively pursues Sir Charles; and Lady Sforza, who sets the Porretta family against marrying their daughter Clementina to Sir Charles in order to facilitate devolution of the family property to her daughter Laurana. In two instances, the interventions of these persecutory figures are indispensable to narrative development. It is Harriet's kidnapping by Hargrave Pollexfen in the novel's first volume that leads to her acquaintance with the Grandison family, and thus to her reticent wooing by Sir Charles. Lady Sforza, meanwhile, exacerbates tensions within the Porretta family regarding Clementina's potential match with Sir Charles. Without her interventions, fewer impediments would stand in the way of the marriage, raising the possibility of a different resolution to the novel's central love triangle. In this way, the function of the central persecutory figure is distributed outward to a constellation of minor persecutors, each making their own modest contribution to the ongoing perturbation of the narrative world. If *Grandison* is Richardson's attempt to decouple masculinity from persecutory violence, this project requires the displacement of the persecutory function to other characters.

Persecution, then, is an indispensable condition of narrative in Richardson's fictions; virtuous as the heroines and heroes may be, eventfulness will never unfold from within the space of the protagonist. In *Clarissa*, this narrative logic is deployed with a rigor, virtuosity, and expansiveness that are probably unmatched in the history of the novel. As a causal agent and source of tragic harm, Lovelace is quite simply omnipresent in the narrative. Lovelace's first letter does not appear until two months into the action of the novel, after many torturous scenes of domestic drama among the Harlowes. Yet these agonized debates stem from sibling rivalry—Arabella's jealousy of Lovelace's preference for Clarissa over herself, and especially James's peremptory insistence that Clarissa marry the odious Solmes—that has its final cause in Lovelace. James is hostile to Lovelace due to events that occur well before the novel's first letter, a college rivalry culminating in a duel in which the former is humiliated. In the novel's first episodes, then, James acts as a kind of surrogate persecutor: the impossible demands he makes of Clarissa can be traced back to the figure of Lovelace.[16]

Furthermore, Lovelace's causal dominance of the narrative continues even after Clarissa is no longer directly under his power. As Sandra Macpherson has brilliantly demonstrated, Richardson insists on the causal links between Lovelace's actions and their unintended outcomes: Clarissa's imprisonment and eventual death.[17] If Lovelace does not intend for Mrs. Sinclair's prostitutes to have Clarissa arrested for debt, or for Clarissa to subsequently pine away, these outcomes nevertheless inexorably unfold from his acts. The causal filaments extending from Lovelace's pursuit of Clarissa thus penetrate the novel in its full breadth; Lovelace's desire is the engine of the entire narrative, from the first letter to the last. Readers of *Clarissa* have often noted with puzzlement the fact that the novel extends for over a hundred pages after its apparent tragic denouement, the death of the heroine. Less often noticed is the austere logic that determines the point at which it does end: the very same page as Lovelace's death.

These persecutory figures are the engines of plot throughout Richardson's canon. If such "strong, manly" (and, *pace* Sade, occasionally female) persecutory figures are "playthings and victims" of their own passions, they also produce plot by causing the victimization of others. Such victimization, as Richardson constructs his narratives, is necessary for something to happen. A Pamela, a Clarissa, a Harriet Byron, or a Charles Grandison, with their diffidence, their difficulty in even discovering what it is they want let alone pursuing it, is not made of the right stuff to produce a story. As Stephanie Hershinow has argued, Richardson's novels are seminal "fictions of inexperience": they are novels of adolescence without being bildungsromane, novels in which the protagonists are oddly impervious to changing in response to the world around them, let alone mastering it.[18] A Mr. B, a Lovelace, or a Hargrave Pollexfen, in contrast, display such vigor in pursuit of their desire as to continually produce plot—but only in the form of persecution. The resulting narrative form is more unusual than critics have acknowledged. The Richardsonian persecutory plot splits two narrative functions that generally coincide: the protagonist as locus of readerly identification and the protagonist as source of narrative-producing desire. The latter function is displaced to persecutory figures, or more simply, villains.

III

Some of Richardson's most self-conscious writing about his own narrative art, in fact, was prompted by the moral ambiguity of the persecutory plot. A plot deriving its impetus from the desires of a villain rather than a protagonist will, clearly, have a tendency toward tragic resolution. *Clarissa*, as Sade recognized, is a special case among Richardson's novels in that it allows this tendency to fully express itself. Richardson expended much energy defending his decision to end the novel with death for Clarissa and with Lovelace's failure to "expiate," even in death, his crime. After resisting the entreaties of Ladies Bradshaigh and Echlin for a happier outcome, he used the "Postscript" to *Clarissa* to lay out a theory of tragedy justifying his decision. As Richardson recognizes, the task at hand is to excuse his conduct in "deferring to extricate suffering virtue until it meets with its reward"—its reward, that is, in heaven.[19] This deferral, of course, is monumental in duration, leaving virtue at the mercy of vice for hundreds of agonizing pages.

The "Postscript," to justify Clarissa's suffering, mounts a critique of demands for "poetical justice," understood as distribution of earthly outcomes to characters according to their ethical merit. As Alex Hernandez has shown, part of what Richardson objects to in poetic justice is a transactional conception of providence, a proportional doling out of reward to the virtuous and punishment to the vicious.[20] James Smith, situating Richardson in a long history of tragic poetics, argues that there is a radical dimension to Richardson's embrace of tragedy. Reading *Clarissa* through Lacan's *Seminar VII*, Smith shows how its heroine is a kind of eighteenth-century Antigone, refusing to give way on her desire even as her actions place her outside of conventional morality.[21] Having read Sade reading Richardson, we can connect Richardson's theory of tragedy to his unusual, villain-driven narrative form. If Richardson champions tragedy for its ethical content—its refusal of worldly compensation for worldly harms, or of the social norms binding eighteenth-century women—he also does so because his method of plot development exerts an implicit pressure toward the triumph of vice over virtue. To evade this pressure, both *Pamela* and *Grandison* make use of plot elements not strictly probable: Mr. B's rapid conversion into the marrying sort, for example, or Sir Charles Grandison's serendipitous interception of Harriet Byron's kidnapping. In *Clarissa*, however—as Richardson puts it in the "Postscript"—"the catastrophe necessarily follows the natural progress of the story" (*C*, 1495).

Another important articulation of Richardson's thinking about tragedy is buried in the text of *Clarissa*, in a letter in which Belford compares Clarissa's plight to that of the heroine of Nicholas Rowe's *The Fair Penitent*. Richardson, in this letter, seems to betray sensitivity to the fact that the plot he is constructing requires the extraction of suffering from a virtuous protagonist.[22] Belford's commentary on Rowe's she-tragedy occurs after the climactic sexual assault, in the stretch of the novel in which he serves as an epistolary go-between between protagonist and persecutor. Belford, writing to Lovelace, explicitly frames Clarissa's experience within the parameters of tragic narrative: "What a fine subject for tragedy would the injuries of this lady, and her behaviour under them, both with regard to her implacable friends and to her persecutor, make! With a grand objection as to the moral, nevertheless; for here virtue is punished!" (*C*, 1205). Belford, along with Ladies Bradshaigh and Echlin, notices that the punishment of virtue introduces moral ambiguity into Richardson's novel along with pathos. Almost as if his character's criticism rings a bit too true, Richardson interrupts Belford with an editorial footnote chastising his poor understanding of tragedy: "Mr. Belford's objection that virtue ought not to suffer in a tragedy is not well considered . . . *The Orphan* . . . *Venice Preserved* . . . *Theodosius* . . . *King Lear* . . . *Othello* . . . Hamlet, to name no more, are instances that a tragedy could hardly be justly called a tragedy, if virtue did not temporarily suffer, and vice for a while triumph" (*C*, 1205). Richardson's language is oddly close here to that Sade would later use to argue for the importance of persecution in the novel: vice "triumphs," virtue "suffers" and "is punished." As both Belford and the editor acknowledge in continuation, virtue may even triumph over vice only in "the rewards of the HEREAFTER," as is indeed the case in *Clarissa*. Richardson summons Shakespearean and Restoration tragedies to insist that, in Sade's terms, "virtue crushed by vice" is a legitimate organizing principle of tragic narrative. (Interestingly, there is considerable overlap here with the tragic dramas Clarissa quotes in her famous, typographically experimental tenth "mad paper.")[23]

Belford continues with an invidious comparison between Rowe's *The Fair Penitent* and a hypothetical tragedy starring Clarissa. Calista, Rowe's titular heroine, is "a desiring luscious wench, and her penitence is nothing but rage, insolence, and scorn" (*C*, 1205). Having thrown herself away on the rake Lothario, her self-destructive penitence leads to the escalating series of deaths that cap the tragedy. The tragic forces at work in the play, for Belford, stem from Calista's character: "She has no virtue; is all pride; and her devil is as much *within* her as *without* her" (*C*, 1205). Lothario, one notices, is off the hook. This misogynist critique of Rowe's tragic heroine abuts praise for Clarissa, who, according to Belford, does nothing to initiate her own tragic entanglement with Lovelace, and who unlike Calista refrains from taking her own life. Clarissa, it seems, is a fairer penitent than Calista in that she has hardly anything to repent.

Though Belford seems to be offering a brief for feminine passivity here, he is also, crucially, rejecting a classical vision of tragedy in favor of the persecutory narrative with which he has just expressed discomfort. If Calista, as in Sophoclean or Shakespearean tragedy, brings about destruction through her own flaws, Clarissa is a tragic heroine insofar as she absorbs the damage caused by the flaws of others. In this sense, many of the comparisons that Richardson raises in his editorial footnote—Lear, Othello, Hamlet—do not seem quite apt. "The devil," for these tragic sufferers as for Rowe's Calista, is "within" as well as "without." For Clarissa, the devil is without exclusively, and tragedy consists in the way that the most untainted virtue cannot withstand forces hostile to it. Having raised doubts about a form of tragedy in which "virtue is punished," Belford seems to come around to the idea of Clarissa as an exemplary tragic sufferer insofar as she suffers without acting.

Belford concludes his letter by copying out one of Clarissa's "meditations," composed of passages from the Book of Job. As Jonathan Lamb and Thomas Keymer have shown, the figure of Job becomes central to Clarissa's self-understanding in the aftermath of the sexual assault.[24] In this context, however, the Job reference carries a whiff of self-exculpation on Richardson's part. Clarissa's Joban "meditation," addressed to her family, at moments describes her suffering at Lovelace's hands as a natural or existential condition: "*Why will ye* break a leaf driven to and fro? *Why will ye* pursue the dry stubble?" (*C*, 1207). Job's affliction, like that of a leaf before the wind, is ordained by God, which is to say that it might as well be authorless. Clarissa's, however, is the product of a strange kind of narrative which, as Belford exclaims, sets out to punish virtue. The turn to the Job theme here might be read as an evasion of the difficult question Belford has raised about the tragedy of Clarissa, which is also a question about the uses of suffering for narrative.

IV

Sade, in summary, made consistent reference to Richardson as a model in developing his own persecutory theory of the novel. According to Sade, plot should be driven by the noxious desires of villain characters, and narrative tension and affective absorption derived from the ensuing sufferings of virtuous protagonists. Sade's prescription appears to retroactively fit Richardson's fiction, especially *Clarissa*, rather well. We need not snicker, as Praz did, at this alignment between the father of sentimental fiction and the most vicious of the *romanciers libertins*. Rather, we can recognize Sade's championing of the Richardsonian persecutory plot as an insight granted by the happenstance of predilection. Sade glimpses—through a glass, darkly—an important aspect of Richardson's legacy: that much of his power and influence as a novelist stem from an innovative narrative formula, one that elevates the agency of persecutors at the expense of that of protagonists. As Richardson's influence diffused through the fiction of the next half century, this pattern would reappear again and again.

For writers in the sentimental tradition, from Richardson up to Austen, the drama of passive virtue assailed by active vice is a central narrative pattern. In novels like Goldsmith's *Vicar of Wakefield* and Burney's *Evelina*, the vicious rake is indispensable to narrative development. If such novels terminate with wish-fulfillment scenarios for protagonists—such as the impeccable marriages attained by Dr. Primrose's children and Evelina Anville—their narrative action is largely produced by the predatory exertions of rakes like Squire Thornhill and Clement Willoughby. In novels committed to the ideals of ingenuous feminine virtue and cozy middle-class domesticity, and to providing heroines and heroes who can serve as paragons for these ideals, a worldly, striving protagonist won't do. Rakes and other villains therefore play an indispensable role in the production and continuation of narrative. A particularly pure version of the persecutory plot appears in the Radcliffean gothic, the heroines of which wander through southern Europe assailed by a rotating cast of monks, banditti, and decadent aristocrats. The Lewisite variant maintains a similar scenario but shifts its focalization from vulnerable heroine to demonic persecutor. (Sade, naturally, preferred the latter; *CL*, 13.) Sade's picaresque *Justine*, in fact, might be read as a radicalization of the persecutory plot.[25] In *Justine*, the villain's role of tormenting the virtuous is extended to an entire social world and, in the novel's final gesture, to nature itself with Justine's demise via lightning bolt.

In each of these cases, villains are not a mere "impediment" to the desires of the protagonist, as the classic structuralist narratologies of Vladimir Propp and A. J. Greimas would have it.[26] Rather, villains take on the role of desiring subject abdicated by the protagonist. An important strain in the eighteenth-century novel, perhaps *the* important strain, fundamentally differs from the central nineteenth-century narrative patterns. The Richardsonian protagonist is not at home among Scott's mediocre heroes, Austen's whip-smart heroines, or Balzac's cynical social climbers. In each case, the fundamental movement of narrative, as in Propp's Russian folk tales, is a desiring subject's search for a desired object; for example, a blonde or brunette heroine, a marriage both respectable and emotionally fulfilling, clout among the Parisian *salons*. Clarissa is a different kind of protagonist. She is indeed remarkable for her refusal to desire anything, implacably choosing the "single life" over the narrative coherence of the marriage plot, declaring of Lovelace that "THIS man is not THE man," and in the end refusing even sustenance (*C*, 72).[27]

Sade's reading of his English forebear, then, offers a narratological approach to one of the eternally recurring themes of Richardson criticism: the passive triumph of the heroine. The Richardsonian heroine, it has long been recognized, is remarkable for her ability to say no. The extraordinary power of negation with which Richardson invests Pamela and Clarissa, their ability to refuse offers that can't be refused, is at the core of Richardsonian virtue. Richardson's inertial theory of virtue has been the subject of both pessimistic and optimistic readings in the feminist tradition, from Nancy Armstrong's seminal argument that *Pamela* embalms its heroine in the domestic sphere to Hannah Chaskin's recent contention that Pamela's diffidence marks her imperfect assimilation to the heteronormative marriage plot.[28] Wendy Lee has gone so far as to argue that the "insensibility" of the Richardsonian heroine inaugurates a tradition of impassivity in the novel culminating in Bartleby the scrivener.[29]

From a narratological perspective, the passivity of the heroine—or, more precisely, the confinement of her activity to a refusal to accede to others' actions—appears as a structural necessity. As the persecutory plot splits the identificatory and actantial functions of the protagonist, the heroine remains the locus of readerly identification but not the driving force behind narrative development. One way of understanding the appeal of this narrative form to someone like Richardson—a cautious advocate for certain forms of gender equality, but only within the bounds of the emerging bourgeois private sphere—is that it creates a field for feminine heroism without the necessity of representing feminine agency.

Sade's account of Richardson appeared at the dawn of the nineteenth century, and therefore, ironically, as the golden age of the persecutory plot in sentimental and gothic fiction began to wane. It may be no accident that the most important works of narrative theory centered around the protagonist's desire, in recent decades, have often been resolutely focused on the nineteenth-century novel. In a period when some of the most important work in the study of the eighteenth-century novel centered on a critique of psychology in the theory of character, critics like Franco Moretti and Alex Woloch were forging an account of the desiring protagonist as a creature of nineteenth-century liberalism.[30] In the nineteenth-century bildungsroman, according to this tradition, to be a protagonist is to be a competitive subject, striving within narrative's marketplace to capture the scarce resources of wealth, love, and social recognition. In the eighteenth century, when capitalism was newer and liberalism inchoate, we find a wide array of novelists drawn to a very different organization of narrative space, one in which the subject of insatiable desire can appear only outside the space of the protagonist. The restless striving that would later ground the liberal account of personhood, before its triumph, takes the form of a nightmare.

NOTES

1. Mario Praz, *The Romantic Agony*, trans. Angus Davidson (Cleveland: Meridian, 1956), 95–97.
2. There is a huge range of seminal work on the eighteenth-century culture of sensibility, much of it referred to in the volume's introduction. For some classic overviews, see Janet Todd, *Sensibility: An Introduction* (London: Methuen, 1986), and Markman Ellis, *The Politics of Sensibility: Race, Gender, and Commerce in the Sentimental Novel* (New York: Cambridge University Press, 1996). See also Katherine Binhammer's overview "Sentiment and Sensibility," in *Samuel Richardson in Context*, ed. Peter Sabor and Betty Schellenberg (Cambridge: Cambridge University Press, 2017), 288–295.
3. Margaret Cohen and Carolyn Dever, "Introduction," in *The Literary Channel: The International Invention of the Novel*, ed. Margaret Cohen and Carolyn Dever (Princeton, NJ: Princeton University Press, 2002), 1–34.
4. James Fowler, *The Libertine's Nemesis: The Prude in "Clarissa" and the* roman libertin (Cambridge: Legenda, 2011). Despite recognition of the lineage between Richardson and Sade in classic accounts like those of Praz and R. F. Brissenden, and despite a recent resurgence of interest in Sade's relationship to the eighteenth-century culture of sentiment, Sade's self-expressed debt to Richardson has never, to my knowledge, been fully explored. Brissenden, *Virtue in Distress: Studies in the Novel of Sentiment from Richardson to Sade* (London:

Macmillan, 1974); Kate Parker and Norbert Sclippa, eds., *Sade's Sensibilities* (Lewisburg, PA: Bucknell University Press, 2015).

5. Simone de Beauvoir, "Must We Burn Sade?," trans. Annette Michelson, in Marquis de Sade, *The 120 Days of Sodom and Other Writings*, trans. Austryn Wainhouse and Richard Seaver (New York: Grove Press, 1966), 4.
6. Marquis de Sade, *The Crimes of Love*, trans. David Coward (New York: Oxford University Press, 2005), 305–306. Hereafter cited in the text as *CL*.
7. "Recollections of Dr. Johnson by Miss Reynolds," in James Boswell, *The Life of Samuel Johnson, LL.D.*, ed. John Wilson Croker, vol. 2 (New York: Harper and Brothers, 1846), 491.
8. Sade later strongly recommends against the overuse of episodes in plotting novels, on the basis that they violate the kind of narrative unity he associates with Prévost and by extension Richardson (*CL*, 16).
9. Anna Laetitia Barbauld, "Life of Samuel Richardson, with Remarks on His Writings," in *The Correspondence of Samuel Richardson* (London: Richard Phillips, 1804), lxxxiii. On Barbauld's use of landscape metaphor to describe narrative, see Cynthia Wall, *Grammars of Approach: Landscape, Narrative, and the Linguistic Picturesque* (Chicago: University of Chicago Press, 2019), 40.
10. Roger Chartier, *Inscription and Erasure: Literature and Written Culture from the Eleventh to the Eighteenth Century*, trans. Arthur Goldhammer (Philadelphia: University of Pennsylvania Press, 2007), 105–125.
11. Marquis de Sade, *Justine, or the Misfortunes of Virtue*, trans. John Phillips (New York: Oxford University Press, 2012), 3–4.
12. Paula Backscheider, "The Rise of Gender as a Political Category," in *Revising Women: Eighteenth-Century "Women's Fiction" and Social Engagement*, ed. Paula Backscheider (Baltimore: Johns Hopkins University Press, 2000), 32. See also Helen Thompson, *Ingenuous Subjection: Compliance and Power in the Eighteenth-Century Domestic Novel* (Philadelphia: University of Pennsylvania Press, 2005), 87–123.
13. Vivasvan Soni, *Mourning Happiness: Narrative and the Politics of Modernity* (Ithaca, NY: Cornell University Press, 2010). For a distillation of the narratological portion of Soni's argument, see "Trials and Tragedies: The Literature of Unhappiness (A Model for Reading Narratives of Suffering)," *Comparative Literature* 59, no. 2 (2007): 119–139.
14. Samuel Richardson, *Pamela in Her Exalted Condition*, ed. Albert J. Rivero, vol. 3 of *The Cambridge Edition of the Works and Correspondence of Samuel Richardson*, ed. Thomas Keymer and Peter Sabor (New York: Cambridge University Press, 2012), 50.
15. Margaret Anne Doody, *A Natural Passion: A Study of the Novels of Samuel Richardson* (Oxford: Clarendon Press, 1974), 71.
16. Richardson confirms this reading in his correspondence with Aaron Hill, at whose suggestion he seems to have fleshed out the backstory involving James and Lovelace. Richardson to Hill, Wednesday, October 29, 1746, in *Correspondence with Aaron Hill and the Hill Family*, vol. 1 of *The Cambridge Edition of the Correspondence of Samuel Richardson*, ed. Christine Gerrard (Cambridge: Cambridge University Press, 2013), 223–229.
17. Sandra Macpherson, *Harm's Way: Tragic Responsibility and the Novel Form* (Baltimore: Johns Hopkins University Press, 2009), 57–97.
18. Stephanie Hershinow, *Born Yesterday: Inexperience and the Early Realist Novel* (Baltimore: Johns Hopkins University Press, 2019).
19. Samuel Richardson, *Clarissa, or, The History of a Young Lady*, ed. Angus Ross (New York: Penguin, 2004), 1495. Hereafter cited in the text as *C*.
20. Alex Eric Hernandez, "Tragedy and the Economics of Providence in Richardson's *Clarissa*," *Eighteenth-Century Fiction* 22, no. 4 (2010): 599–630.
21. James Smith, *Samuel Richardson and the Theory of Tragedy: "Clarissa"'s caesuras* (Manchester: Manchester University Press, 2016).
22. Praz, his ear tuned by Sade, seizes on this passage to demonstrate Richardson's hypocritical knack for persecuting virtue. *Romantic Agony*, 95.

23. See Smith, *Samuel Richardson and the Theory of Tragedy*, 68–90.
24. Jonathan Lamb, *The Rhetoric of Suffering: Reading the Book of Job in the Eighteenth Century* (Oxford: Clarendon Press, 1995), 226–247; Thomas Keymer, "Richardson's *Meditations*: Clarissa's *Grandison*," in *Samuel Richardson: Tercentenary Essays*, ed. Margaret Anne Doody and Peter Sabor (New York: Cambridge University Press, 1989), 89–109.
25. On *Justine*, the picaresque, and tort law, see Frances Ferguson, *Pornography, the Theory: What Utilitarianism Did to Action* (Chicago: University of Chicago Press, 2004), 57–74.
26. For a synthesis of the structuralist, "actantial" approach to fictional character, see Mieke Bal, *Narratology: Introduction to the Theory of Narrative*, 3rd ed. (Toronto: University of Toronto Press, 2009), 201–214.
27. On Clarissa's refusal of food, see Maud Ellman, *The Hunger Artists: Starving, Writing, and Imprisonment* (Cambridge, MA: Harvard University Press, 1993).
28. Nancy Armstrong, *Desire and Domestic Fiction: A Political History of the Novel* (New York: Oxford University Press, 1987); Hannah Chaskin, "'Precise, Perverse, Unreasonable': Queer Form and Genre Trouble in Richardson's *Pamela*," *Modern Philology* 117, no. 1 (2019): 70–90. On the theological dimensions of feminine passivity in Richardson, see Peggy Thompson, "Abuse and Atonement: The Passion of Clarissa Harlowe," in *Passion and Virtue: Essays on the Novels of Samuel Richardson*, ed. David Blewett (Toronto: University of Toronto Press, 2001), 152–169.
29. Wendy Anne Lee, *Failures of Feeling: Insensibility and the Novel* (Stanford, CA: Stanford University Press, 2019).
30. Franco Moretti, *The Way of the World: The Bildungsroman in European Culture* (New York: Verso, 1987); Alex Woloch, *The One vs. the Many: Minor Characters and the Space of the Protagonist in the Novel* (Princeton, NJ: Princeton University Press, 2003).

6

CLARISSA AND WHITE SUPREMACY

Race, Gender, and Erasure

Kerry Sinanan

By 1747, the year of *Clarissa*'s publication, Liverpool had overtaken Bristol as Britain's main slave trading port, with vessels making about fifty voyages a year to capture and enslave around 25,000 Africans annually.[1] These cities rivaled each other within the foremost slave-trading nation: between 1726 and 1750 Britain was transporting 554,042 enslaved people, more than any other European nation, and within the twenty-five-years after 1750 it would hugely surpass its nearest rival, Portugal, by more than 300,000 people, from across Africa, captured, enslaved, and shipped to the colonies.[2] Burgeoning Atlantic power and the arising network of global commerce is the historical context for *Clarissa*. The Harlowes, like the Bertrams in Jane Austen's *Mansfield Park* (1814), are new money garnered from this unprecedented economic boom: Clarissa's Uncle Anthony makes his money in sea trade, inevitably bound up with slavery and empire at this time, and their treatment of Clarissa is informed by their insatiable greed for more money, power, and social standing.[3] They embody British imperial desires of their time: domestic cities were booming with the profit of colonized territories and the Harlowes' aims share in a national spirit of commercial expansion and success. Domestic fictions are part of the imperial narrative.

In Clarissa's first letter of the novel, her introduction of Lovelace is within the economic terms of primogeniture: "Mr Lovelace has been introduced. . . . His birth, fortune in possession of a clear 2000 [pounds a year] as Lord M. had assured my uncle; presumptive heir to that nobleman's large estate." Lovelace is initially entertained to solidify the Harlowes' wealth with old money and land. Notwithstanding their subsequent rejection of him, these global economies will have a direct effect on Clarissa: her family becomes obsessed with ensuring her virtue and obedience because of her capacity to secure and transmit wealth. Clarissa's story generates the longest novel in the English language, in epistolary form, and a heroine who, despite her violation, comes to epitomize white female virtue as a "model" and "paragon," thus reversing the misogynistic norms of the day.[4] Placing the novel in the context of colonial trade and transatlantic slavery, this chapter investigates the unacknowledged relationship between Clarissa and the lives of the millions of enslaved women whose labor produced wealth for the Harlowes and their counterparts in reality. As I discuss, Clarissa's very victimhood at the hands of this voracious patriarchy is a powerful racialized and gendered weapon in colonial discourse that enables the material dispossession of enslaved women.

In discussing Clarissa and *Clarissa*, both character and novel, this chapter considers how we analyze what is fragmentary in literary form and how this works to construct gender and race in the long eighteenth century. More broadly I ask, what and who is given form, what and who is denied form, and how do we read both these presences and absences? Here I am invoking Christina Sharpe's *In the Wake: On Blackness and Being* (2016), which asks for new practices in order to undertake the work of keeping faith with the lost Black lives in the long history of the transatlantic slave trade and racial capitalism. Sharpe's call to undertake wake work is primarily for Black scholars whose lives are part of these pasts "not yet past."[5] But the call to center the lives of dispossessed enslaved women of transatlantic slavery comes also from the work of many others: Jenny Sharpe's *Ghosts of Slavery*, Jennifer Morgan's *Laboring Women* and *Reckoning with Slavery*, Marisa Fuentes's *Dispossessed Lives*, Saidiya Hartman's *Lose Your Mother*, Jessica Marie Johnson's *Wicked Flesh*, to name a few, collectively ask many of us to re-examine our disciplinary methodologies to find ways to narrate, remember, and bring out of the willful obscurity of the colonial archive, the lives and experiences of enslaved women without, as Hartman says, trying to "trespass the boundaries of the archive."[6] This chapter attempts that balance by showing that Clarissa herself has a powerful structural relationship to enslaved women that is mediated through literary form and layers of white symbolism and imagery: these literary devices are all the more effective for hiding that very relationship.

I come to *Clarissa* via the Black Atlantic.

FRAGMENTARY SELFHOOD, RACE, AND GENDER

In *Torrid Zones*, Felicity Nussbaum discusses how the "domestic monogamous Englishwoman, who personifies chaste maternal womanhood" is contrasted in colonial discourse with her other, "the African woman," who "was even less likely than the Englishwoman to speak for herself."[7] This absence becomes a matter for historical enquiry and requires approaching the colonial archive as a source of lies about Black women. Edward Long, for example, in his *History of Jamaica* states that "the women here are, in general, common prostitutes," and he accuses enslaved mothers of causing their own miscarriages through cold water bathing and practices he deems poor.[8] Long continues to compare Black women's reproductivity on Jamaican plantations to the productivity of estates, making a direct equivalence between children and hogsheads of sugar: "I will not deny that those Negroes breed the best, whose labour is least, or easiest. Thus the domestic Negroes have more children, in proportion, than those on penns; and the latter, than those who are employed on sugar-plantations."[9] The presence of Black women in the master's archive is always an act of violent silencing and objectification, in fact representing male desire and reversing the blame for the rapacious 1662 act, *Partus Sequitur Ventrem*, which legalized the mass rape of enslaved women by white masters and the enslavement of their children.[10] Black women are blamed for the crimes of their enslavers.

In her opening to *Dispossessed Lives*, Fuentes describes how she must "trace the distortions of enslaved women's lives inherent in the archive," and she asks, "how do we narrate the fleeting glimpses of enslaved subjects in the archives?"[11] This insistence on fragmentariness, on incompleteness, on absence, and yet the urgency to "say more" nevertheless, underlies my approach here.[12] In contrast to the silences and lies of slavery's archives, in which Black women are spoken of by their enslavers, we have Clarissa and her voluminous letters, her excesses, and her textual overproduction, what Rebecca Anne Barr calls "superabundance."[13] And yet *Clarissa*, of course, is often discussed in terms of fragments, scraps, and detritus: the novel, as soon as we consider its form, unravels, splinters, and falls apart from the illusion of wholeness that the textual material object itself suggests. *Clarissa* is famously over one million words gathered together and yet is clearly disjointed and incomplete in many ways. As R. F. Brissenden writes, "The seven volumes of the first edition of *Clarissa* were published in three instalments during the twelve months from December 1747 to December 1748."[14] The single-volume Penguin edition by Angus Ross, which most present-day readers are familiar with, is another layer of textual coherence given to an originally multivolumed novel. And, of course, the epistolary form is inherently fragmentary both textually and temporally as we read a plot that moves along via letters to and from the characters. Moreover, Thomas Keymer describes the questioning of an inherently unstable self that is ultimately referenced by the supposedly confessional epistolary mode: "Can it be assumed . . . that the conscious mind is ever in full possession of its own internal processes, or that the individual response to the evidence of his unconscious will involve no measure of resistance, suppression, or displacement?"[15] The point to be clear about, however, is that the fragmentariness that constitutes both Clarissa as character and *Clarissa* as novel, and the fragmentariness that characterizes the archives of enslaved women, and that formally constitutes their experiences, are not the same.

Thus, in her letter to Anna Howe written upon her final escape from Lovelace, while speaking in snatches, and narrating her fragmented selfhood, Clarissa can nevertheless write and tell her story to her friend and know that she will be believed and understood: "Once more have I escaped—but alas! *I*, my best self, have not escaped!—Oh! your poor Clarissa Harlowe! *You* also will hate me, I fear!—Yet you won't, when you know all!—But no more of myself! My *lost* self. . . . Forgive, oh! forgive my rambling. My peace is destroyed. My intellects are touched. And what flighty nonsense must you read, if now you will vouchsafe to correspond with me, as formerly!—."[16] As Barr argues so trenchantly, in *Clarissa* "textual fragments, like the novel itself, become objects whose worth is an index to, and product of, the individual."[17] A white readership makes a whole subject out of Clarissa's fragments: *this* is how such fragmentariness works for the white heroine. Her individualism, her subjectivity, and her narrative all cohere, in the end, to produce an intact woman in every sense of the word that Richardson wants us to consider important. Clarissa certainly offers a moral corrective to rapacious masculinity, exemplified by the enslaver, Captain Inkle of Richard Steele's *Spectator* no. 11 story, *but*, as a paragon of English Protestant morality, she would be completely in the service of a reformed manliness, chaste and monogamous in its imperial endeavors, were she to survive. Indeed, the extended ending of the novel, after Clarissa's death, works to expand and "supplement," as Anna puts it, Clarissa's superlative goodness.[18] In letter 529 Anna extensively details Clarissa's virtues and lifestyle, her sincerity, humility, her honesty, but also her Protestant practices that made her an "excellent ECONOMIST and HOUSEWIFE." Clarissa inculcates in herself the ideals of domestic womanhood, designed to support and complement an idealized masculinity: "Let our sex, therefore (she used to say) seek to make themselves mistresses of all that is excellent and incongruous to their sex in the *other*."[19] Notably, in this letter, Anna quotes Clarissa placing her own position as a virtuous woman within the great Chain of Being, an eighteenth-century taxonomic system that placed white people at the very top of a racially graded schema of all life: "In the great scale of beings, the lowest is as useful, and as much a link of the great chain, as the highest."[20] Even as she exercises an apparent humility regarding her own excellence, Clarissa transmits Enlightenment knowledge that is founded on whiteness and race, and signals her own position within her culture's hierarchy. Clarissa as paragon is white patriarchy's trophy, and her violation is wielded to prevent its most abject victims from access to white justice, white sympathy, and white rights.[21]

As Nicole Aljoe reminds us, in order to find ways to understand what enslaved people might have experienced and lived, we have to read "the mediated stories of enslavement that exist as fragments or 'textual splinters' in the archive."[22] This phrase, "textual splinters," is quoted from Jon Sensbach and describes the literary, textual form that stories and histories of enslaved women's lives take. What has not been put into form from the enslaved, what remains fragmentary and scattered shards, fragments, absences, gaps, is *not* to be compared to the collated, entire form of the novel which, however internally fragmented it might be, is nevertheless physically coherent. *Clarissa*'s fragmentariness is not at all like the scattered, mediated slivers of enslaved women's lives. White patriarchal colonial capitalism *requires* and *produces* white women and Black women distinctly in these textual formations. Clarissa is produced by settler-colonial/imperial British culture that requires her violation in order to gather a virtuous white community emboldened by their moral superiority. As Clarissa herself declares in a letter to Reverend Lewen after her rape, "It has not hurt my morals. . . . My will is unviolated."[23] Clarissa's relative vulnerability and fragmentation *consolidates* the imaginative role and moral power of the virtuous white woman of empire who is so central to the forces that destroyed and decimated millions of lives of enslaved women. Clarissa becomes, as Lovelace tells us, a metonymy for all women's virtue: the novel's act of narrative justice in favor of wronged women is indeed Richardson's agenda. Clarissa's violated virginity as idealized, white, virtuous femininity is a tool of white supremacy.

BLACK AND WHITE BINARIES IN *CLARISSA*

Overriding this fragmentariness, then, is the construction of Clarissa as an inherently whole imperial subject. Lovelace's frequent appellation of Clarissa as "my Gloriana" links her to the "virgin queen," Elizabeth I, who authorized the first slave trading voyage by John Hawkins.[24] Even in her plans to escape, Clarissa mentions several times going to the "English colonies," where she could be safe from her family, a trajectory and destination that is the opposite to a place of safety for Black women.[25] And symbolically, despite its oppositions and its proliferating pieces, *Clarissa* participates in the logic of colonial sameness in terms of whiteness, which is in fact constructed by hovering binarism. As Julie Park argues, the novel is constructed from many binary oppositions "inside and outside, absence and presence, self and other, abstract and material, public and private."[26] Crucially, throughout the novel white and black are put into various oppositions surrounding morality, intentions, sincerity, designs, and purpose: Lovelace compares Clarissa's family to "black angels" and "white" ones,[27] Anna considers that her investigations regarding Rosebud that make Lovelace out to be apparently "innocent," could be "a plot set on foot to wash a blackamoor white," Lovelace being the blackened figure in terms of race, as well as in terms of purpose.[28] Clarissa herself cannot account for Lovelace's chameleon-like character: "And tho' *black* seems to be his natural colour, yet has he taken great pains to make me think him nothing but *white*."[29]

While Park focuses on binaries more generally as central to the novel's production of fetish, I think of the binaries in *Clarissa* as constitutive of an embedded racialized, colonial discourse in the novel. As Homi Bhabha explains, these very binaries in colonial discourse ultimately aspire to "the horizon of holism": "The colonial signifier—neither one nor the other—is, however, an act of ambivalent signification literally splitting the difference between the binary oppositions or polarities through which we think cultural difference. It is in the enunciatory act of splitting that the colonial signifier creates its strategies of differentiation that produce an undecidability between contraries or oppositions."[30] The novel's binaries are a strategy of colonialism and part of the eighteenth century's expanding hegemonic power, even if—or especially because—they are never declared to be such. In this way white power appears to be the natural order.

Laura Doyle, Raymond Hilliard, and others have also noted the imperial, racialized binaries throughout *Clarissa*. In letter 31, Lovelace writes to Belford, detailing his motives for pursuing Clarissa when she seems to reject him, or as he tellingly puts it, "How then can she be so impenetrable?" Lovelace is clear that his pride is a prime motivation in ensuring that Clarissa does not prefer "such a wretch as Solmes" to him. And this leads him to express an intensive possessive jealousy: "That her indifference to me is not owing to the superior liking she has for *any* other man is what rivets my chains." This pride is swiftly racialized as Lovelace then casts himself as Othello: "Perdition catch my soul, but I do love her." Here, not only does Lovelace foreshadow that Clarissa is in mortal danger from his "love," but he entwines himself in a racialized discourse about excessive jealousy and revenge that assigns all these destructive qualities to Black men. Lovelace's sexual desire and his need to dominate and own Clarissa are now racialized. Crucially, he also entangles Clarissa in the narratives of *Othello* woven by Iago that created the illusion of Desdemona's deceit. Lovelace is now no longer only metaphorically blackening his ideals, but figuring himself as a physically Black man who might be duped by a white woman. This heightens the idea that Clarissa (as Desdemona) is the violated pure white woman, casting the blame on Black men figured as Othello-like in their extreme passions. The structural work of this comparative web is again to conceal the fact that it is white men who are violating enslaved women to benefit patriarchal capitalism, and Clarissa sits at the center as the wronged pure white woman.

Lovelace then continues to quote from Abraham Cowley's poem "Beauty" in *The Mistress* (1656):

> *Beauty*, thou wilde fantastick Ape,
> Who dost in ev'ry Country change thy shape!
> Here black, there brown, here tawny, and there white;
> Thou *Flatt'rer* which compli'st with every sight!
>   Thou *Babel* which confoundst the Ey
> With unintelligible *variety*!
>   Who hast no certain *What*, nor *Where*,
> But vary'st still, and dost thy self declare
> Inconstant, as thy *she-Possessors* are.[31]

The comparison of beauty to an ape is certainly a conceit that conjoins woman to the bestial, undertaking a taxonomical survey of different colors of women. But in his quoting of Cowley, Lovelace casts himself as having an imperial eye surveying this global range of women who are all "inconstant." Richardson's agenda is to remove Clarissa from this imputation of inconstancy and sexual availability and to assert her as a pure white woman even as she is possessively gazed upon. Natalie Zacek describes this process as part of settler-colonial logic; as "white women [were] placed on such a pedestal, black and mixed-race women both enslaved and free, had to assume the blame for all varieties of sexual immorality, to be denigrated universally as libidinous creatures whose innate depravity lured white men to fall into dissipation."[32] And of course part of Lovelace's stated purpose is to prove that Clarissa would indeed provide him with his own heirs should they be married. Purity becomes synonymous with whiteness, and both are conjoined in Clarissa.

When describing her to Belford after he has captured her, Lovelace's emphasis of Clarissa's whiteness reaches superlative heights:

> Her wax-like flesh (for, after all, flesh and blood I think she is!) by its delicacy and firmness, answers for the soundness of her health. Thou hast often heard me launch out in praise of her complexion. I never in my life beheld a skin so *illustriously* fair. The lily and the driven snow it is nonsense to talk of: her lawn and her laces one might indeed compare to those; but what a whited wall would a woman appear to be, who had a complexion which would justify such unnatural comparisons? But this lady is all glowing, all charming flesh and blood, yet so clear, that every meandring vein is to be seen in all the lovely parts of her which custom permits to be visible.[33]

Body, form, whiteness, and moral purity are all fused here, not just by Lovelace, but by the discourse throughout the novel. Because her skin is almost transparent, her desires and thoughts are legible and revealed as pure. And Clarissa is increasingly whitened as the plot progresses, her linens and lawns impossibly clean and white. When Belford visits her toward the end he describes her as "Dressed, as I told you before, in her virgin white. . . . One faded cheek rested upon the good woman's bosom, the kindly warmth of which had overspread it with a faint, but charming flush; the other paler and hollow, as if already iced over by death. Her hands white as the lily, with her meandering veins more transparently blue than ever I had seen even hers."[34] Even the inside of her black coffin is "lined with white satin"[35] from which will rise her "transparent white" angel form, as Lovelace describes it.[36] These two passages, one before Clarissa's rape and the other after it, clearly emphasize Richardson's point: Clarissa, as a white woman, is more pure *after*: she remains inviolable, rising above male violence in ways refused to Black women.

The degrees of Clarissa's whitening move her from the embodied temptress to the disembodied epitome of transcendent purity that becomes a trope for white women in the English novel. Thus, in the 1808 novel *The Woman of Colour*, Augustus Merton similarly asserts his reliance on hyperwhiteness as an index to female purity. Augustus is to marry Olivia, who is his cousin and the daughter of his uncle, Mr. Fairfield, an enslaver. Olivia's mother was Marcia, an enslaved woman owned by Fairfield, and according to her father's will, Olivia must marry Augustus and transfer her inheritance back to the white male line. Augustus describes his feeling upon seeing Olivia's dark "skin" as "disgust." Remembering his former wife, Angelina, who he believes to be dead, he continues, "*I* that had been used to contemplate a countenance, and a transparent skin of ivory, where Suckling's expression of 'even her body thought' might have aptly originated."[37] Olivia quickly impresses Augustus with a powerful sense of her moral superiority, but we never recover from his confession of revulsion at Olivia's nonwhiteness, nor from his insistence on white female skin as definitive of pure morality. Clarissa provides the blueprint for the fetishization of female whiteness, contrasted with the impurity of colonized women, in English fiction.

These binaries of race are never really resolved but repeatedly asserted, and the endless vacillations that characterize not just Lovelace but also Clarissa—her infamous ambivalence, which Tita Chico in *Designing Women* reads as part of Richardson's satire—therefore make a lot of sense if we read her as more than a product of, but also a *tool* of colonial discourse for which ambivalence is a central strategy of domination.[38] Clarissa, like the imperial power she is within, emphatically proffers principles of sincerity, steadfastness, and honesty as aspirational and discursive, rather than wholly achievable. As Anna repeatedly asserts, Clarissa is not able to fully acknowledge her own desires within domestic strictures: "it is no manner of argument that because you would not be in love, you are not," and Clarissa herself notes that she likes Lovelace more than she should early in the novel.[39] Her purity is constructed out of the ambivalence of her desire. These oppositions in play are vital to establishing the gendered binary central to the novel: "Innocence so triumphant: villainy so debased."[40] Thus Clarissa's virtuous suffering is not simply or only productive of her victimhood at the hands of patriarchy but is *also* a vital component and prop of that very patriarchy, white and imperial in its power.

Clarissa has more integrity *after* her violation, and thus Richardson's plot, especially the extended part after her death, consolidates Clarissa's violations and fragmentations. As Park states, "In Clarissa, we see a woman who becomes an icon for virtuous femininity, despite—and indeed, through—her disturbing need to validate her virtue by dying."[41] Lovelace emphasizes this when he realizes that on his last occasion of seeing Clarissa "her innocence [was] so triumphant over my premeditated guilt."[42] Crucially, though, Clarissa's consolidation is dependent on her class, which she herself notes in her final direct address to Lovelace: "I am a person though thus vilely betrayed, of rank and fortune."[43] And in Clarissa's threatening to take her own life should Lovelace attempt to violate her again, Richardson draws upon the substantial machinery of Western womanhood, epitomized by Dido and Lucretia, both founding figures for Pamela and Clarissa. Henry Fuseli's later paintings of both women capture the sense of transcendence and the phantasmagoric qualities ascribed to their almost disembodied femininity asserted by whiteness. Consolidated, racialized purity arises out of violated white womanhood.

CLARISSA AS WOMAN OF EMPIRE

This angelic icon of virtue, we have long known, is central to empire, and yet despite her enormous importance in English literary history, Clarissa herself is barely discussed in terms of her imperial function. Nussbaum has shown how the making of "domestic English womanhood" was central to imagining a "sexualized woman of empire."[44] In *The Limits of the Human*, Nussbaum extensively discusses how Thomas Southerne's staging of *Oronooko*'s Imoninda as white "has much to do with positing a white European femininity in opposition to the developing stereotypes of black womanhood . . . the color of complexion was an index to virtue by the eighteenth century."[45] In *Torrid Zones*, Nussbaum focuses on both volumes of *Pamela* in a discussion of how polygamy was figured in colonial discourse. Pamela herself, Nussbaum argues, becomes the virtuous case for "monogamy at home," it being understood that colonial masculinity would behave with voracious consumption abroad: "The Englishwoman is contained within the boundaries of marriage and nation, and her superiority is confirmed by her difference from the sexuality of empire's polygamous women."[46] Lovelace, we all know, has no intention of ever being monogamous but insists on testing Clarissa's virtue repeatedly and obsessively: "Libertines are nicer, if at all nice, than other men. They seldom meet with the stand of virtue in the women whom they attempt. And, by the frailty of those they have triumphed over, they judge of all the rest."[47] Female virtue is of course the necessity of primogeniture, which requires that domestic inheritance be consolidated while global empire expands. The first demands monogamy and female purity, and the latter the mass violation of enslaved and colonized women and the denial of them and their children the rights of "humans."

Clarissa, of course, does not want to be married at all, and she and Anna wish to be able to live together, outside of the business of marriage, but still as representatives of virtuous womanhood. Early in their correspondence Anna asserts, "How charmingly might you and I live together, and despise them all!"[48] The estate that Clarissa's grandfather has willed her gives her potential independence allowing the suggested, alternative plot via which Richardson can show that rational, moral women could be property inheritors and could share in the project of Britain alongside primogeniture, if allowed. This alternative social strand does not undermine patriarchal empire, but rather stabilizes and corrects it from its own worst excesses. Moreover, Clarissa's relationships with land and estates via colonialism give her a clear power that is invoked throughout the novel. After Clarissa is raped, Arabella says that the family wants her to "think of going to Pennsylvania, to reside there for some few years, till all is blown over." The Harlowes know a colonial family there, who might be Quakers or Anglicans: "Mr Hartley has a widow sister at Pennsylvania, with whom he will undertake you may board, and who is a sober, sensible, and well-read woman."[49] Charles II had granted the land renamed as Pennsylvania to Sir William Penn in lieu of a debt in 1681. The Hartley family would likely have used enslaved labor: "Despite Quaker opposition to slavery, about 4,000 slaves had been brought to Pennsylvania by 1730, most of them owned by English, Welsh, and Scotch-Irish colonists."[50] Clarissa agrees to go there if she does not die "within a month."[51] The English colonies, land stolen from Indigenous people and worked by enslaved Africans, are a place of refuge and putative moral sustenance for Clarissa.

I am therefore extending the dynamic that both Nussbaum and Nancy Armstrong detail to the kind of purity and virtue Clarissa embodies *outside* of marriage: Richardson in fact asserts an emphatic white female resistance to rape, and a model of pure female monogamy/virginity at the heart of empire that does not require marriage: "I am no wife of *this* man . . . I am not his wife. He has no authority over me."[52] Critics have written about the progression of virtue from *Pamela* to *Clarissa* culminating in *Sir Charles Grandison*, where moral ambivalence is expunged. In her chapter for this volume, Barr notes Sir Charles's chastity as prefiguring the pure man of empire that we see in *Jane Eyre*'s St. John Rivers. Such purity, with imperial dimensions, I argue, is also part of Clarissa's significance. Laura Doyle states that, prior to her trauma, "Clarissa embodies the Atlantic, Anglo-Protestant ideal in her will to transparency."[53] While Doyle reads Clarissa's trials as a critique of the forces she exists within, and that prevent her full embodiment of Protestant liberty, I read Clarissa's violation as *necessary* to that expression of a freedom that has settler-colonial dimensions.

As Doyle explains, Clarissa inherits her landed wealth, which goes back, "time immemorial," from her grandfather, but John her brother inherits "the new colonial wealth."[54] Doyle's reading of *Clarissa* and other novels in the context of Anglicanism forged in the Atlantic offers a vital global context to the heroine's story, and she names that James Harlowe's pursuit of old money is the product of the instability of burgeoning imperial economies. Doyle argues that Richardson exposes the unravelling of gendered Protestant liberty within an imperial context in his figuring of Clarissa's violation and her subsequent fragmentation: "Readers have found themselves 'undone' by this rape and its aftermath—powerfully moved as Clarissa's self temporarily splits wide open. In her post-rape incoherence, Richardson dramatizes the self, broken and scattered under liberty's centrifugal force."[55] However, the conclusion that Doyle reaches regarding Clarissa's fragmented subjectivity omits the heroine's whiteness and her position of power from within colonial culture. Doyle continues to read the fragmentation of Clarissa's selfhood and textual production after she has been raped as correlating "exactly with the ruinous, unanchoring experience of [enslaved people]," "here subsumed within the story of a pure, Anglo-Atlantic martyr."[56] The sea metaphors of Clarissa's Paper X, Doyle argues, specifically "resonated" with the experiences of the Middle Passage: Clarissa describes being pursued by "waves" and as having to "row the galley." While it is undoubtedly the case that Richardson is drawing on these metaphors from the Black Atlantic world, it is vital to read these appropriations as *central* to imperial power's necessary ambivalence and, I would argue, as literary figures that work to bolster, rather than fragment, whiteness. Doyle reads this intersection as "an Atlantic pattern" of "not just a shared imagery but a shared imaginary" between authors of "African and Anglo descent" that reveals a supposedly shared crisis, and with Clarissa, a kind of slavery in common between white and Black Atlantic subjects within modernity.[57] In contrast, I argue that this textual appropriation and representation in form within an epistolary novel is a colonial tactic of *Clarissa* and produces its heroine as the necessary white female victim who strategically obscures the real victims en masse of colonial apocalypse. While Doyle sees the Protestant will to transparency as under pressure and in crisis from the ravages of modernity, I read it as the formally strategic production of what Gerald Horne names "a Pan-European initiative," the "devastating whiteness project," "the elongated process whereby religion was supplanted by 'race' as the animating axis of society which reached its zenith in the Americas," a whiteness that is not sharing anything at all but will appropriate, extract, possess, and command.[58] Clarissa's fragments are not the fragments that M. NourbeSe Philip rearranges for her rendition of *Zong!* These are fragments that NourbeSe Philip must gather and rearrange from the colonial archive precisely because the enslaved victims of the Zong—flung overboard so that the shipping company could reclaim the insurance money on their human cargo—could *not* put their experience into form. Clarissa's fragments do indeed, as Doyle puts it, draw "emotional power from a disavowed slavery," but this disavowal marks not a *shared* crisis at all, but precisely the boundary of power that appropriates from the stolen and scattered lives of enslaved Africans forced to cross the Middle Passage.[59]

ENSLAVED WOMEN IN THE ARCHIVES

A crucial difference between Clarissa and enslaved women is that she is written out of a plot that might make her a mother and offered an emphatic moral inviolability, despite her physical violation, by Richardson, who is ultimately the patriarchal superintendent of plot, form, and character. In contrast, the Virginia law,

Partus Sequitur Ventrem, "that which is brought forth follows the belly," established white male "property rights rooted in maternal descent through the bodies of African women."[60] Black women's mass violation was the necessary "belly" of white empire.[61] The shards of the experiences of enslaved women may be read in the diaries of English enslaver Thomas Thistlewood, who went to Jamaica in 1748 and remained there until his death in 1786. He kept copious written accounts of his time as an overseer and as a slave master himself. Throughout these pages, enslaved women frequently appear, most often as victims of Thistlewood's sexual violence and severe physical discipline: what their lives and experiences were is hard to know through this archive. Hartman's words in "Venus in Two Acts" capture both the difficulty of looking for enslaved women in the archives and the fact that sexual violation characterizes their experience: "the stories that exist are not about them . . . the archive is a death sentence, a tomb, a display of the violated body, an inventory."[62] Hartman's use of the name Venus for enslaved women conveys their already captured sexuality as they were brought across the Middle Passage for consumption of their labor and reproduction.

Thistlewood arrived in Jamaica from England in need of work and left behind a considerable archive of over ten thousand pages. As Douglas Hall and Trevor Burnard show, Thistlewood details his everyday rape of enslaved women.[63] I also note that it is very hard to name the full range of sexual encounters that enslaved women had, given the dynamics of slavery. As Fuentes writes when discussing the sexual labor of enslaved women, "even as we search for 'in between' categories inhabiting space between rape and consent, we are in effect reinscribing the very terms that fundamentally fail to account for the sexual experiences of enslaved women."[64] Most of Thistlewood's recordings are with enslaved women laboring on the plantation he owns or manages and occur as interruptions of their ascribed work. In the Thistlewood archive, diary 3 begins on the Egypt Plantation, where he was overseer in 1752, and he notes the full list of enslaved people. Entry 39 in the inventory is Abba, 42 is Betty, 43 is Marina, and he notes their color and their size.[65] Aiming to trace Abba, bought as a child, through the multiple manuscript diaries requires enormous amounts of time and work: reading her fragments and shards in Thistlewood's difficult script is much harder than reading through *Clarissa*'s million words: and Abba, like all the women Thistlewood lists having sex with, makes no response through his pen. Abba was to work in the kitchen and is clearly part of Thistlewood's everyday life. In 1758, Wednesday, April 19, Thistlewood writes, "About 2 P.M. *Cum mea* Abba, *Sup Lect,* (*sed non bene*)." Hall notes that this is the first time Thistlewood violated "his own" as he usually lists sex with enslaved women owned by other masters. Reading this line feels like a rupture, a violence in the archive that remains only partially legible and that enacts a further violence on Abba as it records her rape. Thistlewood's "*mea*" in this sentence is terrifying: Abba is his property and has now been subject to the full violence of what that means for her life. Abba would go on to have children and to work for many years in Thistlewood's cookhouse. In methodological terms, and in other ways too, how much more difficult it is to sift through leaves and leaves of manuscripts in faded eighteenth-century script, to gather what has never been gathered, than to search for a quotation in *Clarissa*. How much more slender are these fragments, how much more violent. Thistlewood does not speculate on the thoughts or feelings of the enslaved women he violates regularly, noting his sexual activities in Latin, "*Cum*" before the name of multiple women over decades. As Hall and Burnard note, Thistlewood had a long, complex relationship with Phibbah, head of the cook room at the Egypt plantation, whom he called his "wife." A sample of extracts from Thistlewood's 1754 diary records a sequence of consecutive nights in February that note, "At night *Cum* Phibbah" but on the sixth night, "Phibbah kept away" but then returns again. Such fragments disclose an extremely limited account of what Phibbah's life was, and we cannot tell what she thought and felt. We note her presence, consider her actions, and see that she exercised some degree of will and independence, even within slavery's dynamics. As Fuentes notes in an essay that interrogates her own and others' methods for reading the archival silences of enslaved women, "As a historian I am required to work through archival limitations and epistemic violence as I attend to the lives and deaths of the enslaved in the seventeenth- and eighteenth-century Caribbean. My work has aimed to think about (enslaved) black women's lives and their gendered configurations through the violent system in which they were entrapped. How can their desires, thoughts, and concerns be represented when records conspired to obliterate their voices? The archive is a failure in this effort."[66] Every time Thistlewood names and records Abba, Phibbah, and other women in his diaries, their appearance is also a mark of their silencing and of their being outside white rights and white designations of morality.

In contrast to this, Lovelace is forced to record Clarissa's outright, absolute rejection of him after he has attacked her in their last meeting, and after which Clarissa escapes: "but I have my SENSES Lovelace: and from my heart I despise thee, thou very poor Lovelace."[67] Clarissa's words forge her virtue, and she is allowed to reject Lovelace's claims on her. As Terry Eagleton argues, for Clarissa, it is the "ideology of representation which characterizes Clarissa herself." "I always speak and write the sincere dictates of my heart."[68] Clarissa herself pursues what Eagleton terms "the transparent communication of morally useful meaning": this Puritan *transparency* of intention creates a holistic, virtuous self and cannot be divorced from the nearly transparent quality of Clarissa's body, which also mediates her virtue after her rape: "a majesty in her person and manner that is *natural* to her: but which then shone out in all its glory! . . . Such the glorious power of innocence exerted at that awful moment!"[69] I situate Clarissa as a white woman of empire in the much broader historical context outlined by Horne in *The Apocalypse of Settler*

Colonialism, in which he charts the making of whiteness out of the religious strife of sixteenth- and seventeenth-century Europe. For settler colonialism, "The stakes were so large—swathes of land taken illicitly from indigenes, to then be 'stocked' by enslaved Africans—and the ideology so suffused with lingering religious and accelerating racial bigotry that the victimized would ineluctably be numerous. Assuredly, 'whiteness' or 'race' was a more sturdy identity politics for implanting settler colonialism, than religion, which often served to split the settlers."[70] While Black women are not present in the novel, they are indexed by Clarissa herself, who could not exist, materially or symbolically, without her discursively constructed opposite.

Richardson may hide the structural link between Clarissa and her enslaved opposites, but his readers are invited to make Chain of Being links between an emphatically virtuous Clarissa, who remains pure despite her violation, and enslaved women. We can see these structures at work in William Blake's engraving for Stedman's published *Narrative of a five years expedition against the revolted Negroes of Surinam* (1790), depicting *Europe Supported by Africa and America*, which is a visual correlative to Lovelace's quotation from Cowley discussed above. This is the last of eighty plates that Joseph Johnson commissioned for the lengthy history/travelogue narrative that Stedman put together based on his notes and diaries while stationed in Suriname as a paid mercenary for the Dutch, to quash the Maroon rebels. Stedman frames this image with what sounds like a present-day colorblind appeal to shared humanity:

> Feeling reader, I will Close the Scene with an Emblematical Picture of *Europe* Supported by *Africa and America* Accompanied by an Ardent Wish that in the friendly manner as they are Represented they may henceforth & to all Eternity be the Prop of each other; I might have included *Asia* but this I omitted as having no Connection with the Present Narrative—we All only differ in the Colour but we are Certainly Created by the same hand & After the Same Mould thus if it has not pleas'd fortune to make us equal in Authority, let us at least use that Superiority With Moderation & not only Profes that Happiness which we have to bestow on our Superiors and Equals, but with Cheerfulness to the very Lowest of our dependants—[71]

It is very clear that as soon as Stedman attempts to abolish a biologically essentialist raced hierarchy based on skin color (we are all human) he immediately reinstates it through a structured racism that assigns women to their hierarchized position based on skin color—there is, after all, a "natural order": this is in effect racialized gender, clearly laid out for us. The Black and Indigenous women have slave bonds around their arms, are clearly propping up Europe, and are entwined by a rope vine that the white woman holds. She is central, they are to the side. The echoes of Botticelli's Venus are clear, but only the white figure is allowed the modesty of her hair covering her body. At the same time, all women are made for a consuming and appropriating white male gaze. Their gender renders them vulnerable, but the hierarchy under male imperialism is clear too: the women of color are making direct eye contact with the male viewer, while the white figure looks modestly down with a blush on her cheeks, so often the sign of female virtue. The women of color have no blushes. While supposedly being joined by gender, the women are separated by race, but womanness is mythically performed under this sign of whiteness. The image lays bare the entanglements of white femininity with racial capitalism, and Stedman's accompanying words make it clear that his print is an allegory for global empire. The white woman is the vessel of male primogeniture, which will transfer the profits and property generated by colonialism through white generations, forging global white ownership.

And *Clarissa* criticism tends to replicate these very dynamics by insisting on Clarissa's virtue, her resistance, and her victimization, as a female predicament that erases race. In her recent book, *Born Yesterday*, Stephanie Insley Hershinow joins with others who read the narrative form of *Clarissa* as moving away from realism rooted in empirically gleaned fact, to an "aspirational" truth that might be better than "the real world." Clarissa's "moral authority" is forged in her "isolation from experience." Such feminist insistences on Clarissa's morality as "based on ignorance and innocence" need also to name that it is the *white* woman who is produced as innocent and untouched and therefore moral.[72] The binary opposite of this is the overly (sexually) experienced, violated enslaved woman who may have no such escape from lived reality. The weaponization of innocent white womanhood in racial violence against Black people continues today in a hideous history from before Emmett Till, onward. In his last physical sighting of Clarissa, Lovelace's act of rape is morally nullified as he claims, "taking one of the lights, she turned from us; and away she went, unmolested. Not a soul was *able* to molest her."[73] From Pamela to Clarissa, Richardson's emphasis moves from female chastity to innate unassailable virtue—a white feminine virtue that becomes palpable *because* of the threat of rape and sexual violence—and this susceptibility constructs the virtuous white woman of empire.

Oyèrónkẹ́ Oyěwùmí names the gendering of hierarchy in Western discourse as "Sisterarchy," which perfectly describes the work of Blake's print of *Europe Supported by Africa and America*. She argues that African, and specifically Yoruba studies, must decolonize themselves of imported Western gender theory that, despite its insistence on gender as construction rather than biological fact, nevertheless returns cross-cultural gender studies to universal gender categories. Often, "the categorization of women in feminist discourse as a homogeneous, bioanatomically determined group which is always constituted as powerless and victimized does not reflect the fact that gender relations are social relations and, therefore, historically grounded and culturally bound."[74] In Blake's print we see the exportation of the category of "woman" to those others being appropriated by Western culture: they are being colonized by gender as well as by race. As Oyěwùmí asks us, "On what basis are Western conceptual categories exportable or transferable to other cultures that have a different cultural logic?"[75] And so, when we discuss Richardson's feminist commitments in *Clarissa,* it is vital to ensure that we are not exporting, as Stedman does, specifically white, imperial womanhood as a universal. Kathleen Lubey extends readings of Richardson's examinations of "sexualized commerce" in the novel to show us how he minutely details "the systematic instrumentalization of women's bodies to support socio-political institutions that both disenfranchise them and delimit their ontological possibilities."[76] The key point to make explicit, however, is that the novel constructs the *white* woman, specifically and exclusively out of these violations and victimizations, and she then becomes a handmaiden of empire whose role is one of racialized domination over colonized and enslaved women of empire who have no such access, either to the minute descriptions of their depredations, or to the concomitant assertions of their moral superiority.

In *Neither Black nor White yet Both,* Werner Sollors notes that Stedman's description of Joanna, a mixed-race enslaved woman in Suriname, echoes Lovelace's description of Clarissa.[77] Stedman claims that her white father failed to secure her manumission but that he was able to enter into a "Surinam marriage" with her, and he depicts their cohabitation in Edenic terms: "Not Adam and Eve in Paradise could Enjoy a greater Share of felicity, than we did now." The passage in which Stedman describes Joanna for the first time has received much attention for its stylized sentimentalism drawing on "the whole arsenal of neo-Petrarchan description." Casting Joanna as the perfect "Goddess," Stedman injects eroticism into the picture:

> Her face was full of Native Modesty and the most distinguished Sweetness—Her eyes as black as Ebony were large and full of expression, bespeaking the Goodness of her heart. With Cheeks through which glow'd/in spite of her olive Complexion/a beautiful tinge of vermillion when gazed upon—her nose was perfectly well formed rather small, her lips a little prominent which when she spoke discovered two regular rows of pearls as white as Mountain Snow—her hair was a dark brown—next to black, forming a beauteous Glob of small ringlets, ornamented with flowers and gold Spangles—round her neck and Arms and her ancles she wore Gold Chain rings and Medals—while a Shaul of finest indian Muslin the end of which was negligently thrown over her polished Shoulder gracefuly covered part of her lovely bosom.[78]

Sollors draws our attention to the passage's echoes of Lovelace's description of Clarissa in which her "lovely bosom" is exposed to the ravisher. The allusion to *Clarissa* immediately injects the scene with ambivalence, for Stedman becomes the licentious seducer as well as the Petrarchan lover. This eroticism is fully expressed in Holloway's engraving of Joanna, which indeed exposed her bosom for an erotic and appropriative gaze. Their son, Johnny, is in the background. We note that Stedman emphasizes Joanna's ability to blush, for her body to speak, "in spite of her olive Complexion."

I have traced the evolution of the Joanna story through the pages of Stedman's original diaries, to the manuscript "Narrative" in the archive of his materials held at the James Ford Bell library. The realities of such a relationship, bound up within the power dynamics of slavery, were transformed to become a romantic story in the published *Narrative*. This is a violent formal representation of Joanna that transforms Stedman's fragments and scraps in his diaries, into this neoclassical, Western version of an eroticized Black woman. Stedman's first mention of Joanna in his Surinam diary is from March 1, 1773: "receive a cordial and two fine oranges from a mulatto girl." He then notes on April 23, 1773, "J__a comes to stay with me. I give her presents to the value of about ten pounds sterling and am perfectly happy—." On May 8 he says, "at Mr Gordons—give me wedding." This is the "plot" of Stedman's appropriation of Joanna in his primary manuscripts: these are Joanna's fragments. Stedman records having sex with other enslaved women after this point in his diaries. How do we read Joanna through these slivers of archive? Joanna dies soon after Stedman leaves Suriname, unable to purchase her freedom, and it was reported that she was poisoned. The fragments are written by Stedman: she never speaks. Joanna is a captive in a way that Clarissa is not because it is not out of Clarissa's "belly" that the labor and profits will flow—she is not "captive" as Hortense Spillers describes enslaved women; she is not "fungible" in the same way.[79] Joanna's death and her life become no symbol of womanhood but another life lost in the white apocalypse.

The segregation between *Clarissa* and enslaved women has been manufactured to ensure the prime place of white femininity at the heart of empire; the separation is required to maintain white supremacy as apparently independent of material and symbolic contexts. Such segregation begins to collapse once we allow even the archival fragments that are the traces of enslaved women's captured lives to feature in our narratives of the eighteenth century.

NOTES

1. See, for example, the archives of the prominent Liverpool enslaver William Davenport, *The Papers of William Davenport & Co. 1745–1797*, British Online Archives, https://britishonlinearchives.com/collections/12/slave-trading-records-from-william-davenport-co-1745-1797.
2. Slave Voyages, "Trans-Atlantic Slave Trade—Estimates," https://www.slavevoyages.org/assessment/estimates/.

3. For a full discussion of colonial and sea trade and the profits accruing, see Robin Blackburn, "Colonial Slavery and the Eighteenth-Century Boom," in *The Making of New World Slavery: From the Baroque to the Modern, 1492–1800* (London: Verso, 1997). See also Eric Williams, *Capitalism and Slavery* (Richmond, VA: William Byrd Press, 1944).
4. Angus Ross, "Introduction," in Samuel Richardson, *Clarissa, or, The History of a Young Lady*, ed. Angus Ross (London: Penguin, 1985, rep. 2004), 18–19. All quotations are from this edition. See also Laura Doyle, *Freedom's Empire: Race and the Rise of the Novel in Atlantic Modernity, 1640–1940* (Durham, NC: Duke University Press, 2007): "In the fiction of Eliza Haywood and Samuel Richardson, the Atlantic is nowhere to be seen; and yet these two authors are innovative fashioners of the interior selves and conflicts over consent spawned by Atlantic modernity—the conditions of which are implicitly embedded in their novels" (118).
5. Christina Sharpe, *In the Wake: On Blackness and Being* (Durham, NC: Duke University Press, 2016), 13.
6. Saidiya Hartman, "Venus in Two Acts," *Small Axe* 12, no. 2 (2008): 1–14, 9.
7. Felicity Nussbaum, *Torrid Zones: Maternity, Sexuality and Empire in Eighteenth-Century English Narratives* (Baltimore: Johns Hopkins University Press, 1995), 73.
8. Edward Long, *The History of Jamaica or, General Survey of the Antient and Modern State of that Island: With Reflections on its Situation, Settlements, Inhabitants, Climate, Products, Commerce, Laws, and Government*, vol. 2 (London: T. Lowndes, 1774), 436.
9. Long, *The History of Jamaica*, 437.
10. See Jennifer L. Morgan, "*Partus sequitur ventrem:* Law, Race, and Reproduction in Colonial Slavery," *Small Axe* 55 (March 2018): 1–17.
11. Marisa J. Fuentes, *Dispossessed Lives: Enslaved Women, Violence, and the Archive* (Philadelphia: University of Pennsylvania Press, 2016).
12. See also Hartman, "Venus in Two Acts": "I want to say more than this" (2).
13. Rebecca Anne Barr, "Black Transactions: Waste and Abundance in Samuel Richardson's *Clarissa*," in *The Afterlife of Used Things: Recycling in the Eighteenth Century*, ed. Ariane Fennetaux, Amélie Junqua, and Sophie Vasset (London: Routledge, 2014), 199–211, 199.
14. R. F. Brissenden, *Clarissa: Preface, Hints of Prefaces, and Postscript* (Los Angeles: William Andrews Clark Memorial Library, University of California, Los Angeles, 1964), i.
15. Thomas Keymer, *Richardson's "Clarissa" and the Eighteenth-Century Reader* (Cambridge: Cambridge University Press, 2004), 11.
16. *Clarissa*, 974, letter 295 (hereafter L).
17. Barr, "Black Transactions," 205.
18. *Clarissa*, 1465, L 529.
19. *Clarissa*, 1468, L 529.
20. *Clarissa*, 1466, L 529.
21. For a full discussion of white rights in particular, see Charles W. Mills, *The Racial Contract* (Ithaca, NY: Cornell University Press, 1997): "What is needed, in other words, is a recognition that racism (or, as I will argue, global white supremacy) is itself a political system, a particular power structure of formal or informal rule, socioeconomic privilege, and norms for the differential distribution of material wealth and opportunities, benefits and burdens, rights and duties" (3).
22. Nicole Aljoe, "Reading the 'Memoirs of the Life of Florence Hall' through *The Long Song* of the Caribbean Colonial Archive," *American Literary History* 32, no. 4 (2020): 623–644, 624.
23. *Clarissa*, 1254, L 428.
24. *Clarissa*, 542, L 160.
25. *Clarissa*, 754–755, L 230.
26. Julie Park, "I Shall Enter Her Heart: Fetishizing Feeling in *Clarissa*," *Studies in the Novel* 37, no. 4 (2005): 371–393, 373.

27. *Clarissa*, 518, L 152.
28. *Clarissa*, 287, L 73.
29. This is one of the addenda made by Richardson to the first and second editions of *Clarissa*, *Letters and Passages Restored from the Original Manuscripts of the History of "Clarissa," 1751*, introduction by Peter Sabor, bibliographic essay by O. M. Brack, vol. 2 of *Samuel Richardson's Published Commentary on "Clarissa," 1747–65* (London: Pickering & Chatto, 1998), 34.
30. Homi Bhabha, *The Location of Culture* (London: Routledge, 1992), 128.
31. Abraham Cowley, *Poems Written by A. Cowley* (London: Humphrey Moseley, 1656), 48.
32. Natalie A. Zacek, *Settler Society in the English Leeward Islands, 1670–1776* (Cambridge: Cambridge University Press, 2015), 171. See also Jennifer Morgan, *Laboring Women: Reproduction and Gender in New World Slavery* (Philadelphia: University of Pennsylvania Press, 2004), 16: "The struggle with perceptions of beauty and assertions of monstrosity . . . exemplified a much larger process through which the familiar became unfamiliar as beauty became beastliness and mothers became monstrous, all ultimately in the service of racial distinctions. Writers who articulated religious and moral justifications for the slave trade simultaneously grappled with the character of the female African body-a body both desirable and repulsive, available and untouchable, productive and reproductive, beautiful and black."
33. *Clarissa*, 399, L 99.
34. *Clarissa*, 1351, L 474.
35. *Clarissa*, 1306, L 451.
36. *Clarissa*, 1218, L 417.
37. Anonymous, *The Woman of Colour* (1808), ed. Dominique Lyndon (Peterborough, ON: Broadview Press, 2016), 102.
38. Tita Chico, *Designing Women: The Dressing Room in Eighteenth-Century English Literature and Culture* (Lewisburg, PA: Bucknell University Press, 2005).
39. *Clarissa*, 73, L12.
40. *Clarissa*, 951, L 281.
41. Park, "I Shall Enter Her Heart," 373.
42. *Clarissa*, 1310, L 454.
43. *Clarissa*, 949, L 281.
44. Nussbaum, *Torrid Zones*, 1.
45. Felicity Nussbaum, *The Limits of the Human: Fictions of Anomaly, Race and Gender in the Long Eighteenth Century* (Cambridge: Cambridge University Press, 2003), 157–158.
46. Nussbaum, *Torrid Zones*, 93.
47. *Clarissa*, 426, L 110.
48. *Clarissa*, 133, L 27.
49. *Clarissa*, 1256, L 429.
50. Pennsylvania Historical & Museum Commission, "1681–1776: The Quaker Province. The Founding of Pennsylvania," http://www.phmc.state.pa.us/portal/communities/pa-history/1681-1776.html/.
51. *Clarissa*, 1257, L 430.
52. *Clarissa*, 95, L 251.
53. Doyle, *Freedom's Empire*, 139.
54. Doyle, *Freedom's Empire*, 118.
55. Doyle, *Freedom's Empire*, 140.
56. Doyle, *Freedom's Empire*, 142.
57. Doyle, *Freedom's Empire*, 146.
58. Gerald Horne, *The Apocalypse of Settler Colonialism: The Roots of Slavery, White Supremacy and Capitalism in Seventeenth-Century North America and the Caribbean* (New York: Monthly Review Press, 2017), 23.
59. Doyle, *Freedom's Empire*, 143.
60. Morgan, "*Partus sequitur ventrem*," 4.

61. See Saidiya Hartman, "The Belly of the World: A Note on Black Women's Labors, Souls," *Souls* 18, no. 1 (2016): 166–173.
62. Hartman, "Venus in Two Acts," 2.
63. See Douglas Hall, *In Miserable Slavery: Thomas Thistlewood in Jamaica 1750–86* (Kingston, Jamaica: University of the West Indies Press, 1999); Trevor Burnard, *Mastery, Tyranny and Desire: Thomas Thistlewood and His Slaves in the Anglo-Jamaican World* (Chapel Hill: University of North Carolina Press, 2004).
64. Fuentes, *Dispossessed Lives*, 64.
65. Thomas Thistlewood Papers, James Marshall and Marie-Louise Osborn Collection, Beinecke Rare Book and Manuscript Library, Yale University.
66. Marisa Fuentes, "Genres of History and the Practice of Loss: Attending to Silence in Hazel Carby's *Imperial Intimacies*," *Small Axe* 25, no. 1 (2021): 171.
67. *Clarissa*, 950, L 281.
68. Terry Eagleton, *The Rape of Clarissa: Writing, Sexuality and Class Struggle in Samuel Richardson* (Oxford: Blackwell, 1982), 41.
69. *Clarissa*, 949, L 281.
70. Horne, *The Apocalypse of Settler Colonialism*, 174.
71. John Gabriel Stedman, *Narrative of a Five Years Expedition against the Revolted Negroes of Surinam*, ed. Richard Price and Sally Price (London: Open Road, 2016), 618.
72. Stephanie Insley Hershinow, *Born Yesterday: Inexperience and the Early Realist Novel* (Baltimore: Johns Hopkins University Press, 2019), 52, 54.
73. *Clarissa*, 951, L 281.
74. Oyèrónkẹ́ Oyěwùmí, *The Invention of Women: Making an African Sense of Western Gender Discourses* (Minneapolis: University of Minnesota Press, 1997), 10.
75. Oyěwùmí, *The Invention of Women*, 11.
76. Kathleen Lubey, "Sexual Remembrance in *Clarissa*," *Eighteenth-Century Fiction* 29, no. 2 (2016–2017): 151–178, 164.
77. Cited in Werner Sollors, *Neither Black nor White yet Both: Thematic Explorations of Interracial Literature* (New York: Oxford University Press, 1999), 190; see *Clarissa*, 725.
78. Stedman, *Narrative of a Five Years Expedition*, 260, 96, 88.
79. Hortense J. Spillers, "Mama's Baby, Papa's Maybe: An American Grammar Book," *Diacritics* 17 (Summer 1987): 64–81, 67. Though Spillers does not explicitly use "fungible" as a term, her work explains "the transformation of bodies into objects precisely through this logic of fungibility," tracing "blackness as a category that emerges out of the economic ontology that trades in the exchange of commodities." Shannon Winnubst, "The Many Lives of Fungibility: Anti-Blackness in Neoliberal Times," *Journal of Gender Studies* 29, no. 1 (2020): 102–112, 105.

7

MISOGYNY AND THE MALE VIRGIN IN *SIR CHARLES GRANDISON*

Rebecca Anne Barr

THE VIRGIN HERO of Samuel Richardson's final novel, *Sir Charles Grandison* (1753–1754), is more remarkable than all the chaste heroines that went before him. Designed as "the Completion of [the author's] whole Plan," Sir Charles's virginal status is clearly neither incidental or meaningless.[1] As "one of the first virtues" the author considered in creating his "good man," male virginity is integral to *Grandison* and fundamental to the novel's rethinking of sexual power relations.[2] Before *Grandison*, Richardson's plots were driven by a male heterosexuality whose sexual satiation (whether through marriage or rapine) was a presumed prerogative of manliness. Despite eighteenth-century culture's fetishization of women's virginity as key in transferring property and ordering patrilineal succession, no corresponding premium was placed on men's chastity.[3] Instead, as Rachel Gevlin notes, "men were not only excused from but expected to have premarital sex, and adultery was also normalized—so long as all of these pre- and extramarital relations were with lower-class women."[4] It is no wonder that Richard Steele lamented that "Our Sex has usurped a certain Authority to exclude Chastity out of the Catalogue of Masculine Virtues." Citing the almost-customary ruination of educated women (lower rank women clearly deemed disposable), Steele urged "Chastity as the noblest Male Qualification."[5] Acknowledging such an unfashionable opinion risked "the Raillery of the World," Steele claimed that he would happily provide "Examples of Heroic Chastity, were I not afraid of having my Paper thrown away by the Modish Part of the Town." Stories of chaste men were clearly not only a patent absurdity and laughingstock, but also potentially alienated one's audience. As Colley Cibber's response to the novel suggests, this was a high-risk representational strategy: "A male-virgin, said he—ha, ha, ha, hah! . . . and he laughed me quite out of countenance!"[6] But it is this exceptional virtue that distinguishes its exemplary hero from all others. Sir Charles's virginity is key to his omni-attractiveness: his superlative virtue engaging not merely the heart of the lovely Harriet Byron but also the worthy Clementina della Porretta and every family he chances upon. Virginity vouchsafes a male paragon who becomes the linchpin of an extended familial unit and the domestic guarantor of an extended "family of love" that patterns out a stable society.[7]

But even scholarship that understands *Grandison* as an important experiment in remodeling masculinity continues to treat Sir Charles's virginity as unimportant: a quaint oddity of pious Christianity, of which is said, the less the better.[8] In *The Rape of Clarissa*, Terry Eagleton astutely identifies the hero's virginity as a key reason for *Grandison*'s scholarly marginalization. While earlier novels focused on the "passive suffering woman," Richardson's final novel is an example of "the tide of feminization recuperated by patriarchy." In the virginal Sir Charles, *Grandison* attempts no less than "the production of a new kind of male subject." But Eagleton's prognosis on the novel's radical ideology is bleak. "Where *Grandison* is most progressive is in its massive strike on the patriarchal 'double standard.' Having written a novel about a chaste woman, Richardson will show how such chastity is equally essential for men . . . [but] the blunt truth is that in patriarchal society it does not matter whether men are chaste or not. *Grandison*'s virginity has no price, no exchange value: unlike Clarissa, he is not a commodity on the sex or property market. . . . *His virtue is no more than a personal affair, nobody's business but his own*."[9] Eagleton diagnoses the critical indifference to men's sexual behavior as a symptom of patriarchal capitalism invested in female virginity as the means of social reproduction: men's virtue, he bemoans, is "nobody's business." But it *was* of profound concern, and of capital importance, to the enterprising Richardson. His earliest extant works are didactic manuals for young men, with a distinct emphasis on the profit to be made from carnal continence; his early correspondence with "a gentleman" formed his polite style and ideas of masculine virtue, parlaying them into a successful writing career.[10] Richardson's consultative correspondence about his Christian hero is a collaborative attempt to promote men's chastity.[11] Criticism has too frequently colluded with patriarchal codes of sexuality in dismissing the allure of its good man. Now, in the wake of #MeToo, when men's virtue is *everybody's* business, we ought to be reading *Grandison*.[12]

While *Clarissa* endeavors to disprove the "dangerous, but too commonly received Notion, *That a Reformed Rake makes the best Husband*," *Grandison* goes further by promulgating the idea that a male virgin makes the *best* husband.[13] Lisabeth During's definition of the "chastity plot" helps illuminate the significance of Sir Charles's sexual state.[14] A narrative that refuses marriage, the chastity plot pits the integrity of the pure individual against the sordid pragmatism of the world. In such narratives, the virgin asserts a transcendent power and transformative resistance. While During focusses almost exclusively on female virginity, with *Clarissa* as terminal template, *Grandison* possesses many of the chastity plot's key characteristics. Refusing to succumb to either his own or others' desire, the virgin hero's unavailability stimulates women's interest. His is a personal honor that simultaneously solicits and reproves readers' erotic energies. Rather than a "progressive" dissolution of the "sexed double standard," the elevation of male virginity is "socially coercive and psychologically unhealthy," with a "remarkable bond between misogyny and sexual purity, a contract as intimate as it is pervasive."[15] This misogyny suffuses *Grandison*, where the awestruck shame of the women who surround Sir Charles makes visible his power and superiority. In attempting to forestall interpretations of chastity as effeminacy—a moral delicacy *too like* that of the "fair sex"—the novel strategically overdetermines the potency of its male virgin through the coercive control of its female characters. As Daniel Krahn notes, "inclusion within the [Grandisonian] circle comes from submission."[16]

Sir Charles's heroic chastity might seem to finally raise the bar for men's morality, doing away with sexual double standards. But instead, the sexual perfection of his hero sponsors an ambience of inadequacy and abjection for the women supposed to benefit from this exceptional virtue. "The art of virginity," as During notes, has the tendency to become a "violent code" rather than a liberation from the urges of sexual desire. Rather than liberating women, Richardson's virgin hero increases the pressure on them, by appropriating the merits of chastity, surpassing women's performance of passive virtue, and casting them into a state of conscious inferiority. Male virginity thus helps "reproduce patriarchy" and to exacerbate its inequities.[17] By attending to Richardson's programmatic elevation of male virginity, this chapter reveals the price women pay for the creation of such a paragon. Subsequent novels use the Grandisonian model of male virginity to critique the ways in which its overweening libidinal and legal authority actively oppresses female sexuality and subjectivity. In Elizabeth Inchbald's *A Simple Story* (1791) and Charlotte Brontë's *Jane Eyre* (1847), the forbiddingly virginal Dorriforth and St. John Rivers develop the allure of the male virgin, while exposing him as an avatar of militant patriarchy. Rather than redistributing the psychic burden of sexual continence, male virgins in the novel redouble women's repression: enforcing obedience to male-controlled purity and its perpetuation.

SEXING UP THE MALE VIRGIN

Richardson's anxious consultations over *Grandison* confirm the risk of writing a male virgin. Writing to the fourteen-year-old son of a clergyman, he asked for his father to "give me some Sketches from the Knowledge he has of his own Heart. If I see the Materials rise upon me, they may encourage . . . [I am faced with] the Difficulty of drawing a good Man, that the Ladies will not despise, and the Gentlemen laugh at."[18] Cibber's mockery in mind, Richardson prepared to defend his male virgin against men's derision and women's contempt. His anxiety was justified. As E. Derek Taylor observes, "The path to the eighteenth-century's quintessential 'good man' . . . begins with . . . a failed prototype" in *Clarissa*: Hickman,

Anna Howe's suitor.[19] Despite his happy ending (he marries and survives the aftermath of the heroine's death), Hickman is a comic figure on the margins, whose stolid decency offsets the quicksilver sex appeal of Lovelace. Anna Howe finds him thoroughly underwhelming:

> The man, is honest: is of family: has a clear and good estate; and may one day be a baronet, and please you. He is humane and benevolent, tolerably generous, as people say . . . he is sober; modest; they *say*, virtuous. . . .
>
> Nevertheless, to own the truth, I cannot say I love the man; nor ever shall, I believe. . . . For honest Hickman, the good man is so *generally* meek, . . . And then, when I rate him, he seems to be so naturally fitted for rebuke, and so much expects it, that I know not how to disappoint him, whether he just then deserve it, or not. I am sure he has puzzled me many a time when I have seen him look penitent for faults he has not committed, whether to pity or laugh at him.[20]

Her paratactic enumeration of the good man's virtues fails to coalesce into manly attractiveness. Less than the sum of his parts, Hickman has a maiden bashfulness at odds with the braggadocio of hegemonic manhood: his "meekness" suggesting sexual incompetence and even impotence. Anna's catalogue of faint praise climaxes with a bathetic conclusion: "nevertheless . . . I cannot love the man," knowing not "whether to pity or laugh at him."

Surprisingly, Lovelace's description of the "virtuous" Hickman as "a *male-virgin*" is less derisive.[21] The libertine's diagnosis has more than a modicum of sympathy, instead blaming women for rakish preferences. "Women, Jack, like not novices. Two maidenheads meeting together in wedlock, the first child must be a fool, is their common aphorism.[22] They are pleased with a love of the sex that is founded in the knowledge of it. . . . [Yet] these sheepish fellows are sly. I myself was modest once: and this . . . has better enabled me to judge of both."[23] Carnal knowledge, Lovelace argues, equips men with a necessary deidealization of women. Women prefer libertines because sexually experienced partners can best satisfy them, but also because rakes already know women's lustful nature: women can give up the pretense of spiritual superiority. For Lovelace, modesty is stratagem or lack of opportunity. Both his own "sheepishness" and Hickman's virginity are "sly," secretly cunning. The "male-virgin" triggers self-reflection in Lovelace, and epistolary referentiality in the novel, with an editorial interjection referring readers back to letter 115: "I was *originally* a bashful mortal. Indeed I am bashful still with regard to this lady—Bashful, yet know the sex so well!—But that indeed is the reason that I know it so well:—For, Jack, I have had abundant cause, when I have looked into *myself*, by way of comparison with the *other* sex, to conclude that a bashful man has a good deal of the soul of a woman; and so, like Tiresias, can tell what they think, and what they drive at, as well as themselves."[24] Lovelace's sexual cynicism brands a "*male-virgin*" like Hickman simply an "inactive rake."[25] Inferring women's desires from his own "original bashfulness," he dismisses female modesty as a socially produced façade—virginity is merely a Mandevillian "artificial Chastity."[26]

Lovelace's reflexivity and Richardson's editorial interruption not only "compel a certain readerly self-examination" but also act as metafictional markers reframing the earlier novels.[27] Describing Charlotte and her "submissive husband" Lord G as "A very Miss Howe" and "a very Mr. Hickman," *Grandison*'s comic continuation of tragedy becomes explicit.[28] Meditating on "the worthy women betrayed" by the "commonly received notion" that "*a reformed rake makes the best husband*," Clarissa's executor John Belford laments the "total revolution of manners" needed to make a libertine into "a good husband, a worthy father, and true friend."[29] Women can do only so much. *Pamela in Her Exalted Condition* (which Richardson was revising while writing *Grandison*) gives a signal instance of the Herculean feminine labor required to effect such a revolution: well after marriage, Mr. B is still a moral work in progress. The sequel shows the emotional toll moral rehabilitation takes on women. Pamela, eighteenth-century pop culture's favorite militant virgin, pungently refutes the notion that seduction solely dishonors the woman. "How it comes to pass," she fulminates, "that a Woman's Virtue is her Glory, and that a Man's shall not be his? . . . Why [do] you think Virtue in a Man is not as requisite as in a Woman?"[30] Pamela's Pauline attack arises not from protofeminist sympathy (despite the simmering personal resentment), but from her belief in patriarchal superiority and property rights.[31] A gentleman, she argues, is "the Head of his Family. . . . Is it not incumbent upon him then to set a good Example? And will he plead it as a Fashion, that he may do by the dearest Relatives of another Man's Family, what, if any one should attempt to do by his, he would mortally resent?"[32] Though "the chastity and continence of women are absolutely and indispensably necessary" to prevent "families, inheritances, and distinctions of ranks and orders" "from falling into confusion," Richardson's work increasingly makes men responsible for social reproduction.[33] Men's virtue, Pamela insists, *is* everybody's business.

The male virgin offers a social-sexual solution that eases the onus on women as reformers. But it also sidelines, and potentially undermines, women's moral authority and their social value. Male virginity becomes a crowning virtue that eclipses those that have gone before. But for the logic of virginal elevation to work the novel must "first assert the [male] self as great in the world's eyes . . . [since] otherwise [there would] be nothing to truly offer God."[34] Sir Charles's chastity must be shown to be an active choice, a statement of supreme independence, rather than a symptom of asexuality or inadequacy. *Grandison* labors to deactivate risibility by fulsomely accrediting Sir Charles's superlative heterosexual glamour. Harriet and Clementina love him; his ward Emily Jervois is besotted; Lady Olivia pursues him; marriageable-age women and whole families of all ages adore him. From this matrix of adulation, desire, and inaccessibility, the novel fashions a male virgin whose outward conformity masks an impenetrable spiritual self-sufficiency:

> [Sir Charles] is above quarrelling with the world for trifles: but he is still more above making such compliances with it, as would impeach his honour or conscience. . . . My brother is valued by those who know him best, not so much for being an handsome man; not so much for his birth and fortune; nor this or that single worthiness as for being, in that great and comprehensive sense of the word, a *good man* . . . he lived to himself, and to his own heart; and that tho' he had the happiness to please every-body, yet he made the judgment or approbation of the world matter but of secondary consideration. . . . Sir Charles Grandison . . . is not to be misled either by false glory, or false shame, which he calls, The great snares of Virtue! (1:182)

Politic accommodation of sublunary "trifles" allows Sir Charles to flout the "false shame" of virginity in a man.[35] While Hickman's anemic virtues lose propulsion in enumeration, Sir Charles's acquire force by relative negation and combinatory modification: "not so much" his physical attractiveness, not his elite status and wealth, but the alchemical interaction of all possible virtues. Attractive to all, "no singularity appears" (1:181) in his person. Sir Charles's corroborating perfections refuse mere performativity, ramifying the potent invisibility of masculine norms.

The male virgin himself is never advertised. Indeed, in the first two volumes there are scarcely any hints. Sir Charles's coxcomb cousin crassly insinuates the hero's "*pious* turn" requires a trip to town to "make a *man*" (1:360) of him, but such raillery only highlights the weakness of Everard's character. Given virginity's "recessive quality," it must be coaxed into legibility by modest women: professed but not performed.[36] Discreet code words and networked circumlocution suffice to imply Sir Charles's status. Harriet confides, "Miss Grandison means by . . . a good man, what I, and what you, my Lucy, would understand by the word" (1:183). In an "age of Petits Maîtres, and Insignificants," the male virgin signals his difference from "modern men" who "pay their court by the exterior appearance, rather than interiour worth" (1:80). In a novel of compulsive frankness and epistolary exhibitionism, Sir Charles's virginity is an open secret. At the novel's midpoint, Charlotte confesses that "the man [is] virtuous, even, as I believe, to chastity. . . . Don't let the Ladies around you, nor the Gentlemen neither, hear this grace supposed to be my brother's. Nobody about us shall for *me*. I would not have my brother made the jest of one Sex, and the aversion of the other; and be thought so singular a young man" (2:497). The elliptical delicacy of Charlotte's almost-revelation ("this grace *supposed* to be my brother's") respects Sir Charles's aura of purity. But such sotto voce speculation also invites excitable speculation about the untouched body of the hero. Sir Charles's sexual exceptionalism spurs a collective sexual fantasy.

Richardson's "sexy book" reverses gendered dynamics of sexual pursuit so that the hero's "major dilemma in the novel is how to cope with all the women who fancy him."[37] Its "great dearth of good men" (2:348) fuels sexual fixation and feminine insecurity: poor Harriet must cope with constant competition. Women hunger for Sir Charles, not merely on his Italian tour but in polite society and in the close confines of his own household. He lacks neither opportunity nor temptation. Yet Sir Charles "has nothing to reproach himself for" (2:325): his "virtue is virtue upon full proof, and against sensibilities, that it is heroic to overcome" (2:325, 2:326). These proofs of a heroic virginity are now disseminated by his awestruck apostles. Harriet writes, "Let me in confidence hint, what I have gathered from several intimations from Dr Bartlett, tho' as tenderly made by him as possible, that had Sir Charles Grandison been a man capable of taking advantage of the violence of a Lady's passion for him, the unhappy Olivia would not have scrupled, great, haughty, and noble as she is, by birth and fortune, to have been his, without conditions, if she could not have been so with: The Italian world is of this opinion, at least" (2:376). English apophasis confirms Olivia's wanton offer, marshaling discreet traces to evince sexual integrity. Harriet reasons from her own feelings: like her, Olivia "admired him for his virtue . . . he had resisted the greatest temptations that ever man was tried with. I hope, poor woman, that none of them were from her" (2:492). Given the impossibility of verifying his virginity, the hero's silence is taken to confirm that the rumor is true: he "has not, even to [Bartlett], revealed a secret so disgraceful." The vivid charms of Italian noblewomen are no match for buttoned-up English sexlessness, it seems.[38] But Harriet's sympathy for Olivia's sexual longing conveys her own incipient abjection: the precariousness of her claim to a man unnervingly immune to feminine power.

Despite the logic of sexual scarcity, Richardson claimed his final novel was written to please a multitude of women: "teazed by a dozen ladies of note and virtue, to give them a good man, as they say I have been partial to their sex."[39] Several blue-blood correspondents were "contributing authors" to *Grandison*: classicist Elizabeth Carter was understandably proprietorial about "her hero," labeling herself and Catherine Talbot "two Pigmalionesses" responsible for "traits of his good man's character," which Richardson combined with his "own charming ideas . . . [to] form a Sir Charles Grandison."[40] Sir Charles may rightly be termed the product "simultaneously of [female] audience desire and a controlling artist."[41] But Richardson's rhetorical deference to women, and his incorporation of their writing, is counterbalanced by consultation with men: a paternalist committee checks female fantasies. The correspondence of Irish clergyman Philip Skelton echoes these "ladies of note and virtues," in wishing this "good man" as "good a Christian, as a fine gentleman can be." But he adds darker shades: "Your good man will be out of nature, if he is not persecuted: nay, he will be no very good man, if the world does not give him this testimony . . . give us [also] a bad woman, expensive, imperious, lewd, and at last a drammer. This is a fruitful and a necessary subject, which will strike, and entertain to a miracle. You are so safe already with the sex, that nothing you can say of a bad woman will hinder you being a favourite."[42] Disregarding the ferocious samples of "bad women" found in *Pamela* and *Clarissa* (Mrs. Jewkes, Mrs. Sinclair), Skelton argues that the Christian hero demands not merely worldly opposition but also a backdrop of female sinners to throw his virtues into relief. Richardson complied—the errant Mrs. Jervois matches Skelton's demand that one be the "worst of women. A termagant, a swearer, a drinker, unchaste" (1:385). Despite its levity, *Grandison* is populated with immoral mothers, lustful women, disobedient wives, conniving stepmothers, and violent female stalkers.

Introducing a male virgin into the sexed balance sheet of virtue generates an excess of flawed females. *Grandison* "exalts [its] object and lowers, if not . . . debases" (2:78) women characters in an act of imaginative reparation for Richardson's supposed previous partiality. Even after Harriet and Sir Charles's long-delayed nuptials, the novel retains Clementina as a platonically polyamorous supplement to companionate marriage. The hero declares the two women "Sweet sisters! Lovely friends! . . . Kindred souls . . . always near" (3:454), an exacting "triple friendship" (3:191) that suggests the hero's disconcertingly selfish self-approbation.[43] Resolved "to have nothing to reproach himself with," Sir Charles's vaunted infallibility triggers crises of conscience and of confidence. This is coercive perfection. Harriet trembles "Since if there be a fault *between* them it must *all* be that person's; and he will not, if it be possible for him to avoid it, be a sharer in it?" (2:609, also 3:148). Imaginatively and erotically invested in a "fantasy of an integrity so innate as to be untouchable, an identity resilient against all doubt, something both craved and despaired of," *Grandison* prostrates its female characters as a result.[44] Craving and despair mingle comically in Harriet's recasting of her beloved as an improved Adam. Unlike his uxorious forebear, Richardson's hero would not have been "so complaisant to his Eve as *Milton makes Adam*." "[Sir Charles] would have had gallantry enough to his fallen spouse to have made him extremely regret her lapse; but that he would have done *his own duty* . . . and left it to the Almighty, if such had been his pleasure, to have annihilated his first Eve, and given him the second" (2:609). Harriet's Sir Charles is impervious; coldly "gallant" to the fallible female who was his Edenic spouse; absolute in his autonomy, freed from contingency.[45] Despite the humor, Harriet's vision of her beloved's superior manliness ruefully renders her a "Second Eve," resigned to "a second-place Love" (3:14) after Clementina rescinds her engagement. Sir Charles's virginal status is the key to this irresistibility: an inviolability that betokens "an integrity nobody has but everyone desires."[46]

LOVING, HATING, REWRITING THE MALE VIRGIN

Literary criticism's "business-as-usual denigration of *Grandison*" might dismiss its pure hero as unfashionable and obsolete.[47] But the desirable male virgin has reemerged in contemporary mass-market and historical romance, proving that Richardson, as is so frequently the case, created a culturally powerfully and cannily marketable romantic fantasy.[48] Jamie Fraser, for instance, the hero of Diana Gabaldon's blockbuster *Outlander* series, is a virginal Jacobite solider and an international object of desire.[49] Mia Sheridan's best-selling *Archer's Voice* (2014) likewise features a virginal hero whose love salvages the (sexually experienced but emotionally traumatized) heroine. Influential user-generated sites like Reddit and GoodReads compile lists of romances featuring male virgins for avid readers.[50] In contemporary romance, then, the male virgin's traditional moral sensibility is no prudish oddity but fodder for eroticism. Jamie Fraser and his ilk are fantasy incarnations of a sexual integrity and innocence unsullied by contemporary porn culture: figures whose lack of experience proffers heterosexual women readers, in particular, a degree of sexual agency and control. Some contemporary readers—but certainly not all—may also have religious reasons for preferring to read about a "man of probity." Twenty-two-year-old American Muslim reviewer Ayman testifies to the adulation such a man can inspire in 2022: "Archer Hales is single-handedly the most innocent, kind, selfless, caring, thoughtful, loving, and courageous fictional man to ever exist. and it quite frankly makes me sad af because i know a man like him will never exist. they simply don't make his kind in the real world. i'd never say this about any man and maybe not even a fictional one but for Archer Hale, i would lay my life down for him if i have to . . . god he deserves the world and nothing less."[51] Awareness of the hero's dual fictionality and exemplarity—the best "fictional man to ever exist," a "man like him will never exist . . . they don't make his kind in the real world"—does not diminish this intense attachment, a romance instance of the "kind of Historical Faith which Fiction is generally read with, though we know it to be Fiction."[52]

Women's fantasies of respect, empowerment, and desire are licensed by contemporary romance male virgins. But these texts also overwhelmingly affirm normative hegemonic manhood in their plot trajectories—once tutored, the erstwhile male virgin usually assumes a sexually dominant, traditional, and protective role in the relationship. Unlike these romances, Inchbald and Brontë's novels rewire the marriage plot, rejecting or sidelining the Grandisonian figures as suitable spouses. Taken together, these rewritings suggest that the female self-laceration and subordination that seem a mere side effect of Grandisonian chastity are in fact a necessary condition of its misogynist moral structure. It requires women's abjection for its paragon to prosper and rule. As a "priestly Grandison," the magnetic virtues of *A Simple Story*'s Dorriforth prompted Maria Edgeworth to rejoice she never met with such "for I must inevitably have fallen desperately in love with him; and destitute of . . . [the] power of charming, I might have died in despair."[53] Such destitution always looms in Grandisonian novels, as the fetishization of Christian righteousness prostrates the lowly. Like Emily Jervois, Dorriforth's ward Miss Milner is drawn not to physical attractiveness but to a moral authority that diminishes her transient attractions: "in the calendar of love, a solemn lord chief justice, or a devout archbishop ranks before a licentious king," she avers.[54] Altering Grandison's confessional status, Inchbald draws on Catholicism's Gothic strains to provide a religious rationale for Dorriforth's chastity, intensifies the extremity of repression and creates an inquisitorial double in the character of his mentor and fellow Jesuit Sandford. As Barbara Judson beautifully observes, the first two volumes carry "the seeds of hauteur that disfigure [Dorriforth's] behavior . . . when he has perfected his system of polite constraint into a form of intimidation so elegant he can disavow any coercion."[55] Instead, Sandford programmatically humiliates Miss Milner on his behalf. An "expert" in the "mortifications of slight," Sandford is "eager to draw upon him her detestation, in the hope he could also make her abominate herself" (39). Her lessons in spiritual insufficiency make self-loathing habitual. It is no accident that the "inward nothingness" (40) Sandford instills resonates with Miss Milner's first stirrings of love for Dorriforth: neither joy nor excitement, but a sense of being "annihilated" (83) in the presence of her beloved.

Though Barker claims that, unlike the benign Sir Charles, Dorriforth "nourishes animosity" only when his virtue is "combined with his intimidating hostility," his militant virginity imposes a hierarchical and brutalizing relation from the outset.[56] His ward attests that his "tenderness . . . frightens me, . . . intimidates, and strikes me dumb— . . . what can I do but stand before him like a guilty creature, acknowledging my faults" (49). When inexorable purity is consecrated as male, simply to be an attractive young woman feels incriminating. Paradoxically, Miss Milner's passion is the fruit of what pains her: "his being faultless, was the first cause of my passion" (149) she confesses. It is only when Dorriforth becomes a landowner and thus requires a spouse to ensure inheritance that Miss Milner becomes a potential bride. Her sense of having overcome male virginity adduces a momentary power that is intoxicating: she believes she has transformed "Dorriforth, the grave, the sanctified, the anchorite Dorriforth . . . the proud Priest, the austere guardian" into "the most impassioned lover" (138), "the veriest slave of love."

Inchbald disables *Grandison*'s "comic-romantic . . . collusion between providential plots based on the Fall and patriarchy" by breaking the novel into two shocking acts.[57] Shifting from romantic union to spousal dereliction, female exile, and disgrace, *A Simple Story* "insists on abjection as implicit in the position of the female in the patriarchal order."[58] Miss Milner's "experiment in being beloved in spite of her faults" (138) fails not due to her sexuality, as many critics have argued, but as a result of the faults inherent in the type of desire Dorriforth/Elmwood's virginity created. Through the novel's unhappily-ever-after Inchbald attacks the premise of perfection that Richardson's hero retailed. While Sir Charles's marriage inaugurates firm domestic governance, Dorriforth/Elmwood leaves England and his wife after only four years, called away to his "large estate in the West Indies" (196). It is this three-year desertion that precipitates his wife's fall. Banal neglect and loneliness, not dissipation, cause Lady Elmwood's adultery. Sandford's training in mortification and shame ensures she exiles herself, and she dies in a remote retreat. No detail is given of Elmwood's Caribbean business, other than that he is detained there by "a severe and dangerous illness" (196) and that he returns "a hard-hearted tyrant" (195). The colonial enterprise is not merely a "narrative link between two disparate tales but a specific encoding of political meaning," as Miriam Wallace notes.[59] It is crucial in accounting for *A Simple Story*'s generic rupture, its critique of paternalist authority, and its disenchantment with the transformative possibilities of the male virgin. Volumes 3 and 4 were composed in the late 1780s, at the height of British's debates on abolition, where the extremes of imperialist exploitation of the West Indies were impossible to ignore. If Miss Milner flexed her meager power via coquetry, Lord Elmwood's mature authoritarianism is seasoned by lucrative inhumanity. "Tainted" by slaveholding, and "by such close proximity with the absolute authority of the slave-holder," the tendencies toward extreme inhumanity in Elmwood's character are cemented, rather than instilled.[60] The terminal volumes undo the romance of the male virgin, revealing the "good man" not as a benevolent patriarch but as a tyrant who demands too much of a vulnerable spouse while bitterly expecting her to fail, and whose subsequent militant authoritarianism requires the total passivity of his daughter and an unquestioning submission from his family. *A Simple Story* draws out the relationship between cruelty and masochism in *Grandison*'s fair-sexed subordination.

In Brontë's *Jane Eyre*, St. John Rivers demands female self-sacrifice in service to an imperial project. Through his religious righteousness, the novel highlights the coercive power of the male virgin when it is part of a rhetoric of feminized labor and civic utility: where love is women's service to God and empire. Given the virile flamboyance of Rochester, critics are liable to overlook Brontë's evocation of the young clergyman's suitability as a romantic partner.[61] But as a preacher, St. John's clerical charisma is powerful. Jane remarks his "strictly restrained zeal . . . compressed, condensed, controlled. The heart was thrilled, the mind astonished, by the power of the preacher: neither were softened."[62] Harriet's discomfort at her imperfections relative to the "good man" resonates with Jane's sense of "inexpressible sadness" at hearing her cousin's sermonizing. Jane senses in him "turbid dregs of disappointment . . . impulses of insatiate yearnings and disquieting aspirations," which unsettle in their similitude to her own restricted agency.[63]

St. John's nominated "second Eve" is horrified by his suppression of natural desire and the redirection of marital intentions toward her. While *Grandison*'s pragmatic offering of Sir Charles's "second-placed love" (2:647) is laudable, Brontë casts such renunciation as perversity. While Sir Charles's "divided heart" symptomatized sensibility, St. John's eagerness to quench *his* first love seems a chilling inhumanity. He loves "with all the intensity, indeed, of a first passion, the object of which is exquisitely beautiful, graceful, fascinating," while maintaining "a calm, unwarped consciousness" that his beloved "would not make . . . a good wife."[64] Sir Charles's dutiful resignation of his first partner is treated with light comedy, but St. John's unstinting conviction of his superior moral destiny makes him as "inexorable as death."[65] His moral authority deprives Jane of "liberty of mind," but she recognizes that she does "not love my servitude . . . I daily wished more to please him: but to do so, I felt daily more and more that I must disown half my nature."[66] While Sir Charles compels prostration, intersecting mid-Victorian ideologies of empire, gender, and nation ironically grant Jane the "adamantine authority" to refuse this particular form of sacrifice.[67] Made "of the material from which nature hews her heroes—Christian and Pagan—her lawgivers, her statesmen, her conquerors," "it would be a trying thing to be [the] wife" of such a Christian hero.[68]

> "I can imagine the possibility of conceiving an inevitable, strange, torturing kind of love for him, because he is so talented. . . . In that case, my lot would become unspeakably wretched. He would not want me to love him; and if I showed the feeling, he would make me sensible that it was a superfluity, unrequired by him, unbecoming in me. I know he would."
>
> "And yet St. John is a good man," said Diana.
>
> "He is a good and a great man; but he forgets, pitilessly, the feelings and claims of little people, in pursuing his own large views. It is better, therefore, for the insignificant to keep out of his way, lest, in his progress, he should trample them down."[69]

Jane's wary counterfactual identifies admiration's proximity to desire, recognizing the cold disgust that love would prompt in this good man. In its Victorian iteration, the unassailability of the Grandisonian "good man" is a chilling prerequisite of imperial Christianity.

Jane Eyre crystallizes the psychopathology of Grandisonian romance. By rejecting St. John's offer of companionate service, the novel refuses the masochistic contract entailed in loving the "good man" and returns, paradoxically, to women's moral role in redeeming fallen men. As Deirdre David observes, "rehabilitating the colonizer seems to have come first, and converting the colonized second" during the 1830s and 1840s, making domestic reform a legitimate priority for women.[70] So though she rejects the evangelical self-immolation of St. John's

Indian mission, Jane's love for Rochester is nonetheless a form of sacrifice. Marriage becomes a moral vocation harnessing her disciplinary energies to render this "man of pleasure" "a good husband, a worthy father, and true friend," in Belford's terms. Much like *Pamela in Her Exalted Condition*, Jane has the comfort of knowing she's far too good for her spouse. Like Harriet Byron, too, Jane "implicitly accepts her unhappiness, subordination, and restriction" as the price of moral authority.[71] Refusing the self-annihilating love of St. John, *Jane Eyre* nonetheless remains enthralled by him, acknowledging his value for the moral justifications of Empire. In the novel's final perplexing lines the narrator's thoughts fly to her cousin. "St. John is unmarried," she states, "he never will marry now." "Resolute, indefatigable. . . . Firm, faithful, and devoted, full of energy, and zeal, and truth, he labours for his race."[72] Directed away from companionate union, where it would suffocate "feminist individualism," St. John's zeal is harnessed instead by white Christian supremacy.[73] That magnetic pull of the "eunuch's sublimity" intensifies the "interdependent relationship between [the novel's] erotic power dynamics, female agency, and xenophobic and colonial rhetorics" while allowing Brontë to calibrate the real "pleasures of submission" in Jane's marriage to Rochester.[74]

In its final, unnerving ventriloquizing of St. John Rivers's terminal ecstasy, the novel apotheosizes the hero it seemingly rejected. The clergyman's purity and desire for disincarnation recall Clarissa Harlowe: both are eager to meet their maker and "stand without fault before the throne of the Lord."[75] St. John's ascension irradiates the closure of a marriage plot in which the reformed rake *does* make the best husband: confirming Jane's spiritual insufficiency for the mission acts as an ironic benediction for her marriage to a reassuringly imperfect man. Inchbald and Brontë's rewritings of *Grandison* draw out the ways in Richardson's model of male virginity actively retrenches and consolidates patriarchal authority. These novels expose the retaliatory motivations underlying *Grandison*'s project. Their chaste men of feeling devolve into tyranny, in Elmwood's case, or "punitive detachment," with St. John Rivers: the rise of Richardson's "good man," they suggest, depends on an extreme subordination of women.[76] Narrative arcs that stigmatize female desire and that threaten the extinction of female agency suggest that virginity's "radical passion for renunciation" requires the repression of women.[77] By depicting male virgins whose judgments on women are cold, unsparing, and sometimes cruel, these texts direct our attention to *Grandison*'s strain of misogyny: its use of fair-sex crowdsourcing to deprecate the very "*Femalities*" (3:95) whose desire sponsored the self-sufficient pride and transcendent morals of the hero. But even as they resist Richardson's virginal paramour by replotting heroines away from marital abjection, the very persistence of the Grandisonian figure in late eighteenth- and nineteenth-century novels, and his afterlives in male virgin erotica, confirms him—for better or worse—as an influential template for heterosexual fantasy.

NOTES

1. S. R. to Aaron Hill, October 29, 1746, *CECSR 1*:223. For the argument that *Grandison* encapsulates Richardson's didactic vision, see Emily Friedman, "The End(s) of Richardson's Sir Charles Grandison," *Studies in English Literature 1500–1900* 52, no. 3 (2012): 651–667; Bonnie Latimer, *Making Gender, Culture, and the Self in the Fiction of Samuel Richardson: The Novel Individual* (Burlington, VT: Ashgate, 2013).
2. Samuel Richardson, *The History of Sir Charles Grandison*, vol. 4, ed. E. Derek Taylor, Melvyn New, and Elizabeth Kraft (Cambridge: Cambridge University Press, 2022), footnote 130, 2035.
3. See Laurence Stone, *The Family, Sex and Marriage in England 1500–1800* (London: Penguin, 1977), 502–504.
4. Rachel Gevlin, "Adulterous Austen: Educating the Rake in *Sense and Sensibility* and *Mansfield Park*," *English Literary History* 87, no. 4 (2020): 1055–1078, 1060.
5. Richard Steele and Joseph Addison, *The Guardian*, ed. John Calhoun Stephen (Lexington: University Press of Kentucky, 1982), no. 45, May 2, 1707, 179–180.
6. Louise Curran, *Samuel Richardson and the Art of Letter-Writing* (Cambridge: Cambridge University Press, 2016), 138–139; Richardson to Lady Bradshaigh, March 14, 1751, *CECSR 5*:170. See Michael Orange, "Prudes, Lusciousness and Joseph Andrews," *Sydney Studies* 17 (1991): 46–66, for a study of the comic dimensions of Fielding's male virgin.
7. Samuel Richardson, *The History of Sir Charles Grandison*, ed. Jocelyn Harris, 3 vols. (Oxford: Oxford University Press, 1972), 1:133. All further citations are to this edition and are given parenthetically in the text.
8. See, for instance, Tassie Gwilliam's *Samuel Richardson's Fictions of Gender* (Stanford, CA: Stanford University Press, 1995), which discusses *Grandison* in the third chapter, "'The Good Man, Alas!': *The History of Sir Charles Grandison* and the Triumph of Masculinity"; Elaine McGirr, "Manly Lessons: *Sir Charles Grandison*, the Rake and the Man of Sentiment," *Studies in the Novel* 39, no. 3 (2007): 267–283; Jeremy W. Webster, "Sentimentalizing Patriarchy: Patriarchal Anxiety and Filial Obligation in *Sir Charles Grandison*," *Eighteenth-Century Fiction* 17, no. 3 (2005): 425–442; Helen Thompson, "Secondary Qualities and Masculine Form in *Clarissa* and *Sir Charles Grandison*," *Eighteenth-Century Fiction* 24, no. 2 (Winter 2011–2012): 195–226.
9. Terry Eagleton, *The Rape of Clarissa: Writing, Sexuality and Class Struggle in Samuel Richardson* (Oxford: Blackwell, 1982), 95, 99, 96; emphasis added.
10. See Bonnie Latimer's contribution to this collection. Curran, *Samuel Richardson and the Art of Letter-Writing*, 128.
11. Curran, *Samuel Richardson and the Art of Letter-Writing*, 124–156.
12. See Tarana Burke, *Unbound: My Story of Liberation and the Birth of the Me Too Movement* (London: Headline Books, 2021), for the dynamics of patriarchy, race, and misogyny.
13. *Samuel Richardson's Published Commentary on "Clarissa," 1747–65*, vol. 1: *Prefaces, Postscripts and Related Writings*, intro. Jocelyn Harris, ed. Thomas Keymer (London: Pickering and Chatto, 1998), 18.
14. Martha J. Koehler, "The Problem of Suspense in Richardson's *Sir Charles Grandison*," *The Eighteenth Century*, 54, no. 3 (2013): 317–338.
15. Lisabeth During, *The Chastity Plot* (London: University of Chicago Press, 2021), 37. During's classification of what she calls "the eunuch's plot" as "metaphysical and (often) masculine . . . too good for the world" (27) almost applies to *Grandison*. Sir Charles's sexual renunciation is not a rejection of the world, but the performance of authoritative self-discipline, which fits him as its governor. Instead, it intervenes in character and plot, stimulating and organizing readerly desire and admiration.
16. Daniel Krahn, "Secrets and Selves: Theorizing a 'Grandisonian' Self," *Philological Quarterly* 96, no. 1 (2017): 55–76.

17. Michel Foucault, *The History of Sexuality*, vol. 4: *The Confessions of the Flesh*, trans. Robert Hurley (London: Penguin, 2022); During, *The Chastity Plot*, 16; Corinne Harol, *Enlightened Virginity in Eighteenth-Century Literature* (Basingstoke, UK: Palgrave Macmillan, 2006), 2.
18. Samuel Richardson to William Lobb, London, April 10, 1750, in *Correspondence Primarily on Sir Charles Grandison*, ed. Betty Schellenberg (Cambridge: Cambridge University Press, 2015), 9.
19. E. Derek Taylor, "General Introduction," in *The History of Sir Charles Grandison*, 1:xliii.
20. Samuel Richardson, *Clarissa, or, the History of a Young Lady*, ed. Angus Ross (New York: Penguin, 1984, repr. 2005), 209.
21. *Clarissa*, 802.
22. See, for example, George Wilkins, *The Miseries of Inforced Marriage* (1607): "The wise and ancient fathers know this rule, / Should both wed maids, the child would be a fool."
23. *Clarissa*, 802.
24. *Clarissa*, 440–441.
25. Patricia McKee, *Heroic Commitment in Richardson, Eliot, and James* (Princeton, NJ: Princeton University Press, 1986), 135.
26. Johnson glosses bashful as "vitiously modest," sly as "Meanly artful; secretly insidious; cunning"—with an example from *Clarissa*. *A Dictionary of the English Language*, by Samuel Johnson (1755), https://johnsonsdictionaryonline.com/1755/bashful_adj; Bernard Mandeville, *A Modest Defence of the Publick Stews* (London: A. Moore, 1724), 75.
27. Terry Castle, *Clarissa's Cyphers: Meaning and Disruption in Richardson's "Clarissa"* (Ithaca, NY: Cornell University Press, 1982), 29.
28. Alan Dugald McKillop, *Samuel Richardson: Printer and Novelist* (1936; repr., Chapel Hill: University of North Carolina Press, 1960), 212; *Grandison*, 1:229.
29. *Clarissa*, 1393; James Smith, *Samuel Richardson and the Theory of Tragedy: "Clarissa"'s caesuras* (Manchester: Manchester University Press, 2016), 2.
30. Samuel Richardson, *Pamela in Her Exalted Condition*, ed. Albert J. Rivero (Cambridge: Cambridge University Press, 2012), 152.
31. John Milton's gloss brings out the misogyny in Pauline's formulations of male chastity: "if unchastity in a woman whom Saint Paul termes the glory of man, be such a scandall and dishonour, then certainly in a man who is both the image and glory of God, it must, though commonly not so thought, be much more deflouring and dishonourable. In that he sins both against his owne body which is the perfeter sex, and his own glory which is in the woman, and that which is worst, against the image and glory of God which is in himselfe." *An Apology against a Pamphlet Call'd A Modest Confutation of the Animadversions upon the Remonstrant against Smectymnuus* (London: John Rothwell, 1642; Ann Arbor: Text Creation Partnership, 2011), 18, https://quod.lib.umich.edu/e/eebo/A70588.0001.001?rgn=main;view=fulltext.
32. Richardson, *Pamela in Her Exalted Condition*, 152.
33. Anonymous, *Critical Remarks on Sir Charles Grandison, Clarissa, and Pamela*, intro. Alan D. McKillop (London: J. Dowse, 1754), Augustan Reprint Society, 29–30, 32–33.
34. Bonnie Lander Johnson, *Chastity in Early-Modern Stuart Literature and Culture* (Cambridge: Cambridge University Press, 2015), 144.
35. William Hazlitt notes that "her brother Sir Charles lived to himself" "passes into a proverb among the fair correspondents." Hazlitt characterizes such self-sufficiency as a form of self-absorption: "Sir Charles Grandison was the counterpart of Clarissa Harlowe," he "never admired any one but himself, and was the God of his own idolatry." William Hazlitt, "On Living to One's Self," in *Table Talk, or, Original Essays on Men and Manners*, vol. 1 (London: Henry Colburn, 1824), 209–234, 213–214.
36. During, *The Chastity Plot*, 288.
37. Juliet McMaster, "*Sir Charles Grandison*: Richardson on Body and Character," *Eighteenth-Century Fiction* 1, no. 2 (1989): 83–102, 89; Erin Mackie, *Rakes, Highwaymen, and Pirates:*

The Making of the Modern Gentleman in the Eighteenth Century (Baltimore: Johns Hopkins University Press, 2009), 172.

38. *Grandison* anticipates the sexless decorum of Jane Austen's heroes, whose buttoned-up politeness "explicitly and directly . . . promotes particular ideas of Englishness." Roger Sales, *Jane Austen and Representations of Regency England* (London: Routledge, 1996), 11.
39. Richardson to his translator du Freval, 1751, in Schellenberg, *Correspondence Primarily on Sir Charles Grandison*, 8.
40. Catherine Talbot to Elizabeth Carter, December 23, 1751, 2:64, and Elizabeth Carter, December 23, 1750, 1:374, both in *A Series of Letters between Mrs. Elizabeth Carter and Miss Talbot*, 3 vols. (London, 1809); Natasha Simonova, "Living Clarissas: The Grey Family Papers and Women's Contribution to Literary History" (unpublished paper, Faculty of English, University of Cambridge, February 13, 2020). Simonova suggests that Talbot revised the entire manuscript.
41. Hilary Havens, *Revising the Eighteenth-Century Novel: Authorship from Manuscript to Print* (Cambridge: Cambridge University Press, 2019), 2; Betty A. Schellenberg, "Using 'Femalities' to 'Make Fine Men': Richardson's Sir Charles Grandison and the Feminization of Narrative," *Studies in English Literature 1500–1900* 34, no. 3 (1994): 599–616, 599, https://doi.org/10.2307/450884.
42. Friday, May 10, 1751, in Schellenberg, *Correspondence Primarily on Sir Charles Grandison*, 51–52.
43. See David Macey, "'Business for the Lovers of Business': Sir Charles Grandison, Hardwicke's Marriage Act and the Specter of Bigamy," *Philological Quarterly* 84, no. 3 (2005): 333–335.
44. During, *The Chastity Plot*, 55.
45. As Gillian Beer notes, both Milton and Richardson treat "chastity—both the moral state, and, by extension, as the type of integrity—[as] an absolute." Gillian Beer, "Richardson, Milton, and the Status of Evil," *Review of English Studies* 19, no. 75 (August 1968): 261–270, 262.
46. During, *The Chastity Plot*, 54.
47. Toni Bowers, *Force or Fraud: British Seduction Stories and the Problem of Resistance, 1660–1760* (Oxford: Oxford University Press, 2011), 305.
48. See Jonathan A. Allen, "Theorising Male Virginity in Popular Romance Novels," *Journal of Popular Romance Studies* 2, no. 1 (2011): 1–14.
49. Diana Gabaldon's *Virgins: An Outlander Short Story* (London: Century, 2016) develops the fact of Jamie's virginity (a subject of much debate on online forums), providing a meta-commentary on his decision to refrain from sex before marriage for religious reasons.
50. On the r/RomanceBooks list (160,000 readers), for example, there are multiple threads on "male virgins in romance," "Blushing Virgin or Celibate Hero"; GoodReads has "Male Virgins" with 547 titles and "Best Virgin Male Romance" with *Archer's Voice* at number 1 in both: https://www.goodreads.com/shelf/show/male-virgin; https://www.goodreads.com/list/show/108487.The_best_virgin_male_romance.
51. Ayman, review of October 22, 2022, https://www.goodreads.com/book/show/32822135-archer-s-voice.
52. Richardson, *Selected Letters*, 85.
53. Gerard Barker, *Grandison's Heirs: The Paragon's Progress in the Late Eighteenth-Century Novel* (Newark: University of Delaware Press, 1985), 87; Maria Edgeworth, letter to Elizabeth Inchbald, January 14, 1810, in *Women Critics 1660–1820*, ed. Folger Collective on Early Women Critics (Bloomington: Indiana University Press, 1995), 376–377.
54. Elizabeth Inchbald, *A Simple Story*, ed. J. M. S. Tompkins, introduction by Jane Spencer (Oxford: Oxford World's Classics, 1988), 120. All further citations are to this edition and are given parenthetically in the text.
55. Barbara Judson, "The Psychology of Satan: Elizabeth Inchbald's *A Simple Story*," *English Literary History* 76 (2009): 599–624; Barker, *Grandison's Heirs*, 89–90.
56. Barker, *Grandison's Heirs*, 95.

57. John Morillo, "Editing Eve: Rewriting the Fall in Austen's *Persuasion* and Inchbald's *A Simple Story*," *Eighteenth-Century Fiction* 23, no. 1 (2010): 195–223, 196.
58. G. E. Haggerty, "Female Abjection in Inchbald's *A Simple Story*," *Studies in English Literature 1500–1900* 36, no. 3 (1996): 655–671, https://doi.org/10.2307/450804/.
59. Miriam Wallace, "Wit and Revolution: Cultural Resistance in Elizabeth Inchbald's *A Simple Story*," *European Romantic Review* 12, no. 1 (2001): 92–121, 103.
60. Wallace, "Wit and Revolution," 104.
61. For the romance appeal of St. John Rivers and an argument for his own sexual motivations, see Michelle Thurlow, "Marble under a Strange Spell: St. John Rivers' 'Long-Cherished Scheme' to Wed Jane Eyre," *Journal of Popular Romance Studies*, September 19, 2017, 1–21, https://www.jprstudies.org/2017/09/marble-under-a-strange-spell-st-john-rivers-long-cherished-scheme-to-wed-jane-eyreby-michelle-thurlow/.
62. Charlotte Brontë, *Jane Eyre* (Oxford: Clarendon Press, 1969), 449.
63. Brontë, *Jane Eyre*, 449.
64. Brontë, *Jane Eyre*, 476–477.
65. Brontë, *Jane Eyre*, 455.
66. Brontë, *Jane Eyre*, 339.
67. Deirdre David, *Rule Britannia: Women, Empire, and Victorian Writing* (Ithaca, NY: Cornell University Press, 2018), 80.
68. Brontë, *Jane Eyre*, 502, 501.
69. Brontë, *Jane Eyre*, 531.
70. David, *Rule Britannia*, 85.
71. David, *Rule Britannia*, 80.
72. Brontë, *Jane Eyre*, 578.
73. Gayatri Chakravorty Spivak, "Three Women's Texts and a Critique of Imperialism," *Critical Inquiry* 12 (Autumn 1985): 263–264.
74. During, *The Chastity Plot*, 29; M. A. Davis, "'On the Extreme Brink' with Charlotte Brontë: Revisiting *Jane Eyre*'s Erotics of Power," *Papers on Language and Literature* 52, no. 2 (2016): 115–148, 206.
75. Brontë, *Jane Eyre*, 578. See Kerry Sinanan's "*Clarissa* and White Supremacy: Race, Gender, and Erasure," chapter 6 in this volume, for the imperial dimensions of *Clarissa*'s purity.
76. David, *Rule Britannia*, 90.
77. During, *The Chastity Plot*, 293. For Brett Kavanaugh's invocation of male virginity as claim to moral authority, see Rebecca Anne Barr, "The Good Man on Trial, or, Male Virginity and the Politics of Misogyny" (Online Digital Seminar in Eighteenth-Century Studies, 2020), https://www.youtube.com/watch?v=D_PzV-v_zLQ/.

8

SOLVING FOR Y

Fictive Kinship and Character in *The History of Sir Charles Grandison*

SARAH BERKOWITZ

HOW MANY CHILDREN had Sir Charles Grandison? Julian Bere essentially asked this question when she wrote to Samuel Richardson about the conclusion of *The History of Sir Charles Grandison.* Bere felt the novel unfinished and wanted to "see Sir Charles in the Parental Character."[1] Richardson's reply explains why an extension to his novel is both unnecessary and impossible. Unnecessary because, after cataloging the endings for all of the major and some of the minor characters in the novel, he concludes that their stories had already achieved satisfactory resolutions. The only character who remained unaccounted for is Lady Olivia, and she alone would not be worth another volume (3:469). Impossible because the novel takes place in "pretty near the present time," and any additional writing would carry his characters into the future. Richardson thought it improper to speculate, even in fiction.

But even if Richardson cannot or will not predict his characters' futures, he concludes that his readers already have the information they need to imagine Sir Charles as a father. Attentive readers could already anticipate Sir Charles's "parental character" by watching him interact with other people's children: "See we not, from his tenderness to Mrs. Reeve's little boy; from his goodness to Lady L's son; and to Lady G's little girl; from the observation of his Lady, that the Brave are always tender and humane; from his general prudence, as well as from his own duty to a blameable Father, whose failings he occasionally deplored with a piety worthy of himself; that he would have shone in every part of the parental character? [Who ever knew a dutiful Son that made not a good Father?]" (3:469–470; brackets in original). L. C. Knights might conclude that only the most naive readers could imagine a family life for Lady Macbeth, but Richardson actively encourages this kind of imaginative speculation about Sir Charles. If we rely on Richardson's response to Bere, it's how his characters are meant to be read.

Richardson is encouraging his readers to play a version of "If X were your Y," a series that used to run on the late, great humor website The Toast. "If X were your Y" was a recurring feature that began with editor Nicole Cliffe imagining what would happen "if Channing Tatum were your boyfriend," and providing a list of imagined interactions between "you" and an idealized Channing Tatum ("If Channing Tatum were your boyfriend he would NEVER try to tell you about Slavoj Žižek"). The feature spurred a slew of reader contributions leading to such posts as "If Barack Obama were your father . . . ," "If Natalie Dormer were your girlfriend . . . ," "If Justin Bieber were your son . . . ," and so on. What I find interesting about the formula is that there is as much variability in Y as there is in X: the goal is for the author to match the right celebrity with the right relationship to an imagined reader. Stanley Tucci is an imaginary boyfriend, but Stephen Colbert is an imaginary father; Kristen Stewart is an imaginary girlfriend, but Cobie Smulders is an "ostensibly platonic gym buddy you have conflicted feelings about." The type of relationship between the author and the celebrity creates as much room for imaginative projection as the actual celebrity.

When critics write about character, they generally focus on how authors conceptualize X: *Who* is this imagined figure, and how does the novel get us to imagine their thoughts and feelings? But *Grandison*, I argue, does character differently, and Richardson is much more interested in the imaginative potential of Y: Is Sir Charles meant to be an ideal husband? Brother? Father? Richardson insists that we have all the information we need about Sir Charles's character to know the answer—if X is a fixed variable, then we have all the information we need to solve for Y.

In this chapter, I argue that *Grandison* uses literary character to prompt readers to prioritize imaginative speculation about relationships over interiority. Richardson does this both through characterization of his "good man" Sir Charles and by employing metaphors of family relationships between characters who are unrelated to each other. All of the novel's main characters are prone to claiming proto-family relationships by asking other characters to think of them "as a sister" or "like a father," ultimately forming sentimental extended families. Sir Charles starts the novel with two legitimate biological sisters and acquires two brothers-in-law by the end. But by my count, at the end of the book Sir Charles has eight sisters and ten brothers, and that doesn't include the sentimental siblings adopted in turn by his real and imagined siblings. By emphasizing the rhetorical family over the conjugal or consanguineal family, *Grandison* presents a fantasy of community that is infinitely adaptable and expandable while still retaining hierarchy. Sir Charles's character, then, manifests not only through his interiority but through the sentimental family he creates.

CHARACTER

Richardson's place in the history-of-the-novel canon comes from his innovations in character. In *The Rise of the Novel*, Ian Watt credits Richardson for the creation of individualized characters with subjectivity in realist fiction.[2] Watt describes Richardson's novels as having "a direction . . . towards the delineation of the domestic life and the private experience of the characters who belong to it: the two go together—we get inside their minds as well as their houses."[3] Nancy Armstrong uses Pamela Andrews as blueprint for subjectivity itself, essentially arguing that Richardson invented subjectivity as we know it.[4] Richardson critics interested in individuality and subjectivity have a difficult time accounting for *Grandison*, whose titular protagonist seems to lack the interiority of Pamela Andrews and Clarissa Harlowe. This has always made Sir Charles the odd man out in Richardson's oeuvre.[5] Although his novel enjoyed immense popularity when it was first published and was famously the favorite novel of Jane Austen, *Grandison* oscillated in and out of readers' awareness over the following centuries, and by the mid-twentieth century was downright out of fashion.

Critics offer two explanations for *Grandison*'s relative unpopularity, both having to do with the ways character functions in the novel. The first explanation comes from the novel's prioritizing of communal harmony over individual subjectivity. Rather than plumbing the depths of a fictional psyche, *Grandison* presents a world where the needs of individual characters are intentionally subverted to an extraordinary morality for the good of the greater community. Betty Schellenberg claims it as an example of a genre of conservative fiction from the mid- to late eighteenth century that prioritizes "the circumscription of socially threatening individualistic desire in a plot structure that models a community of consensus as the ideal unit from which a stable society is constructed."[6] She considers *Grandison* as one of "the most fully developed and the most optimistic" examples of the genre (52). The pleasures of these novels are not those of identifying with a single, extraordinary individual, but rather come from watching a community form itself.[7]

Yet the community forms itself around an extraordinary individual. The second explanation for the novel's unpopularity comes from Sir Charles's perfection, which is often dismissed as a form of pandering to female audiences. In *Grandison's Heirs*, Gerard Barker argues that the success of the Sir Charles figure comes from his status as "the feminine wish dream of the ideal male suitor," but because women's expectations were unrealistic, Sir Charles is ultimately doomed to be an "imaginative failure."[8] Richardson himself was aware of the narrative challenges posed by his title character. In a famous letter to Lady Bradshaigh, he complains of the difficulties of writing about a "good man": "I own that a good woman is my favourite character. . . . I can do twenty agreeable things for her, none of which would appear in a striking light in a man. Softness of heart, gentleness of manners, tears, beauty, will allow of pathetic scenes in the story of one, which cannot have place in that of the other. Philanthropy, humanity is all he can properly rise to" (March 24, 1751, in *Correspondence with Lady Bradshaigh and Lady Echlin*,

1:174). There simply weren't as many ways to make philanthropy and humanity narratively interesting, partially because, as civic goods, they lead us away from the world inside the mind and inside the house.

But Richardson's "imaginative failure" springs from a desire to preserve what I would call Sir Charles's imaginative potential. In *Grandison*'s preface, Richardson describes his hero as "the Example of Man acting uniformly well thro' a variety of trying Scenes" (1:4). His uniformity assures us that even if circumstances change, his character will remain steady. It's this very characteristic consistency that makes him especially attractive to women. When Sir Rowland argues that masculine bad behavior is justifiable, as long as it is kept out of sight of ladies, Harriet rebukes him: "A pure heart, whether in man or woman, will be always, in every company, on every occasion, pure" (1:41). Richardson imagines *Grandison* as a kind of writing prompt: fan fiction in the form of a conduct book. The same qualities that assure us we *can* imagine Sir Charles's parental character also suggest it is a moral imperative that we do so.

GRANDI-STANS: IMAGINATIVE EXPANSION AND CHARACTER FORMATION

Fandom is not an inapt metaphor for the way character operates in *Grandison*. Sir Charles is a moral pinup, and the other characters comprise his fan club—writing to one another about his good deeds and exemplary character. Because of the novel's epistolary format, Sir Charles is a textual creation even to the other characters within *Grandison*. Characters such as the Selbys and the Porrettas, who become fixtures of Sir Charles's moral community and his fictive kin, read about Sir Charles in letters long before they meet him in the flesh. Perhaps because of his textuality, I find the most useful tools for understanding character in *Grandison* come from the literature on eighteenth-century reading practices.

In "The Rise of Fictionality," Catherine Gallagher argues "the novel provided its reader a seemingly free space in which to temporarily indulge imaginative play."[9] Gallagher, following Hume, believes that the appeal of fictional characters stems from the dissolution of the barriers between reader and character: "The body of the other person, although it conveys the original sense data and serves as the basis for all the modes of relationship that supposedly allow sympathetic identification, is also paradoxically imagined to be a barrier . . . This proprietary barrier of the other's body is what fiction freely dispenses with, by representing feelings that belong to no other body, fiction actually facilitates the process of sympathy."[10] Gallagher's model of fictionality theorizes a kind of energy created by the potential embedded in the form of character. The space created by the "nobody" in the text is a vacuum that begs to be filled by the reader's imagination.

Grandison transfers the potential energy generated by character onto the relationships between the characters. One of the cases Gallagher presents in "The Rise of Fictionality" is of a young woman of marriageable age engaging in "affective speculation," about a potential suitor. Experience of fictional character gives the woman the "ironic credulity," necessary to see beyond "the literal truth of a representation."[11] Young women of marriageable age abound in *Grandison*, but because Sir Charles "acts uniformly," his intentions and motives are almost always legible. Harriet baldly states, "I am sure I should not esteem him, were he not the good man he is," and she is never given any reason to doubt his sincerity (2:13). Instead, the imaginative speculation comes from picturing the different relationships she might possibly have with Sir Charles. When she fears marriage will never be an option, she accepts a role as his "third sister."

Harriet's unrequited love for Sir Charles reveals the central problem at the core of *Grandison*: there's simply not enough Sir Charles to go around. Sir Charles would be the perfect husband for any of the marriageable young ladies in the novel but can ultimately marry only one person. Writing in 1754, a man who identifies himself as "A Lover of Virtue" takes Richardson to task for making Sir Charles's *such* an exemplary character: "In Grandison, you have endeavoured to give an example of universal goodness and benevolence. But I am afraid you have strained and stretched that character too far; you have furnished him with too great a variety of accomplishments, some of them destructive, at least not so consistent with the principal and most shining virtue. *The man is every thing*, as Lucy or Harriet says; which no man ever was or will be."[12] Actually, it's Mrs. Shirley who says he is "every thing," but the lover of virtue is not alone in objecting to the sentiment. This critique, that the character of Sir Charles was "unrealistic," is the same one Barker makes when he accuses Richardson of imaginative failure. So many good qualities could never fit into a single, Sir Charles–sized container.

Sir Charles's physical body is limited, but his character seems to be infinite, and he has the economic resources to match his benevolence. When Mrs. Curzon shows the newly married Harriet around Grandison Hall, she explains how he looks after his tenants. He does his duty keeping up the estate and managing the grounds. Sir Charles also provides poor relief and medical care to anyone on his lands (provided Dr. Bartlett will vouch for his or her character). Although we are constantly told that Sir Charles is an excellent manager and economist (he has spent his time abroad learning "Husbandry and law" that he might become "his father's steward" (3:288), we never see those skills tested. Dr. Bartlett assures Harriet that Sir Charles will "be the friend of every worthy man and woman. He will find out the sighing heart before it is overwhelmed with calamity" (3:288). His estate is not only self-sustaining but constantly expanding and able to support "every man and woman." I draw attention to the connection between Sir Charles's ability to generate wealth (moral and economic) and his "stretched" character. The two enable each other—the better he is, the further his goodness "stretches."

In *The Afterlife of Character*, David Brewer coins the term "imaginative expansion" to describe certain eighteenth-century reading practices "by which the characters in broadly successful texts were treated as if they were both fundamentally incomplete and the common property of all."[13] Brewer traces what I would call eighteenth-century fan fiction: reader-generated content about certain favorite characters that continues their stories outside the pages of their own novels or plays. Brewer writes about real readers' treatment of fictional characters, but "imaginative expansion" is also a shockingly accurate model of the way Sir Charles's character operates within his own novel.

Sir Charles, too, is "incomplete and the property of all," and a moral community forms around him as the other characters swap "Sir Charles stories." Again, the relationship between characters here seems more like the relationship between readers as Brewer imagines it: "Readers who imagine characters as common, and hence available to the public, also imagine themselves as part of a public, a virtual community interested in the same things as they are, which in turn requires a common object to rally around even as it enhances that object's felt value . . . by making it the commons around which the virtual community organized itself" (14). Circulating tales of Sir Charles creates a fan club, a community of people writing to each other about Sir Charles.

Imaginative expansion is thus what allows Sir Charles to be "every thing." Brewer uses Simon Stern's model of an "economy of abundance" to describe the way circulation creates value: "Any future use becomes a form of increase . . . value is added merely by additional iteration and circulation" (11). The more people who describe Sir Charles's exploits, the more impressive those exploits become. After her tour of Grandison House, Harriet explains that she has minutely described Sir Charles's land management because, "Every-thing he *has* done, *does* and *intends* to do, is proper for you, and for all the world to know. I wish all the world were to know him, as I do; not for his sake, but for their own" (3:289). In an economy of abundance Sir Charles can marry Harriet and still be available to all the world. In fact, the more people who admire Sir Charles, the better the position of Sir Charles's wife.

In the same speech where she calls Sir Charles "every thing," Mrs. Shirley assures Harriet that she has made a wise choice: "There was a time that I thought no man on earth could deserve you: Now it is my prayer, and will be, that you will deserve this man. . . . Yesterday's transaction is your Glory; glory in it, my Harriet!" (3:239). Mrs. Shirley imagines marriage to Sir Charles as a transaction that leaves everybody richer. In the world of *Grandison* the moral community is also a prosperous one: Sir Charles oversees a Sir Charles–backed economy (based on the Sir Charles standard), where his moral character acts as guarantor for the worth of other individuals in his social sphere.

But fandom is notoriously fickle, and the danger for the Sir Charles–backed economy is that some eighteenth-century hipster will come along and claim that Sir Charles is overrated. Richardson needs to show that Sir Charles's moral worth is underwritten by something of real value in addition to infinite social approbation. His social and economic power fall short here, not because they are worthless but because they have an intrinsic value that can be separated from Sir Charles. The symbiotic relationship between Sir Charles and his moral community is essentially tautological: the community models itself around Sir Charles because he is virtuous, but we know Sir Charles is virtuous because so many members of the community model their behavior on his. Fandom provides the form of community in *Grandison*, but it is not sufficient to justify the function.

EXTENDING FAMILY

Richardson manages to write his way out of this chicken and egg problem by using metaphors of nuclear family to describe Sir Charles's relationships with the characters who surround him. "Families are little communities," writes Harriet, early in the novel, "there are but few solid friendships out of them; and that they help to make up worthily, and to secure, the great community, of which they are so many miniatures" (1:25). In the world of *Grandison*, the family is the most important social unit, responsible for meeting all the emotional, economic, and social needs of the individual. As such, one would expect the family to be treated like female virtue: dangerously permeable and always under siege. But if anything, the worry in *Grandison* seems to be that family boundaries are not permeable enough so that the consanguine characters are constantly looking for ways to expand their family circle and enlarge their little community.

As Richardson was writing *Grandison*, the eighteenth-century family was in transition. With the rise of market capitalism, the affective family created by marriage began to eclipse the family of origin as the most important social and economic "kin structure."[14] Ruth Perry describes this shift as moving from "consanguinity to conjugality. . . . That is the biologically given family into which one was born was gradually becoming secondary to the chosen family constructed by marriage."[15] At first, *Grandison*'s conception of the family seems to align with this shift: Sir Charles successfully ignores the confines of the biological family and claims kinship with men, women, and Italians who are not related to him by birth.

But Sir Charles's chosen family is not the conjugal family as Perry conceptualizes it. It's no coincidence that Richardson's novels about extraordinary heroines are stories about the dangers and pleasures of marriage, and that such a narrative is insufficient for his extraordinary hero. When Harriet realizes that she has romantic feelings for Sir Charles, she experiences jealousy for the first time. "Is love, if I must own love, a narrower of the heart?" (1:387). The fantasy of the conjugal family is that of one unique individual recognizing another individual's particularity, of the heart narrowing to gratify romantic and sexual interest. But, if Sir Charles's story were about a unique individual with a soul that only Harriet could comprehend, he would no longer be "incomplete and the property of all," and thus no longer able to function as the linchpin of a moral community.

Instead, *Grandison* presents us with a third model of family that's based primarily on imaginative adoption and is more capacious than either conjugality or consanguinity. Anthropologists call this kind of adoption "fictive kinship," and use it to describe "public validation of a special kind of association."[16] These are relationships that do not have the heft of law but nevertheless validate an emotional connection between unrelated people to the community at large. Olivia Cook describes the epistolary format of Richardson's novels as "mimic[ing] the literary sphere" and creating a "quasi-public" space, "modelled on the relations of the affective family."[17] Fictive kinship establishes the "quasi-public" nature of the moral community: just public enough that Sir Charles Grandison can influence more people than he is biologically related to, but not so public that his influence becomes formalized political power.

It's easy to read this kind of community formation as coercive. Naomi Tadmor argues convincingly that family in this period essentially meant a group of people who shared a residence and owed allegiance to the same authority.[18] As such, the relationship between the "head of house" and the family members was always necessarily transactional. From the marriage contract to the servant's employment agreement, the family was created through transactional exchanges where two parties consented to an unequal relationship. Once relationships are acknowledged to be transactional the motivation of both parties becomes suspect, investing family ties with a similar narrative frisson to romantic ties: What, exactly, are Sir Charles's intentions in claiming that Harriet and Clementina are his "sisters"?

While I agree that this kind of adoptive relationship is not uncoercive, there's more at play here than just Sir Charles Grandison railroading his family and friends into submission. The adopted family relationships have real weight in the novel, but how much weight remains deliberately unclear. When Charlotte thinks Sir Charles has proposed to Harriet, whom the Grandisons have long claimed as a fourth sibling, she asks, "Do I, or do I not, embrace my sister, my *real* sister, my sister Grandison?" (2:132). Charlotte knows that the fictive sisterhood she feels for Harriet is less *real* than a legal relationship constructed through Harriet's marriage to Sir Charles would be. But the potential to acquire fictive siblings also destabilizes the value of the real sibling tie. Charlotte especially is constantly in danger of being labeled unworthy of her consanguineal relationship to Sir Charles. She fears "that he would think her unworthy of that tender relation to him" (1:416). The question for the other characters (and for the reader) is how well their own behavior conforms to Sir Charles's standard, which means their position in the extended family remains contingent.

But oddly, within *Grandison*'s framework, this contingency does not necessarily translate into vulnerability. When the novel begins, Harriet finds herself in a common position for a novel's heroine: unmarried and orphaned, in between her father's house and some imagined future husband's. As a woman without a male protector, Harriet should be vulnerable, but her fictive kinship ties are so strong that she never feels helpless. She has managed to build up an extended family around her consisting of grandparents, aunts, uncle, and cousins who allow her an appropriate degree of both autonomy and protection. In his correspondence, Richardson claims that his aim in creating Harriet was "to make her what I would have supposed Clarissa to be, had she not met with such persecutions at home."[19] Harriet's extended family trusts her judgment, and she responds to them with an appropriate reverence. After a barrage of advice from her family about how to handle her budding attraction to Sir Charles, she playfully replies,

> And now let me take it a little unkindly, that you call me your *orphan-girl!* You two, and my honoured uncle, have supplied all wanting relations to me: My father then, my grandmamma, and my other mamma, continue to pray for, and to bless, not your orphan, but your real, daughter in all love and reverence, . . .
>
> —Harriet Byron-Shirley-Selby (1:309)

The hyphenated last name is indicative of the way family functions as a characterological device in *Grandison*. Harriet's metaphorical family is cumulative, and she imagines herself as a child with more than two parents. Harriet feels cared for because Mrs. Shirley and the Selbys have offered her prudent advice when she needs it most, substituting a practical morality for nearer blood relationships.

Cynical readers may see this kind of adoption as nothing more than an excuse for intimacy under the guise of fraternal affection ("What business had he to take my hand? But indeed, the character of *brother* might warrant the freedom"; 1:391), but it has a major structural advantage over marriage: it radically reshapes the community the characters share. Fictive kinship not only expands the number of young women and men who can be intimate with each other—and, crucially for the novel, write to one another—but also allows for an exponential increase in the size of the total community. After Harriet rejects Lord D, he requests friendship with her partially so that he may become friends with Sir Charles by proxy. He assures her that even if she marries someone else, the bonds between all would be secure: "Dearest Miss Byron, take another worthy young man into your friendship but with a tender name: I shall then claim the fourth place in it for myself. O my dear! What a quadruple knot will you tie!" (2:385). Marriage, the narrower of the heart, will only ever tie two people together, but the brother and sister alliances that the characters form substitute sentiment for blood relations, giving the sentimental family infinite room to grow.

FAMILY VALUE: FICTIVE KINSHIP AND THE ECONOMY OF PLENTY

Two different models of family value and their relationship to patriarchal character are on display in the generational divide between Sir Charles and his "blameable father," Sir Thomas. Sir Thomas is a rake and a spendthrift who cannot access the moral community of fictive kinship ties because he can imagine the consanguineal family and the conjugal family only as mutually exclusive. Sir Charles's ability to reconcile the two models becomes the ultimate marker of his moral worth and upright character.

When he returns from Italy, Sir Charles's first task is to rescue his family from the moral, emotional, and financial mess his father has made of it. His father has, Harlowe-like, refused to provide for his daughters, prioritizing his own pleasure over their security. When Lord L asks about his oldest daughter's dowry, Sir Thomas refuses to give her anything: "I have a good share of health: I have not quitted the world so entirely, nor think I ought, as to look upon myself as the necessary tool of my children, to promote their happiness at the expence of my own" (1:326). Sir Thomas has taught his children to think of the family as an economy of scarcity. When Sir Charles returns from Italy, he is under no legal obligation to provide for his sisters, and Charlotte and Caroline are rightly apprehensive. They are now "in the worldly-wise way of thinking," thanks to their father, and know their provision can come only at the expense of their brother, "it was now . . . become his *interest* to keep up the distance which their unhappy father had been solicitous to create between them" (1:358).

But, true to form, their brother upends their expectations. He greets them warmly, mourns his father piously, and then goes about setting the estate to rights. In one typical scene, when the three are dividing their mother's jewels, they come across various bonds and denominations of money that she has set aside for each child, and a "miniature picture of his mother, set in gold" (1:368). Sir Charles "took [his sisters' purses]; and emptying them on the table, mingled the contents of both together: There may be a difference in the value of each: Thus mingled, you, my sisters, will equally divide them between you. This picture . . . is of infinite more value than all the three purses contained besides" (1:369). The purses allow Sir Charles to literalize the sentimental value he places on his female relations. He mingles the purses to show that Charlotte and Caroline are not in competition for his affection, or his resources—he plans to treat them equally. And just in case they still have doubts, he makes sure they know he values the portrait of his mother over pecuniary gain.

Eschewing his own economic self-interest in favor of family cohesion marks Sir Charles as what John Barrell calls "the disinterested gentleman."[20] Disinterest here means freedom from any kind of self-interest that might come before the good of the nation as a whole. Setting himself up as the disinterested patriarch who puts family love before worldly goods gives Sir Charles the kinds of moral bona fides that simply aren't available to the other characters. Perry claims that the relationship between brother and sister was "a moral litmus test" because brothers were expected but not obligated to provide for their unmarried sisters, and if that's the case then Sir Charles passes with flying colors.[21] Restoring the family harmony, then, is about restoring patriarchal disinterest.

Nowhere is Sir Thomas's self-interest more evident than in his relationship with Mrs. Oldham, his housekeeper and mistress. Taking a mistress means his daughters cannot live under his roof because Mrs. Oldham's presence would automatically tarnish the sisters' reputations. Sir Thomas has again structured his family so that he literally has to choose between his mistress and his daughters. After Sir Thomas's death, it seems that Caroline and Charlotte with their "real" consanguineal ties to the estate have finally triumphed over their rival. Mrs. Oldham is thrown out of the house with only "one suit of cloaths, besides those she had on," and Caroline and Charlotte are confident their brother will applaud their actions (1:356).

If Sir Charles were another Sir Thomas, they would have been right, but Richardson shows that substituting a disinterested patriarch for an interested one fundamentally reorganizes the family. When Sir Charles arrives to adjudicate, he is in a structural position to do justice to all without harm to himself. Sir Charles injects imaginative potential into the relationship between Sir Thomas and Mrs. Oldham, thus allowing a number of generously tactful misreadings that allow him to reconcile the various interests of all the parties. He claims that because his father made no will, they can never truly know his intentions toward Mrs. Oldham or his daughters. His father's lack of clarity allows for a certain amount of productive presumption. He reasons that if his father had made a will, he would have provided for Mrs. Oldham. And not necessarily for lascivious reasons; rather, the relationship between housekeeper and master requires the kind of consideration Mrs. Oldham lays claim to: "I dare say, that my father's bounty enabled even his meanest servants to save money. I would not keep one, that I thought did not" (1:371). This is sentimental family expansion in reverse—by legitimizing the economic tie between Mrs. Oldham and Sir Thomas, Sir Charles can obscure the emotional tie that existed between his father and mistress.

But imposing the sentimental family on Sir Thomas's relationship with Mrs. Oldham comes at a human cost. It's telling that even with the striking number of adoptive "siblings" in the novel, Sir Charles never recognizes Mrs. Oldham's illegitimate children as his family, despite the fact that they share a father. (Although he does provide for them economically and designate Dr. Bartlett to see to their education.) The one relationship fictive kinship has difficulty accounting for is the parent/child relationship. Under normal circumstances, marriage and heterosexual reproduction would be the only ways to expand the "little community" of the family. But if fictive kinship is imagined as a series of consensual contractual relationships between characters who share a moral code, reproduction bypasses the contract. As Tadmor illustrates, children are the only people whose relationship to a family is not (initially) contractual. And Mrs. Oldham's illegitimate children dispel the imaginative potential of her relationship to the larger Grandison family: she can benefit from Sir Charles's generosity, but she is cut out of any kind of affective tie to the larger community.

The changes in the family around Sir Charles illustrate the symbiosis between the "good man" and the shape of the community that surrounds him. The early scenes in which Sir Charles shows his business acumen by settling his father's estate (and a few more estates besides) are also the scenes where he establishes his moral authority: "After the Anderson, the Danby, the Lord W. affairs, he appeared to me in a much more shining light than an hero would have done, returning in a triumphal car covered with laurels, and dragging captive princess at its wheels. How much more glorious a character is that of *The Friend of Mankind*, than that of *The Conqueror of Nations!*" (2:70). This is Richardson's good man in action: prudent administration as an act of heroism. The private family setting allows him to establish both his appropriate disinterest and his emotional sensibility; displaying to best advantage both his good sense and his good heart.

CONCLUSION: SOLVING FOR Y

Unlike Channing Tatum, if Sir Charles Grandison were your boyfriend he would *undoubtedly* try to tell you about Slavoj Žižek. But he would do the same thing as your father, son, friend, or brother. The question, then, is not "How would Sir Charles act?" but rather "How would I feel about a boyfriend who explicates Žižek?" Because Sir Charles is a moral exemplar, we are never in doubt of the action he would take in any variety of trying situation; what we are unsure about is whether or not we could measure up to his example. Refocusing imaginative potential from X to Y, from character to relationship, allows us to garner more imaginative possibilities from a single X than a fixed Y would. Sir Charles may not be "every thing," but he contains the potential to be anything to you.

NOTES

1. Samuel Richardson, *The History of Sir Charles Grandison*, ed. Jocelyn Harris, 3 vols. (Oxford: Oxford University Press, 1972), 3:467. All further citations are to this edition and appear parenthetically in the text.
2. Ian Watt, *The Rise of the Novel* (Berkeley: University of California Press, 2001).
3. Watt, *The Rise of the Novel*, 175.
4. Nancy Armstrong, *Desire and Domestic Fiction: A Political History of the Novel* (New York: Oxford University Press, 1987).
5. For reception history, see Bonnie Latimer, *Making Gender, Culture, and the Self in the Fiction of Samuel Richardson: The Novel Individual* (Burlington, VT: Ashgate, 2013), 1–2; and Sylvia Kasey Marks, *Sir Charles Grandison: The Compleat Conduct Book* (Cranbury, NJ: Associated University Presses, 1986), 15–18.
6. Betty A. Schellenberg, *The Conversational Circle: Re-reading the English Novel, 1740–1775* (Lexington: University Press of Kentucky, 1996), 4.
7. See also Patricia Meyer Spacks, *Boredom: The Literary History of a State of Mind* (Chicago: University of Chicago Press, 1995), and Rebecca Anne Barr, "Richardson's *Sir Charles Grandison* and the Symptoms of Subjectivity," *The Eighteenth Century* 51, no. 4 (2010): 391–411. Spacks blames *Grandison*'s reputation as a boring novel on its preference for "exemplary rather than unique" characters (138). Barr coins the term "anti-individualist subjectivity" to describe communal character in *Grandison*. She describes the communal formation of character in *Grandison* as "totalitarian": "*Grandison*'s idiosyncratic blend of coercion, subordination to a central figure of power, of constant self-examination and openness mirrors the structure of power and knowledge characteristic of totalitarianism. Reading *Grandison* as a novel of totalitarian morality offers insight into the delights of self-negation, and the appeal of this anti-individualist novel, helps explicate critical rejection" (393).
8. Gerard A. Barker, *Grandison's Heirs: The Paragon's Progress in the Late Eighteenth-Century English Novel* (Newark: University of Delaware Press, 1985), 15, 36.
9. Catherine Gallagher, "The Rise of Fictionality," in *The Novel*, vol. 1: *History, Geography and Culture*, ed. Franco Moretti (Princeton, NJ: Princeton University Press, 2006), 347.
10. Catherine Gallagher, *Nobody's Story: The Vanishing Acts of Women Writers in the Marketplace, 1670–1820* (Berkeley: University of California Press, 1994), 171.
11. Gallagher, "The Rise of Fictionality," 346.
12. Anonymous, *Critical Remarks on Sir Charles Grandison, Clarissa, and Pamela* (London: J. Dowse, 1754), 18.
13. David Brewer, *The Afterlife of Character, 1726–1825* (Philadelphia: University of Pennsylvania Press, 2005), 2.
14. A fully historicized analysis of the shift in kinship structures is outside the scope of this chapter, but the literature on the subject is extensive. In addition to Perry and Tadmor, see Lawrence Stone, *The Family, Sex and Marriage in England, 1500–1800* (London: Penguin, 1977); Randolph Trumbach, *The Rise of the Egalitarian Family* (New York: Academic Press, 1978); and Leonore Davidoff and Catherine Hall, *Family Fortunes: Men and Women of the English Middle Class, 1780–1850*, 3rd ed. (London: Routledge, 2018).
15. Ruth Perry, *Novel Relations: The Transformation of Kinship in English Literature and Culture, 1748–1818* (Cambridge: Cambridge University Press, 2004), 14.
16. Charles A. Ibsen and Patricia Klobus, "Fictive Kin Term Use and Social Relationships: Alternative Interpretations," *Journal of Marriage and Family* 34, no. 4 (1972): 615.
17. Miranda J. Burgess, *British Fiction and the Production of Social Order, 1740–1830* (Cambridge: Cambridge University Press, 2000), 27.
18. Naomi Tadmor, *Family and Friends in Eighteenth-Century England: Household, Kinship, and Patronage* (Cambridge: Cambridge University Press, 2001), 20.

19. Samuel Richardson to Lady Bradshaigh, March 24, 1751, in *The Cambridge Edition of the Correspondence of Samuel Richardson: Correspondence with Lady Bradshaigh and Lady Echlin*, ed. Peter Sabor, vol. 1 (Cambridge: Cambridge University Press, 2016), 173.
20. John Barrell, *English Literature in History, 1730–80: An Equal, Wide Survey* (New York: St. Martin's Press, 1983).
21. Perry, *Novel Relations*, 144.

9

"ONE IN A HUNDRED"

Extending the Influence of Richardson's *Sir Charles Grandison*

E. Derek Taylor

In *Grandison* he has done what has seldom or never been bettered.
—Arthur Conan Doyle, *Through the Magic Door* (1908)

Scholars interested in demonstrating the influence of Richardson's final work of fiction, *The History of Sir Charles Grandison* (1753–1754), on future English novelists have tended to point in the direction of two prominent nineteenth-century admirers: Jane Austen (1775–1817) and George Eliot (1819–1880). *Grandison* is often mentioned in both Austen and Richardson circles as Austen's "favorite novel," inspiring her to write one of her earliest pieces of juvenilia.[1] She read *Grandison* "over and over again," we are told by one biographer, and according to her nephew she knew every detail by heart: "the wedding days of Lady L. and Lady G. were as well remembered," he explained of his aunt, "as if they had been living friends."[2] Direct references to Richardson's novel surface throughout Austen's fiction; indirect effects, from characterization to plot lines and tone, are perhaps more pervasive—and significant.[3] Eliot too admired *Grandison*, and her tellingly defensive comments on it have become nearly as ubiquitous in Richardson scholarship as those of Austen. "The morality is perfect," she marveled to Sara Sophia Hennell in a letter of October 13, 1847, on first reading the novel. Five years later (October 30, 1852) she expressed her "pity" to Bessie Rayner Parkes for any "heathen who did not like that book."[4] Eliot's disappointment in *Grandison*'s length would have delighted its author had he still been living. As opposed to Richardson's contemporary Horace Walpole (1717–1797), who found his interest flagging by the time he reached the fourth of seven volumes, or the anonymous reader who implored Richardson in 1754 "to let Sir Charles Grandison's History be the last of the kind you trouble the Public with," Eliot recalled of her first encounter with *Grandison* that she had been "sorry that the long novel was not longer."[5] Her own "long" novels, as with those of Austen, have likewise been shown to carry clear traces of her interest in Richardson's culminating effort as an author.[6]

And here the story generally ends: George Eliot as the terminus ad quem of *Grandison*'s reach. One could certainly round out this picture by pointing to other Victorian admirers, such as Charlotte Mary Yonge (1823–1901). Characters in her wildly successful *The Heir of Redclyffe* (1853) adduce Sir Charles while arguing over the value of "perfect characters."[7] In 1864, Yonge recommended *Grandison* to a budding writer whose manuscript was not quite capturing the "tone" of the period in which her narrative was set. As late as 1899, she found herself using "Grandisonian" to describe the century before hers.[8] Even less admiring treatments reveal a continued investment in the patterns Richardson established in his last novel. Sven-Johan Spånberg notes that the first edition of George Meredith's *The Ordeal of Richard Feverel* (1859), for instance, includes as a "direct descendant of Richardson's hero" one "Mrs. Grandison," whose primary "ambition in life is to give birth to a son of the same moral stature as his ancestor." Eight daughters later (including ones named Charlotte, Harriet, Clementina, and Carola [feminized version of Charles]), Mrs. Grandison comes to believe that the father of the novel's eponymous protagonist, Sir Austin, "is, in fact, the reincarnation of her hero."[9] That neither he nor his son (the title character) are later-day Sir Charles Grandisons becomes a running undercurrent for the remainder of the novel.[10]

It is telling that Meredith cut all direct references to *Grandison* in subsequent editions of *The Ordeal of Richard Feverel*—a sign, perhaps, of his sense of its dwindling allusive currency. Indeed, for some prominent British authors of this period, Richardson's novel had evidently ceased to register particular importance. Sarah Raff identifies what appears to be Charles Dickens's only direct reference to *Grandison* in one of the *Sketches by Boz*, where Sir Charles serves as a deflating point of comparison for the title character, Mr. Watkins Tottle (he "had a clean-cravatish formality of manner, and kitchen-pokerness of carriage, which Sir Charles Grandison himself might have envied").[11] Wilkie Collins likewise refers to *Grandison* only in passing, and as something of a bygone curiosity—in "Mrs. Zant and the Ghost" (1879), the narrator describes Mr. John Zant's "elaborate gallantry worthy of Sir Charles Grandison."[12] One suspects that Anthony Trollope (1815–1882) speaks for more than a few midcentury authors through the voice of Johnny Eams in *The Last Chronicle of Barset* (1867): "The Sir Charles business is done and gone."[13]

Examples such as these may explain Gerard Barker's suggestion in the preface to his 1985 study of the influence of *Grandison* on the two generations of British novelists that followed. "Someone," he speculates, might one day pursue the influence of Richardson's final novel "well into Victorian fiction"—but not, it is implied, beyond. In what follows, I demonstrate that this circumscribed purview can safely be expanded. As it turns out, at least two decidedly canonical authors of subsequent literary periods—Henry James (1843–1916) and Ford Madox Ford

(1873–1939)—continued to feel the gravitational pull of Richardson's "good man." I conclude with a somewhat speculative suggestion about the surprising line running from *Grandison* to two preeminent authors of detective fiction, Arthur Conan Doyle (1859–1930) and Dorothy Sayers (1893–1957), in the hopes that better prepared scholars of these authors and this genre might discover ways to flesh out an admittedly inchoate sketch. My point throughout is certainly not that these authors were only, or even primarily, indebted to Richardson's final novel in devising their own works of fiction. Indeed, what Barker says of Austen probably goes for these writers as well: "While Austen was genuinely fond of Richardson's novel and valued his artistic genius, she was too much a realist and ironist to accept his preposterously perfect hero uncritically."[14] My model for influence, then, is more in keeping with what Woolf was doing when she published *Mrs. Dalloway* in 1925. Clarissa Dalloway is certainly *not* Clarissa Harlowe; and yet we know from Woolf's diary that the author's most famous literary creation resulted (at least in part) from her quite consciously reworking Richardson's doomed protagonist.[15] I contend that, as with Woolf, James and Ford developed ways of adapting what they found compelling in Richardson for their own unique, and sometimes contrary, purposes.

I

Consider the following summary of a novel published in serial form one year after *Daniel Deronda* (1876), Eliot's final work of fiction:

> An extraordinarily wealthy bachelor of his national type, while travelling in Europe, encounters a charming young woman whose family is equal parts aristocratic, Catholic, and arrogant. A fast, enduring friendship develops between the well-meaning protagonist and the young woman's passionate younger brother; a fast, enduring hostility develops between the protagonist and the young woman's haughty older brother. The younger brother does all in his power to arrange a marriage between his sister and his new friend, though his effectiveness is limited due to a wound he receives in a duel fought despite our hero's best arguments against the custom. The older brother, to the contrary, never ceases to recoil at the prospects of a connection between his family and the title character. The young woman, for her part, would seem inclined toward marrying the protagonist, but, her family's displeasure made clear, she finds her way at last to a convent.

The novel in question is *The American* (1876–1877), an early effort by Henry James (1843–1916), first published by the *Atlantic Monthly*. Yet, with only very slight adjustments, the description here offered applies with remarkable precision to Richardson's *Grandison*. The younger brother in *The American*, Valentine Bellegarde, is wounded in a duel over a foolish love matter and dies with the hero, Christopher

New-man (not *Grandi-son*), at his bedside. In Richardson's novel, the younger brother, Jeronymo della Porretta, is ambushed over a jilted lover but, after months of anguished suffering, is finally saved when Sir Charles appears by his bedside with Mr. Lowther, an English doctor, whose salutary efforts (in what must be the funniest unintended joke in the novel) prove remarkably effective. Both Sir Charles and Newman animadvert at length against dueling, Sir Charles generally to enemies who challenge him, Newman to his headstrong new friend. "There are many bad customs . . . that I grieve for," Sir Charles grimly muses, "but for none so much as this of premeditated duelling."[16] Newman wholeheartedly agrees. "It's d——d barbarous and it's d——d corrupt, both," he fruitlessly insists to the recalcitrant Valentin.[17] Claire de Cintré, who is French, does indeed end up in a convent in James's novel, thwarting both Newman's proposal and her rapacious family's attempts to arrange an economically advantageous match. In *Grandison*, Clementina della Porretta, who is Italian, has one foot wavering over the threshold as the novel ends, leaving her family (and more than a few readers) to wonder whether she will become a nun or the wife of a man she seems not to love.[18]

The most instructive connection, and distinction, between the two novels has to do with their respective authors' attitudes toward the cultural values their protagonists embody. "He believed that Europe was made for him, not he for Europe" (66). This is the narrator of *The American* describing, with at least a modicum of ironic distance, the unfailingly self-secure Newman—a man who, when we meet him, is in the process of offering outlandish sums of money for cheap copies of paintings in the Louvre, and who throughout the novel drops such gems as "Well, I am very rich" without a hint of a blush (128). But Europe *is*, it would appear, made for Sir Charles—Richardson might have entitled his novel *The Englishman* and not gone wrong. It is true that Sir Charles bends toward politeness in accordance with the varying cultural expectations and standards he encounters in his continental travels, but never too far. "He censures not others for complying with fashions established by custom," Harriet Byron admiringly explains of her soon-to-be husband in volume 4, "but he gives not into them" (907). Throughout Richardson's novel it is made clear that Sir Charles and the Englishness he represents set the gold standard against which all things European fall short. French and Italian doctors do all they can to treat Jeronymo's wounds, but Mr. Lowther knows best (see in particular pages 972–975). The della Porrettas' zealous Catholicism has its merits, but Sir Charles's measured Anglicanism is superior.[19] Sir Charles's Italian love interest is perfect, but his English one is more perfect. (One could expand this list ad nauseum.) James, unlike Richardson, had traveled too much and lived abroad for too long to allow his American to exude superiority unchallenged.[20] To Newman's astonished recognition that the Bellegardes believe he is "not good enough" to marry Madame de Cintre, Valentine—or is it James?—responds, "Brutally speaking—yes!" (105). The della Porrettas likewise initially reject the "foreigner" and "heretic" Sir Charles (704, 733), but of course never Richardson. It is telling that, in the end, Sir Charles has so fully converted his potential Italian in-laws to his way of seeing that they not only accede to his marrying their daughter but heartily beg him to do so.

There is more than just internal textual evidence to support the suggestion that James's second novel has something to do with Richardson's last. James was certainly familiar with *Grandison*, as his annoyed review of Dinah Craik's *A Noble Life* (published in *The Nation* in 1866) makes clear: "Sir Charles Grandison, with his wig and his sword, his high heels, his bows, his smiles, his Johnsonian compliments, his irreproachable tone, his moderation, his reverence, his piety, his decency in all the relations of life, was possible to the author, and is tolerable to the reader, only as the product of an age in which nature was represented by majestic generalizations." The twenty-one-year-old James found "something almost awful in the thought of a writer undertaking to give a detailed picture of the actions of a perfectly virtuous being."[21] It is worth noting here that "awful" was a far more slippery term in 1866 than it is today; where twenty-first-century ears are likely to equate the word exclusively with pejorative synonyms such as "dreadful" or "monstrous," James's contemporaries would have been likely to affix a meaning closer to "commanding reverential fear" or "awe-inspiring."[22] That James himself may have been nodding, at least, toward the latter sense of the word is suggested ten years later, when he offered a subtly different critical opinion regarding yet another "perfectly virtuous" character—Eliot's Daniel Deronda: "There is something very fine in the author's own feeling about Deronda. He is a very generous creation. He is, I think, a failure—a brilliant failure. . . . The author meant to do things very handsomely for him; she meant, apparently, to make a faultless human being."[23] Here, in the same year in which *The American* was first appearing in print, the author comes, if not full circle, at least halfway back around in his consideration of the character type Richardson so famously, and infamously, established in *Grandison*.

The connections between Eliot's and Richardson's male paragons have been made many times, and with good reason. As Leslie Stephen put it in 1902, "Daniel Deronda is throughout true to his higher nature, and is, in George Eliot's works, what Sir Charles Grandison is in Richardson's—the type of human perfection."[24] It is difficult to imagine that James would have failed to recognize Deronda's and Sir Charles's shared lineage as "faultless" characters, which may suggest a level of Bloomian anxiety of influence on James's part that allowed him to credit, if in limited measure, in Eliot what in Richardson had to be discounted utterly. It is also possible that James is finding in Eliot's Grandisonian character a way of justifying his own "awful" efforts in *The American*.

Indeed, whatever else may be said of Newman, and for all his differences from Grandison, he is, by the author's own accounting, James's version of a "Good

Man."[25] Richardson had begun his work on *Grandison* with little else but the nature of his main character (and attendant narrative difficulties) in mind, as his first comments on the subject suggest: "To draw a good man—a man who needs not repentance, as the world would think! How tame a character?"[26] This same aspect of James's protagonist—"the moral necessity" of his "practical, but quite unappreciated, magnanimity"—likewise proved central from the start, as James recalled of his "first glimpse" of what would become *The American* ("It had come to me, this happy, halting view of an interesting case, abruptly enough").[27] Newman's fundamental decency represented, for James, the core of his novel—a point he stressed with evident exasperation in a letter of October 24, 1876, to William Dean Howells, who had complained to James about the story ending without a marriage between the hero and his love interest: "In a word, Mme de Cintré doesn't marry Newman, and I couldn't possibly, possibly, have made her do it. . . . My subject was: an American letting the insolent foreigner go, out of his *good nature*, after the insolent foreigner had wronged him and *he* had held him in his power. To show the *good nature* I must show the wrong and the wrong of course is that the American is cheated out of Mme de Cintré."[28] The ending that Howells (and many readers since) identified as a narrative weakness was, for James, a necessary component of what had been his point from the beginning. "Whether it was Christian charity or unregenerate good nature," the narrator of *The American* explains with characteristic wryness at the climactic moment, "I don't pretend to say; but Newman's last thought was that of course he would let the Bellegardes go" (306). Newman's character, as the saying goes, is indeed his destiny—and, as his friend Mrs. Tristram offers in the penultimate paragraph of the novel, his defining characteristic is, simply put, his "remarkable good nature!" (309).

II

The appeal of Richardson and his "Good Man" would not have surprised James's friend Ford Madox Ford, a much more sympathetic reader of Richardson.[29] "For Richardson I have the profoundest respect that amounts as nearly as possible to an affection," Ford wrote in 1929. "You might call him an eighteenth-century Henry James," he continues, "and not go so far wrong."[30] Ford's "affection" for Richardson derived in large measure from his attention to, and struggles with, achieving formal realism in his epistolary fiction. "If," as Ford explains the problem, "Sir Charles Grandison is walking in the Yew Walk how can he know what characters are present in and what conversations are being carried on in the Cedar Parlour . . . ?" Richardson's solutions to such difficulties are "so craftsmanlike," Ford concludes, "that we do well to love him."[31]

But Ford does not only appreciate Richardson's carpenter-like attention to technique. "For me," he explains, "I read Richardson for a hearty and wholesome dose of sentimentality." "It is his sentimentalizing," Ford continues, "that is his E string."[32] Of course, Ford had a particular interest in "sentimentalizing," having written, in 1915, *The Good Soldier*, a novel whose protagonist, Edward Ashburnam, is described repeatedly in these terms. "Good soldiers are sentimentalists," the narrator, John Dowell, explains. Edward, he continues, took a "sentimental view of the cosmos."[33] Like Sir Charles, who refuses to dock his horses' tails (195), takes "tenderly kind notice" of infants (1483), and sheds "tears of compassion" over the sufferings of the sick (1201), Edward "loved, with a sentimental yearning, all children, puppies, and the feeble generally" (26). Sir Charles and Edward share similar civic virtues, too, the first as "the best of brothers, friends, landlords, masters, and the bravest and best of men" (325), the other as "the fine soldier, the excellent landlord, the extraordinarily kind, careful, and industrious magistrate, the upright, honest, fair-dealing, fair-thinking, public character" (69). Perhaps not surprisingly, each man is given to irrepressible acts of heroism. Among the "bitterest quarrels" ever to erupt between Edward and his wife Leonora, we are told, "came after he had, for the second time, jumped overboard from the troop-ship and rescued a private soldier" (186). So frequent are Sir Charles's dangerous interventions on behalf of helpless others that even Richardson's most sympathetic reader, Dorothy, Lady Bradshaigh, threw up her hands in protest.[34]

Roads not taken in *Grandison* provided Ford with productive ways forward. Without question the most controversial aspect of Richardson's novel for contemporary readers was the hero's stated willingness to marry into, and compromise with, a Catholic family. To the horror of much of Richardson's English readership, only male offspring would be raised Protestant according to the terms proposed by Sir Charles—the girls, alongside their mother and her personal confessor, would be free to worship at a Catholic chapel Sir Charles promises to construct on his own estate.[35] While the marriage between Sir Charles and Clementina never comes to pass, in *The Good Soldier* we find the Protestant Edward negotiating with tremendous difficulty a relationship with Leonora, his own Catholic wife—and insisting on a compromise, in case of children: "Edward was perfectly willing that the girls should be Catholic; the boys must be Anglican" (103). Like Sir Charles, Edward proposes building "a Roman Catholic chapel" on his own land—and even expresses some dismay (ever the sentimentalist) that "Leonora's confessor did not make strenuous efforts to convert him" (100). Like Clementina, Leonora expresses "agonizing" concern over the thought of bringing into the world children whose souls would be doomed by "false doctrine" (103).

The tragic denouement of *The Good Soldier* results from Ford's willingness to follow to its conclusion a thread Richardson raises only to let drop. In *Grandison*, Sir Charles's young ward, Emily Jervois, falls desperately, dangerously in love with her much-admired protector—and the increasingly dismayed adults around her respond accordingly, Sir Charles by removing himself as much as possible from her presence, his sister and wife by finding Emily a new living situation entirely, all in hopes (as Lady G. puts it) that the "fire may be smothered in her own heart" before it is too late (1417). Nancy Rufford, Edward's ward, likewise moves quite unconsciously from awe and reverence for her protector to passionate affection. "She had lived with the Ashburnhams ever since she had been of the age of thirteen," Dowell explains, and "had not a thought of evil in her head—the poor girl" (70). Emily escapes just in the nick of time, her sanity (and a relatively clean conscience) in tow; as *Grandison* concludes, her infatuation with Sir Charles appears to have been effectively rerouted toward a fully appropriate suitor, Sir Charles's friend Beauchamp. Nancy is not so lucky. Although, like Sir Charles, Edward takes avoidance measures for fear "of the girl falling in love with him" (139), unlike Sir Charles he very much *is* in love with his ward. Nancy's departure for India at Edward's insistence comes too late for her, too late for him, too late for all involved. "He's dying for love of you," Leonora insists to Nancy in an attempt to prevent her leaving. Nancy's response—"I know it. . . . And I am dying for love of him" (144)—represents precisely the sort of unrecoverable acknowledgment the adults in *Grandison* work so assiduously to avoid.

As with Henry James, Ford's treatment of his "good man" includes significant ironic undercurrents; Richardson's contemporary Laurence Sterne (1713–1768) would surely have appreciated the ways in which Ford teases out the suggestive implications of being a "man of feeling." Where Sir Charles's rakish potential remains latent, if only just—"Had he been a wicked man, he would have been a *very* wicked one!" his sister wryly notes (318)—Edward actualizes that potential in ways equal parts reckless and excessive—whether conducting a series of financially ruinous affairs or spontaneously kissing a nursemaid while riding in a "third-class carriage" in India (104–105).[36] Although Dowell is eager to soften the implications of the picture of his friend emerging in his own recounting—"I trust I have not, in talking of his liabilities, given the impression that poor Edward was a promiscuous libertine. He was not; he was a sentimentalist" (62)—Ford himself well understood that the two categories need not be mutually exclusive. Richardson (citing scriptural precedent) had teased both close correspondents and readers of *Grandison* with the possibility of allowing Sir Charles to embrace a polygamous solution to his romantic difficulties; "I think he should have you both," Lady G. mischievously suggests to Harriet Byron as she ponders her and her rival's seemingly equal claims to Sir Charles's affection (1409).[37] This is Edward's proposed solution as well, only he, predictably enough, is not joking. Dowell explains that as tensions between Edward, his wife, and his potential lover build to a furious head, he "seems about that time to have conceived the naïve idea that he might become a polygamist" (130).

The uniformly good behavior of Richardson's "good man" puts him in position to impose his healing will on a world that seems always on the brink of calamity; it is not an exaggeration to say that every situation Sir Charles touches is somehow improved or "fixed" because of it.[38] As readers of *The Good Soldier* know, Ford's "good man" is often not very good at all. He disrupts, rather than heals, the world around him, and his best intentions almost never have salubrious effects. His life ends in suicide. "There was too much of the sentimentalist about Ashburnam," Dowell explains of a man who slit his own throat, "and society does not need too many sentimentalists" (259). Perhaps we might say that if James provides an exasperated revision of Richardson's "good man," Ford provides something more like a wistful, tragic homage. "*The Good Soldier*," Ford wrote in a dedicatory letter to what he claimed as his "best book," "remains my great auk's egg for me as being something of a race that will have no successors" (3, 4).

III

And here I had thought my story would end. As Jocelyn Harris notes, however, "Richardson has a trick of turning up all over the place."[39] On a hunch, I decided it might be worth pursuing what I have long thought of (and accordingly labeled in my working notes) as the "Superman problem" Richardson encounters in his imagining of Sir Charles Grandison. How can an author generate audience interest in a character whose seeming immunity to evil impulses and actions and whose physical indomitability neuter every ostensible source of narrative conflict? Richardson himself was keenly aware of the self-imposed difficulty and ingeniously surmounted it by introducing two "right" paths forward for his protagonist—Sir Charles must negotiate what amounts to an Escher drawing narrative and arrive, somehow, at outcome 1a (marry the wonderful and deserving Harriet) but avoid, somehow, outcome 1b (marry the wonderful and deserving Clementina). The writers of Superman, recognizing that "invincible characters are boring," eventually hit upon Kryptonite.[40]

In part I took to this comparison because I had decided, during the early stages of writing the introduction to the Cambridge University Press edition of *Grandison*, that Superman provided the logical final destination for representations of Richardson's "good man"—the unreality of the character type could survive into the twentieth century only in a genre that unblinkingly embraced unreality. My thinking on this point was essentially (again) standing on the shoulders of Barker, who had suggested that Sir Charles's "exemplary perfection" could not be reconciled with the "circumstantial realism and psychological analysis" of future novels (no mention of comics).[41] Having fortuitously come across the comment from Arthur Conan Doyle that serves as the epigraph for this chapter, however, it now seems to me that a *different* type of "superman"—one whose "astonishing powers of ratiocination . . . put him beyond humanity"[42]—might better capture the direction in which Sir Charles's perfection could be productively reworked.

Doyle considered himself against the grain in admiring Richardson's artistry over the works of his great eighteenth-century rival, Henry Fielding: "On the whole, my balance inclines towards Richardson, though I dare say I am one in a hundred in thinking so."[43] Did any of that admiration find its way into Doyle's construction of Sherlock Holmes? It is possible, of course, to value Richardson's final novel and write the world's most successful detective series without the one having anything to do with the other. Doyle did not need Sir Charles to imagine a character with "superhuman" powers of deduction.[44] But it is at least worth noting here that one of the underrecognized abilities Sir Charles demonstrates throughout *Grandison* is his own astonishing capacity for sleuthing out hidden truths. Whether ascertaining the truth of his sister's embarrassing love entanglement (429) or detecting the anonymous author of a letter warning of an impending assassination attempt (1394), Sir Charles is not simply never wrong in a passive, parochial sense. He is *always* right in an active, involved sense. (This is not to mention Sir Charles's keen awareness of which hearts have melted for him, and when, and how to respond, frequently even before the persons in question become conscious of their own predicament.) One could imagine Watson saying of Holmes what Harriet claims of Sir Charles: "His is the most delicate of human minds" (811).

And what of the next great English detective, Dorothy Sayers's Lord Peter Wimsey? As it turns out, Sir Charles has indeed been proposed as a model. Though some of the evidence adduced is too general to be persuasive—"both Sir Charles and Lord Peter," Elaine Bander writes, "are aristocratic models of gentlemanly honour, delicacy, courage, and wit"—it is true that "both heroes love" and eventually marry "a Harriet."[45] Furthermore, like Sir Charles, Lord Peter laments his society's treatment of single women—"Thousands of Old Maids, simply bursting with useful energy"—and his establishment and funding of a stable workplace for several of them (the so-called Cattery) is, as Banders suggests, similar in important respects to Sir Charles's proposal for the creation of Protestant "Nunneries."[46] It is worth noting that the reader's first introduction to Lord Peter (chapter 1 of *Whose Body?*) finds him tellingly "looking at himself in the eighteenth-century mirror over the mantlepiece"—a telling bit of symbolism for a character Sayers herself later described as an "eighteenth-century Whig gentleman born a little out of his time."[47]

But perhaps the more important point to make in closing is that in focusing primarily on reverberations of Richardson's "good man," I inadvertently foreclosed the possibility of detecting signs of the continuing appeal of his good *women*. Banders offered her suggestion of an affiliation with *Grandison* despite having "no idea whether Dorothy L. Sayers was acquainted with Richardson's last novel."[48] She was indeed. Whatever Sayers thought of Sir Charles as a model for her male protagonist, the tellingly named Harriet Vane (Lord Peter's female counterpart and eventual wife) would seem to owe a clear debt to Sayers's encounter with *Grandison* as a young woman. "I am toiling through 'Sir Charles Grandison,'" she wrote in 1917, "as usual, the woman of secondary importance (Charlotte Grandison in this case) is much more charming and interesting because Richardson is not bent on making her a paragon of all the virtues, & her love affair with Lord G——is delightful, & amazingly true. He is one of those solemn, creeping kind of creatures, & she is a very whimsical, lively woman, & disgusted by his open adoration. . . . Don't you think Charlotte is rather like me?"[49] Sayers thought herself much like Charlotte Grandison; her eventual readers have tended to see a great deal of Sayers in Harriet Vane. Christine Colón uses the transitive property in finding significant overlap among the three: "While Peter Wimsey certainly shares some qualities with Charles Grandison, I think a stronger connection may exist among Charlotte Grandison, Harriet Vane, and Harriet's creator." Like Sayers herself, both Charlotte and Harriet share a resistance to the traditional marriage plot, and both refuse to "feel or act a certain way simply because it is expected of them as women." Of particular significance, Colón suggests, are the ways in which Harriet's long-standing resistance to Lord Peter's romantic interest replays Charlotte's attempt to achieve "a balance that allows each to maintain a certain level of detachment while still being able to live happily in a relationship with a man who truly loves her."[50]

Ford, writing in 1929, insisted that "Samuel Richardson is still read and read with enthusiasm." Indeed, he concludes with needling good humor, "I have even met persons who were engrossed by the conversations in the Cedar Parlour of *Sir Charles Grandison*."[51] If I were a betting man—Sir Charles's stern admonitions against all forms of gambling notwithstanding—I would wager that further signs of "engrossed" readings of *Grandison* by twentieth-century authors (and twenty-first?) are still to be discovered.

NOTES

Epigraph: Arthur Conan Doyle, *Through the Magic Door* (New York: The McClure Company, 1908), 145. As Andrew Lycett explains, this book pulled together "a series of articles on [Doyle's] favourite authors" printed in *Cassell's Magazine* in 1906—and these articles themselves "recycled some previous material." Andrew Lycett, *The Man Who Created Sherlock Holmes: The Life and Times of Sir Arthur Conan Doyle* (New York: Free Press, 2007), 318.

1. See Brian Southam, *Jane Austen's "Sir Charles Grandison"* (Oxford: Clarendon Press, 1980). Southam convincingly rejects a family tradition granting authorship of the short play to Austen's niece Anna.
2. See Deirdre Le Faye, *Jane Austen: A Family Record*, 2nd ed. (Cambridge: Cambridge University Press, 2004), 57; and J. E. Austen-Leigh, *A Memoir of Jane Austen and Other Family Recollections*, ed. Kathryn Sutherland (Oxford: Oxford University Press, 2002), 71.
3. On these points see, in particular, Gerard A. Barker, *Grandison's Heirs: The Paragon's Progress in the Late Eighteenth-Century English Novel* (Newark: University of Delaware Press, 1985); Park Honan, "Richardson's Influence on Jane Austen," in *Samuel Richardson: Passion and Prudence*, ed. Valerie Grosvenor Myer (London: Vision Press, 1986); and Jocelyn Harris, *Jane Austen's Art of Memory* (Cambridge: Cambridge University Press, 1989).

4. *The George Eliot Letters*, ed. Gordon S. Haight, 9 vols. (New Haven, CT: Yale University Press, 1954–1978), 1:240, 2:65.
5. See Walpole's letter of December 19, 1753, to Richard Bentley: "For my part, I stopped at the fourth; I was so tired of sets of people getting together, and saying, 'Pray, Miss, with whom are you in love?' and of mighty good young men that convert your *Mr M—'s* in the twinkling of a sermon!" (Horace Walpole, *Horace Walpole's Correspondence*, ed. W. S. Lewis, 48 vols. (New Haven, CT: Yale University Press, 1937–1983), xxxv, 160, available online at https://walpole.library.yale.edu/. The anonymous complaint (March 28, 1754) may be found in *Correspondence Primarily on Sir Charles Grandison (1750–1754)*, vol. 10 of *The Cambridge Edition of the Correspondence of Samuel Richardson*, ed. Betty A. Schellenberg (Cambridge: Cambridge University Press, 2015), 201. Eliot's comment may be found in her letter of December 21, 1876, to Mrs. Charles Bray in Haight, *The George Eliot Letters*, 6:320.
6. See especially Mark Kinkead-Weekes, *Samuel Richardson: Dramatic Novelist* (Ithaca, NY: Cornell University Press, 1973), 292–294; and Margaret Anne Doody, "George Eliot and the Eighteenth-Century Novel," *Nineteenth-Century Fiction* 35, no. 3 (1980): 260–291.
7. Charlotte Mary Yonge, *The Heir of Redclyffe*, ed. Barbara Dennis (Oxford: Oxford University Press, 1997), 30.
8. See Yonge's letters of March 31, 1864, to Ann Maria Carter Smith and December 15, 1899, to Maria Edith Walker, https://c21ch.newcastle.edu.au/yonge/.
9. I am quoting from 21 of Sven-Johan Spånberg, *"The Ordeal of Richard Feverel" and the Traditions of Realism* (Uppsala: Uppsala Offsetcenter AB, 1974); chapter 2 is devoted to Meredith's complex parody of *Grandison*.
10. Spånberg points to Sir Austin's "disastrous" attempt to recreate a "Platonic *menage a trois*" along the lines of Sir Charles, Harriet, and Clementina (his wife is seduced by his friend) as well as to the "bitter twist" of the novel's end, in which Richard is seriously wounded in that least Grandisonian of practices, a duel (23, 24).
11. See Sarah Raff, "Ghost of the Guardian in *Sir Charles Grandison* and *Bleak House*," in *The Afterlives of Eighteenth-Century Fiction*, ed. Daniel Cook and Nicholas Seager (Cambridge: Cambridge University Press, 2015), 91–110, 91 and 91n1.
12. Wilkie Collins, *The Complete Shorter Fiction*, ed. Julian Thompson (New York: Carroll & Graf, 1995), 693.
13. Anthony Trollope, *The Last Chronicle of Barset*, ed. Stephen Gill (Oxford: Oxford University Press, 1981), 398.
14. Barker, *Grandison's Heirs*, 147.
15. For an account of Woolf's "thoroughgoing" reimagining of *Clarissa* in *Mrs. Dalloway*, see Jocelyn Harris, "Clarissa Lives! Reading Richardson through Rewritings," in *Approaches to Teaching the Novels of Samuel Richardson*, ed. Lisa Zunshine and Jocelyn Harris (New York: Modern Language Association of America, 2006), 140–146, 143. According to her diary, Woolf decided to dive directly into Richardson's novel relatively late in the process of her composition of *Mrs. Dalloway*, writing on August 3, 1924, "And should I demolish Richardson? whom I've never read? Yes, I'll run through the rain into the house & see if Clarissa is there. But thats a block out of my day, a long long novel" (Virginia Woolf, *The Diary of Virginia Woolf*, ed. Anne Olivier Bell, 5 vols. [London: Hogarth Press, 1978], 2:309). By October 17, 1924, Woolf celebrates writing "the last words of the last page of Mrs. Dalloway" (2:316).
16. Samuel Richardson, *The History of Sir Charles Grandison*, ed. E. Derek Taylor, Melvyn New, and Elizabeth Kraft (Cambridge: Cambridge University Press, 2022), 220. Further references are cited parenthetically in the text.
17. Henry James, *The American*, ed. James W. Tuttleton (New York: Norton, 1978), 211; see 206–211. Further references are cited parenthetically in the text.
18. Cf. Elizabeth Carter's illuminating letter of April 3, 1754, to her friend Catherine Talbot on finishing the novel: "I believe Mr. Richardson was determined to be revenged on the

people who thought him too prolix by finishing his Book in Such a Manner as to make the[m] wish it had been still longer." She continues, "However I am < > per[s]waded the Conclusion is a very judicious one though one cannot help Wishing to know in what Manner, after all, Clementina is disposed of" (*Elizabeth Carter, 1717–1806: An Edition of Some Unpublished Letters*, ed. Gwen Hampshire (Newark: University of Delaware Press, 2005), 146).

19. Richardson makes it a particular point of emphasis in *Grandison* that, as Sir Charles puts it, "We Protestants confine not salvation within the pale of our own church: Catholics do" (1057).
20. See in particular Peter Sabor, "'A Safe Bridge over the Narrow Seas': Crossing the Channel with Samuel Richardson," in *All Before Them: Attitudes to Abroad in English Literature, 1660–1780*, ed. John McVeagh (London: Ashfield Press, 1990), 159–170. Sabor notes that the farthest Richardson ever traveled was as a child, when he and his family moved from Derbyshire to London, "a distance of some 130 miles" (159).
21. Henry James, *Notes and Reviews by Henry James* (Cambridge, MA: Dunster House, 1921), 167.
22. All of the quoted synonyms here may be found in the *OED* entry for "awful."
23. Henry James, "Daniel Deronda: A Conversation" (1876), in *Partial Portraits* (London: Macmillan, 1899), 65–96, 76–77. The quoted assessment is made by one "Constantius" in the course of her conversation with "Pulcharia," whose response is also worth noting: "[Eliot] made a dreadful prig" (77).
24. Leslie Stephen, *English Men of Letters: George Eliot*, ed. John Morley (New York: Macmillan, 1902), 185.
25. Richardson and his circle of correspondents used this phrase repeatedly to describe Richardson's unnamed protagonist in the early stages of writing, to the point that Alan Dugald McKillop suggests that "the original title of the story was *The Good Man*" (*Samuel Richardson: Printer and Novelist* [1936; repr., Chapel Hill: University of North Carolina Press, 1960], 206).
26. Richardson to Lady Bradshaigh, letter of [late November?] 1749, in *Correspondence with Lady Bradshaigh and Lady Echlin*, vols. 5–7 of the *Cambridge Edition of the Correspondence of Samuel Richardson*, ed. Peter Sabor (Cambridge: Cambridge University Press, 2016), 5:81.
27. From "Preface to the New York Edition (1907)," in James, *The American*, 3.
28. Henry James, *Henry James: Selected Letters*, ed. Leon Edel (Cambridge, MA: Harvard University Press, 1987), 137; emphasis added.
29. On the relationship between James and Ford, see in particular Miranda Seymour, *A Ring of Conspirators: Henry James and His Literary Circle* (Boston: Houghton Mifflin, 1988).
30. Ford Madox Ford, "The English Novel," in *Critical Writings of Ford Madox Ford*, ed. Frank MacShane (Lincoln: University of Nebraska Press, 1964), 3, 6. Kinkead-Weekes notes that Richardson's "affinity with Henry James" was underscored by Ford's contemporaries E. M. Forster and Percy Lubbock (vii).
31. Ford, "The English Novel," 8, 9.
32. Ford, "The English Novel," 5, 4.
33. Ford Madox Ford, *The Good Soldier*, ed. Martin Stannard (New York: Norton, 2012), 25, 26. Further references are cited parenthetically in the text.
34. In a letter of November 20, 1753, Bradshaigh wonders skeptically of Sir Charles, "how many lives does he save, as it were by accident?" (*Correspondence with Lady Bradshaigh and Lady Echlin*, 5:311–312).
35. See Richardson, *Grandison*, 635, 1116. For an excellent account of the alarm raised by Sir Charles's evenhanded treatment of the della Porettas, see Patrick Mello, "'Piety and Popishness': Tolerance and the Epistolary Reaction to Richardson's *Sir Charles Grandison*," *Eighteenth-Century Fiction* 25, no. 3 (2013): 511–531.
36. Mary V. Yates, "The Christian Rake in *Sir Charles Grandison*," *Studies in English Literature 1500–1900* 24, no. 3 (1984): 545–561, 551.

37. See, for example, Richardson's letter of December 8, 1753, to Bradshaigh, where he comments on Lady G's suggestive suggestion—"The Apostle says, Woman was made for Man, not Man for Woman" (*Correspondence with Lady Bradshaigh and Lady Echlin*, 5:319).
38. Not all of Sir Charles's manipulations have aged particularly well. For an excellent skeptical reading of Sir Charles's arrangement of a marriage between his elderly and largely incapacitated Uncle W. and the young (and financially strapped) Miss Mansfield, see Bonnie Latimer, "'Apprehensions of Controul': The Family Politics of Marriage, Choice and Consent in *Sir Charles Grandison*," *Journal for Eighteenth-Century Studies* 32, no. 1 (2009): 1–19.
39. Harris, "Clarissa Lives!," 146.
40. For a lively account of this history, see Paul Fairchild, "Kryptonite Is Crap," *The Atlantic*, June 20, 2013, https://www.theatlantic.com/technology/archive/2013/06/kryptonite-is-crap/276984/.
41. Barker, *Grandison's Heirs*, 48.
42. Daniel Cottom, "Sherlock Holmes Meets Dracula," *English Literary History* 79, no. 3 (2012): 537–567, 537–538.
43. Doyle, *Through the Magic Door*, 150.
44. Cottom, "Sherlock Holmes Meets Dracula," 537.
45. Elaine Banders, "The Case for *Sir Charles Grandison*: A Note on Barbara Reynolds's 'The Origin of Lord Peter Wimsey,'" *The Sayers Review* 1, no. 4 (1977): 8–9, 8.
46. Dorothy L. Sayers, *Unnatural Death* (1927; New York: Harper & Row, 1987), 42; Richardson, *Grandison*, 867.
47. See Dorothy L. Sayers, *Whose Body?* (1923; New York: Harper & Row, 1987), 13; and Sayers, *The Mind of the Maker* (1941; New York: Harper & Row, 1979), 131. I am indebted to my colleague Chene Heady for pointing out this reference to me.
48. Banders, "The Case for *Sir Charles Grandison*," 9.
49. Dorothy L. Sayers, *Letter to Family*, 1917 (Wade Center Archives, Wheaton College, 68/81-2), quoted in Christine Colón, "Dorothy L. Sayers and the Construction of Female Identity," in *Persona and Paradox: Issues of Identity for C. S. Lewis, His Friends and Associates*, ed. Suzanne Bray and William Gray (Newcastle upon Tyne: Cambridge Scholars, 2012), 156–167, 159.
50. Colón, "Dorothy L. Sayers and the Construction of Female Identity," 159, 161.
51. Ford, "The English Novel," 5.

ACKNOWLEDGMENTS

First, we'd like to thank James Smith. Although his name doesn't appear among the contributors, this volume would not exist without him. Both editors are deeply grateful for the persistence, good humor, and kind encouragement of all our essayists, who have stuck with us through house and institutional moves, the post-pandemic period, and several revisions of the manuscript. Rebecca is grateful to colleagues and students at the Universities of Cambridge, Edinburgh, and Notre Dame, who gave lively feedback on her chapter in this collection. Thanks also to the Faculty of English, University of Cambridge, for a term of sabbatical leave that helped her complete this project. Bonnie owes a debt of gratitude to friends who originally shaped the thinking for this piece, chiefly James Daybell and Elaine Murphy. Thanks also to my new colleagues at Southampton, who have been extraordinarily welcoming, and to the Leverhulme Trust, who supported part of the work that went into this volume through a 2022 Research Fellowship.

BIBLIOGRAPHY

List of Richardson materials referred to in the text (plus suggested abbreviations where relevant).

THE CAMBRIDGE EDITION OF THE WORKS OF SAMUEL RICHARDSON (CEWSR)

CEWSR 1—The Early Works. Edited by Alexander Pettit. In *The Cambridge Edition of the Works of Samuel Richardson*. Peter Sabor and Tom Keymer, general editors. Cambridge: Cambridge University Press, 2012.

CEWSR 3—Samuel Richardson, *Pamela in Her Exalted Condition*. Edited by Albert J. Rivero. Cambridge: Cambridge University Press, 2012.

CEWSR 8–11—The History of Sir Charles Grandison. Edited by E. Derek Taylor, Melvyn New, and Elizabeth Kraft. Cambridge: Cambridge University Press, 2022.

OTHER EDITIONS OF RICHARDSON'S NOVELS AND WRITINGS

The Apprentice's Vade Mecum (1734). Edited by Alan Dugald McKillop. Los Angeles: William Andrews Clark Memorial Library, 1975.

Pamela—Pamela; or, Virtue Rewarded (1740). Edited by Thomas Keymer and Alice Wakely. Oxford: Oxford University Press, 2001.

Pamela II—Pamela; or, Virtue Rewarded. In a series of familiar letters from a beautiful young damsel to her parents: and afterwards, in her exalted condition, between her, and persons of figure and quality, upon the most Important and Entertaining Subjects, In Genteel Life. The third and fourth volumes. London: Printed for S. Richardson, 1741.

Clarissa—Clarissa, or, The History of a Young Lady. Edited by Angus Ross. New York: Penguin, 1985, reprinted 2004.

Prefaces, Postscripts and Related Writings. Introduction by Jocelyn Harris, edited by Thomas Keymer. Vol. 1 of *Samuel Richardson's Published Commentary on "Clarissa," 1747–65*. London: Pickering & Chatto, 1998.

Letters and Passages Restored from the Original Manuscripts of the History of "Clarissa," 1751. Introduction by Peter Sabor, bibliographic essay by O. M. Brack. Vol. 2 of *Samuel Richardson's Published Commentary on "Clarissa," 1747–65*. London: Pickering & Chatto, 1998.

Grandison—The History of Sir Charles Grandison (1753–1754). Edited by Jocelyn Harris. 3 vols. Oxford: Oxford University Press, 1972.

A Collection of the Moral and Instructive Sentiments, Maxims, Cautions, and Reflections, Contained in the Histories of "Pamela," "Clarissa," and "Sir Charles Grandison" (1755). Introduction by John A. Dussinger, afterword by Ann Jessie Van Sant. Vol. 3 of *Samuel Richardson's Published Commentary on "Clarissa," 1747–65*. London: Pickering and Chatto, 1998.

THE CAMBRIDGE EDITION OF THE CORRESPONDENCE OF SAMUEL RICHARDSON (CECSR)

CECSR 1—Correspondence with Aaron Hill and the Hill Family. Edited by Christine Gerrard. Cambridge: Cambridge University Press, 2013.

CECSR 5–7—Correspondence with Lady Bradshaigh and Lady Echlin. Edited by Peter Sabor. 3 vols. Cambridge: Cambridge University Press, 2016.

CECSR 10—Correspondence Primarily on Sir Charles Grandison (1750–1754). Edited by Betty Schellenberg. Cambridge: Cambridge University Press, 2015.

OTHER RICHARDSON LETTERS AND COLLECTIONS OF LETTERS

Correspondence. Edited by Anna Laetitia Barbauld. 6 vols. London: Phillips, 1804.

Richardson to Thomas Verren Richardson. Reprinted in *The Imperial Review; Or London and Dublin Literary Journal* (August 1804): 609–616.

Selected Letters. Edited by John Carroll. Oxford: Clarendon Press, 1964.

OTHER PRIMARY AND ARCHIVAL MATERIAL

Allestree, Richard. *The Whole Duty of Man.* London, 1657.

Anonymous. *An Amorous Dialogue between Iohn and his Mistris.* London, 1685.

———. *Apprentice's Faithful Monitor.* London, 1733.

———. *Critical Remarks on Sir Charles Grandison, Clarissa, and Pamela.* London: J. Dowse, 1754.

———. *Cruel and Barbarous News from Gheapside* [*sic*] *in London: Being a True and Faithful Relation of an horid* [*sic*] *Fact, acted by an unhuman Mistris upon the body of her Apprentice. . . .* London, 1676.

———. *An excellent Ballad of George Barnwel an Apprentice of London, who was undone by a strumpet, who having thrice robbed his Master, and murdered his Vncle in Ludlow.* London, 1661.

———. *Gods Justice against Murther, or The Bloudy Apprentice Executed.* London, 1668.

———. *The Loyal London Prentice.* London, 1681.

———. "Weekly Miscellany." *The Gentleman's Magazine*, December 8, 1733.

———. *The Woman of Colour.* Edited by Dominique Lyndon. 1808. Peterborough, ON: Broadview Press, 2016.

Armstrong, John. *The Art of Preserving Health.* 3 vols. Dublin: James Rudd, 1756.

Austen-Leigh, J. E. *A Memoir of Jane Austen and Other Family Recollections.* Edited by Kathryn Sutherland. Oxford: Oxford University Press, 2002.

Boswell, James. *The Life of Samuel Johnson, LL.D.* Edited by John Wilson Croker. 2 vols. New York: Harper and Brothers, 1846.

B. P. *The Prentises Practise in Godlinesse, and His True Freedome.* London: Iohn Bach, 1608.

Brontë, Charlotte. *Jane Eyre.* Edited by Juliet Atkinson and Margaret Smith. Oxford: Clarendon Press, 1969.

Burton, Robert. *The Anatomy of Melancholy.* Vol. 1: *Text.* Edited by Thomas C. Faulkner, Nicolas K. Kiessling, and Rhonda L. Blair. Oxford: Clarendon Press, 1989.

Campbell, R. *The London Tradesman. Being a Compendious View of all the Trades, Professions, Arts, both Liberal and Mechanic, Now Practised in the cities of London and Westminster.* London: T. Gardner, 1747.

Carter, Elizabeth. *Elizabeth Carter, 1717–1806: An Edition of Some Unpublished Letters.* Edited by Gwen Hampshire. Newark: University of Delaware Press, 2005.

Cheyne, George. *An Essay of Health and Long Life.* London, 1724.

Chico, Tita. *Designing Women: The Dressing Room in Eighteenth-Century English Literature and Culture.* Lewisburg, PA: Bucknell University Press, 2005.

Churchill, Charles. *The Poetical Works of Charles Churchill*. Edited by Douglas Grant. Oxford: Clarendon Press, 1956.

Collins, Wilkie. *The Complete Shorter Fiction*. Edited by Julian Thompson. New York: Carroll & Graf, 1995.

Cooper, Anthony Ashley (Earl of Shaftesbury). *Characteristics of Men, Manners, Opinions, Times*. Edited by Lawrence E. Klein. Cambridge: Cambridge University Press, 1999.

Crouch, Nathaniel [Richard Burton, pseud.]. *The Apprentices Companion, Containing Plain and Useful Directions for Servants, especially Apprentices; How to Perform Their Particular Duties to Their Masters, So as to Please God*. London: Thomas Mercer, 1681.

Davenport, William. *The Papers of William Davenport & Co. 1745–1797*. British Online Archives. https://britishonlinearchives.com/collections/12/slave-trading-records-from-william-davenport-co-1745-1797.

Davies, Rebecca S. "The Maternal Contradiction: Representing the Fictional Mother in Richardson's Pamela II (1741)." *Journal for Eighteenth-Century Studies* 33, no. 3 (September 2010): 381–397.

Defoe, Daniel. *The Complete English Tradesman*. London: Charles Rivington, 1726.

Doyle, Arthur Conan. *Through the Magic Door*. New York: McClure, 1908.

Dworkin, Craig. *Chapter XXIV—The Missing Chapter*. Salt Lake City, UT: Red Butte Press, 2013.

Dworkin, Craig, Simon Morris, and Nick Thurston. *Do or DIY*. York, UK: information as material, 2012.

Eliot, George. *The George Eliot Letters*. Edited by Gordon S. Haight. 9 vols. New Haven, CT: Yale University Press, 1954–1978.

Fielding, Sarah, and Jane Collier. *The Cry: A New Dramatic Fable*. Edited by Carolyn Woodward. 1754. Lexington: University Press of Kentucky, 2018.

Fielding, Sir John. *The Universal Mentor*. London, 1763.

Ford, Ford Madox. "The English Novel." In *Critical Writings of Ford Madox Ford*, edited by Frank MacShane, 3–20. Lincoln: University of Nebraska Press, 1964.

———. *The Good Soldier*. Edited by Martin Stannard. New York: Norton, 2012.

Gerard, Sarah. "Trisha Low." *Bomb Magazine*, June 3, 2014. https://bombmagazine.org/articles/trisha-low/.

Harkin, Natalie. *Dirty Words*. Melbourne: Cordite Books, 2015.

Hartman, Saidiya. "The Belly of the World: A Note on Black Women's Labors, Souls." *Souls* 18, no. 1 (2016): 166–173.

———. "Venus in Two Acts." *Small Axe* 12, no. 2 (2008): 1–14.

Howe, Susan. *The Liberties*. Guilford, CT: Loon Books, 1980.

Hutcheson, Francis. *An Inquiry into the Origin of Our Ideas of Beauty and Virtue*. London: J. Darby, 1726.

Inchbald, Elizabeth. *A Simple Story*. Edited by J. M. S. Tompkins, introduction by Jane Spencer. 1791. Oxford: Oxford World's Classics, 1988.

James, Henry. *The American*. Edited by James W. Tuttleton. New York: Norton, 1978.

———. "Daniel Deronda: A Conversation" (1876). In *Partial Portraits*, 65–96. London: Macmillan, 1899.

———. *Henry James: Selected Letters*. Edited by Leon Edel. Cambridge, MA: Harvard University Press, 1987.

———. *Notes and Reviews by Henry James*. Cambridge, MA: Dunster House, 1921.

J. S. *The Famous History of Aurelius the Valiant London-Prentice Shewing His Noble Exploits at Home and Abroad, His Love, and Great Success. Very Pleasant and Delightful*. London: J. Bach, 1686.

Keymer, Tom, and Peter Sabor, eds. *The "Pamela" Controversy: Criticisms and Adaptations of Samuel Richardson's "Pamela," 1740–1750*. 6 vols. Cambridge: Cambridge University Press, 2001.

Kirkman, Francis. *The Unlucky Citizen: Experimentally Described in the Various Misfortunes of an Unlucky Londoner.* London, 1673.

Li, Bella. *Argosy.* Sydney: Vagabond Press, 2017.

Long, Edward. *The History of Jamaica or, General Survey of the Antient and Modern State of that Island: With Reflections on its Situation, Settlements, Inhabitants, Climate, Products, Commerce, Laws, and Government.* Vol. 2. London: T. Lowndes, 1774.

Low, Trisha. *The Compleat Purge.* Chicago: Kenning Editions, 2013.

———. "Confessions." In *Against Expression: An Anthology of Conceptual Writing,* edited by Craig Dworkin and Kenneth Goldsmith, 352–358. Evanston, IL: Northwestern University Press, 2011.

———. *Confessions [of a Variety].* Oakland: gauss pdf, 2010.

———. "On Being-Hated: Conceptualism, the Mongrel Coalition, the House That Built Me." Open Space, May 20, 2015. https://openspace.sfmoma.org/2015/05/on-being-hated-conceptualism-the-mongrel-coalition-the-house-that-built-me/.

———. *Socialist Realism.* Minneapolis, MN: Coffee House Press, 2019.

———. "You Guys, We Need to Talk about Felix." In *Notes on Post-Conceptual Poetry,* edited by Felix Bernstein, 9–13. Los Angeles: Insert Blanc Press, 2015.

Low, Trisha, Benjamin Anastas, and Agata Tuszynska. "Better Off Said." Interview by Rachel Riederer. *Guernica,* June 3, 2013. https://www.guernicamag.com/better-off-said/.

Mandeville, Bernard. *A Modest Defence of the Publick Stews.* London: A. Moore, 1724.

Mauclerc, James. *The Christian's Magazine.* London: S. Richardson, 1750.

Milton, John. *An Apology Against a Pamphlet Call'd A Modest Confutation of the Animadversions upon the Remonstrant Against Smectymnuus.* London: John Rothwell, 1642.

Morgan, Jennifer L. "*Partus Sequitur Ventrem:* Law, Race, and Reproduction in Colonial Slavery." *Small Axe* 55 (2018): 1–17.

Nace, Nicholas D. *catch-words.* York, UK: information as material, 2018.

Palmer, Charles. *A Collection of Select Aphorisms and Maxims: With Several Historical Observations: Extracted from the Most Eminent Authors.* London: E. Cave, 1748.

Philip, M. NourbeSe. *Zong!* Middletown, CT: Wesleyan University Press, 2008.

Sade, Marquis de. *The Crimes of Love.* Translated by David Coward. New York: Oxford University Press, 2005.

———. *Justine, or the Misfortunes of Virtue.* Translated by John Phillips. New York: Oxford University Press, 2012.

———. *The 120 Days of Sodom and Other Writings.* Translated by Austryn Wainhouse and Richard Seaver. New York: Grove Press, 1966.

Sayers, Dorothy L. *Letter to Family.* 1917. Norton, MA: Wade Center Archives, Wheaton College, 68/81-2.

———. *The Mind of the Maker.* 1941. New York: Harper & Row, 1979.

———. *Unnatural Death.* 1927. New York: Harper & Row, 1987.

———. *Whose Body?* 1923. New York: Harper & Row, 1987.

Sherrod, Danielle. "An Interview with Trisha Low." *Bookslut,* December 2013. http://www.bookslut.com/features/2013_12_020428.php/.

Slave Voyages. "Trans-Atlantic Slave Trade—Estimates." www.slavevoyages.org/assessment/estimates/.

Smythies, William. *Advice to Apprentices, And other Young Persons, To beware of Evil Company and Evil Courses: And particularly of THEFT.* London, 1687.

Stephen, Leslie. *George Eliot.* Edited by John Morley. New York: Macmillan, 1906.

Sterne, Laurence. *Tristram Shandy.* Edited by James A. Work. New York: Odyssey Press, 1940.

———. *Tristram Shandy: The Text.* Edited by Melvyn New and Joan New. The Florida Edition of the Works of Laurence Sterne. Gainesville: University Press of Florida, 1978.

Thomas Thistlewood Papers, James Marshall and Marie-Louise Osborn Collection, Beinecke Rare Book and Manuscript Library, Yale University.

Trenchfield, Caleb. *A Cap of Gray Hairs for a Green Head: Or, A Fathers Counsel to His Son, an Apprentice in London.* 5th ed. Glasgow, 1692.

Trollope, Anthony. *The Last Chronicle of Barset.* Edited by Stephen Gill. Oxford: Oxford University Press, 1981.

Tryon, Thomas. *A New Method of Educating Children: Or, Rules and Directions for the Ordering and Governing Them during their Younger Years.* London, 1695.

Walpole, Horace. *Horace Walpole's Correspondence.* Edited by W. S. Lewis. 48 vols. New Haven, CT: Yale University Press, 1937–1983. Available online at https://walpole.library.yale.edu/.

Whittaker, Alison. *Blakwork.* Broome, Australia: Magabala Books, 2018.

Woolf, Virginia. *The Diary of Virginia Woolf.* Edited by Anne Olivier Bell. 5 vols. London: Hogarth Press, 1978.

Yonge, Charlotte Mary. *The Heir of Redclyffe.* Edited by Barbara Dennis. Oxford: Oxford University Press, 1997.

———. "Letters of Charlotte Mary Yonge." https://c21ch.newcastle.edu.au/yonge/.

Zinzano, Nicholas. *The Servants Calling; With Some Advice to the Apprentice.* London, 1725.

SECONDARY MATERIAL

Abramowicz, Sarah. "English Child Custody Law, 1660–1839: The Origins of Judicial Intervention in Paternal Custody." *Columbia Law Review* 99, no. 5 (1999): 1344–1392.

Aljoe, Nicole. "Reading the 'Memoirs of the Life of Florence Hall' through *The Long Song* of the Caribbean Colonial Archive." *American Literary History* 32, no. 4 (2020): 623–644.

Allan, David. *Commonplace Books and Reading in Georgian England.* Cambridge: Cambridge University Press, 2010.

Allen, Jonathan A. "Theorizing Male Virginity in Popular Romance Novels." *Journal of Popular Romance Studies* 2, no. 1 (2011): 1–14.

Altieri, Charles, and Nicholas D. Nace, eds. *The Fate of Difficulty in the Poetry of Our Time.* Evaston, IL: Northwestern University Press, 2018.

Aravamudan, Srinivas. "The Return of Anachronism." *Modern Language Quarterly* 62, no. 4 (December 2001): 331–354.

Armstrong, Nancy. *Desire and Domestic Fiction: A Political History of the Novel.* Oxford: Oxford University Press, 1987.

Arrosa, María Laura, and Néstor Gandelman. "Happiness Decomposition: Female Optimism." *Journal of Happiness Studies* 17 (2016): 731–756.

Backscheider, Paula, ed. *Revising Women: Eighteenth-Century "Women's Fiction" and Social Engagement.* Baltimore: Johns Hopkins University Press, 2000.

Bal, Mieke. *Narratology: Introduction to the Theory of Narrative.* 3rd ed. Toronto: University of Toronto Press, 2009.

Banders, Elaine. "The Case for *Sir Charles Grandison*: A Note on Barbara Reynolds's 'The Origin of Lord Peter Wimsey.'" *The Sayers Review* 1, no. 4 (1977): 8–9.

Barchas, Janine. *Graphic Design, Print Culture, and the Eighteenth-Century Novel.* Cambridge: Cambridge University Press, 2003.

Barker, Gerard A. *Grandison's Heirs: The Paragon's Progress in the Late Eighteenth-Century English Novel.* Newark: University of Delaware Press, 1985.

Barkman, Adam. "Negative Happiness." *Kritike: An Online Journal of Philosophy* 3, no. 1 (2009): 72–77.

Barr, Rebecca Anne. "Black Transactions: Waste and Abundance in Samuel Richardson's *Clarissa.*" In *The Afterlife of Used Things: Recycling in the Eighteenth Century*, edited by Ariane Fennetaux, Amélie Junqua, and Sophie Vasset, 199–211. London: Routledge, 2014.

———. "Richardsonian Fiction, Women's Raillery, and Heteropessimist Humour." *Eighteenth-Century Fiction* 33 (2021): 575–600.

———. "Richardson's *Sir Charles Grandison* and the Symptoms of Subjectivity." *The Eighteenth Century* 51, no. 4 (2010): 391–411.

Barrell, John. *English Literature in History, 1730–80: An Equal, Wide Survey*. New York: St. Martin's Press, 1983.

Batchelor, Jennie. *Dress, Distress and Desire: Clothing and the Female Body in Eighteenth-Century Literature*. Basingstoke, UK: Palgrave Macmillan, 2005.

Beer, Gillian. "Richardson, Milton, and the Status of Evil." *Review of English Studies* 19, no. 75 (1968): 261–270.

Ben-Amos, Ilana Krausman. *Adolescence and Youth in Early Modern England*. New Haven, CT: Yale University Press, 1994.

Benedict, Barbara. *Making the Modern Reader: Cultural Mediation in Early Modern Literary Anthologies*. Princeton, NJ: Princeton University Press, 1996.

Bernstein, Felix. *Notes on Post-Conceptual Poetry*. Los Angeles: Insert Blanc Press, 2015.

Bhabha, Homi. *The Location of Culture*. London: Routledge, 1992.

Blackburn, Robin. *The Making of New World Slavery: From the Baroque to the Modern, 1492–1800*. London: Verso, 1997.

Blewett, David, ed. *Passion and Virtue: Essays on the Novels of Samuel Richardson*. Toronto: University of Toronto Press, 2001.

Boe, Ana de Freitas, and Abby Coykendall, eds. *Heteronormativity in Eighteenth-Century Literature and Culture*. Farnham, UK: Ashgate, 2014.

Booker, Kristina. "Richardson's *Pamela*, Defoe's *Roxana*, and Emulation Anxiety in Eighteenth-Century Britain." *Journal for Early Modern Cultural Studies* 14, no. 2 (2014): 41–61.

Bowers, Toni. *Force or Fraud: British Seduction Stories and the Problem of Resistance, 1660–1760*. Oxford: Oxford University Press, 2011.

Brewer, David. *The Afterlife of Character, 1726–1825*. Philadelphia: University of Pennsylvania Press, 2005.

Brissenden, R. F. *Clarissa: Preface, Hints of Prefaces, and Postscript*. Los Angeles: William Andrews Clark Memorial Library, University of California, Los Angeles, 1964.

———. *Virtue in Distress: Studies in the Novel of Sentiment from Richardson to Sade*. London: Macmillan, 1974.

Burgess, Miranda J. *British Fiction and the Production of Social Order, 1740–1830*. Cambridge: Cambridge University Press, 2000.

Burke, Tarana. *Unbound: My Story of Liberation and the Birth of the Me Too Movement*. London: Headline Books, 2021.

Burnard, Trevor. *Mastery, Tyranny and Desire: Thomas Thistlewood and His Slaves in the Anglo-Jamaican World*. Chapel Hill: University of North Carolina Press, 2004.

Busse, Kristina. *Framing Fan Fiction: Literary and Social Practices in Fan Fiction Communities*. Iowa City: University of Iowa Press, 2017.

Carruthers, A. J. *Notational Experiments in North American Long Poems, 1961–2011: Stave Sightings*. Cham, Switzerland: Palgrave Macmillan, 2017.

———. "Sound, Visual, Digital and Conceptual Poetries in Australia." In *The Cambridge Companion to Australian Poetry*, edited by Anne Vickery, 348–349. Cambridge: Cambridge University Press, 2024.

Cascone, Kim. "The Aesthetics of Failure: 'Post-Digital' Tendencies in Contemporary Computer Music." *Computer Music Journal* 24, no. 4 (2000): 12–18.

Castle, Terry. *Clarissa's Cyphers: Meaning and Disruption in Richardson's "Clarissa."* Ithaca, NY: Cornell University Press, 1982.

Chartier, Roger. *Inscription and Erasure: Literature and Written Culture from the Eleventh to the Eighteenth Century*. Translated by Arthur Goldhammer. Philadelphia: University of Pennsylvania Press, 2007.

Chaskin, Hannah. "'Precise, Perverse, Unreasonable': Queer Form and Genre Trouble in Richardson's *Pamela*." *Modern Philology* 117, no. 1 (2019): 70–90.

Clemens, Justin. "After After Finitude: An Afterword." In *Aesthetics After Finitude*, edited by Baylee Brits, Prudence Gibson, and Amy Ireland, 229–235. Melbourne: re.press, 2016.

Cohen, Margaret, and Carolyn Dever, eds. *The Literary Channel: The Inter-national Invention of the Novel.* Princeton, NJ: Princeton University Press, 2002.

Colón, Christine. "Dorothy L. Sayers and the Construction of Female Identity." In *Persona and Paradox: Issues of Identity for C. S. Lewis, His Friends and Associates*, edited by Suzanne Bray and William Gray, 156–167. Newcastle upon Tyne: Cambridge Scholars, 2012.

Cottom, Daniel. "Sherlock Holmes Meets Dracula." *English Literary History* 79, no. 3 (2012): 537–567.

Cramer, Florian. "What Is 'Post-Digital?'" *APRJA* 3, no. 1 (2014): 10–24.

Cressy, David. *Literacy and the Social Order: Reading and Writing in Tudor and Stuart England.* 1980. Reprint, Cambridge: Cambridge University Press, 2006.

Curran, Louise. *Samuel Richardson and the Art of Letter-Writing.* Cambridge: Cambridge University Press, 2016.

Curran, Louise, and Sören Hammerschmidt. "Mediation, Authorship, and Samuel Richardson: An Introduction." In "Mediating Richardson," special issue, *Eighteenth-Century Fiction* 29 no. 2 (2016): 121–129.

Dale, Amelia. "Black Page: *Tristram Shandy* after Conceptualism." *The Shandean* 33 (2022): 101–131.

———. "Contemporary Art and the Eighteenth-Century Novel." In *The Edinburgh Companion to the Eighteenth-Century British Novel and the Arts*, edited by Jakub Lipski and M-C. Newbould, 488–491. Edinburgh: Edinburgh University Press, 2024.

David, Deirdre. *Rule Britannia: Women, Empire, and Victorian Writing.* Ithaca, NY: Cornell University Press, 2018.

Davidoff, Leonore, and Catherine Hall. *Family Fortunes: Men and Women of the English Middle Class, 1780–1850.* 3rd ed. London: Routledge, 2018.

Davis, M. A. "'On the Extreme Brink' with Charlotte Brontë: Revisiting *Jane Eyre*'s Erotics of Power." *Papers on Language and Literature* 52, no. 2 (2016): 115–148.

DeGabriele, Peter. *Sovereign Power and the Enlightenment: Eighteenth-Century Literature and the Problem of the Political.* Lewisburg, PA: Bucknell University Press, 2015.

DeRitter, Jones. "A Cult of Dependence: The Social Context of *The London Merchant*." *Comparative Drama* 21, no. 4 (1987–1988): 374–386.

Dinshaw, Carolyn, Lee Edelman, Roderick A. Ferguson, Carla Freccero, Elizabeth Freeman, Judith (Jack) Halberstam, Annamarie Jagose, Christopher Nealon, and Nguyen Tan Hoang. "Theorizing Queer Temporalities: A Roundtable Discussion." *GLQ: A Journal of Lesbian and Gay Studies* 13, no. 2–3 (2007): 177–195.

Domingo, Darryl. "Richardson's Unfamiliar Quotations: *Clarissa* and Early-Eighteenth-Century Comedy." *Review of English Studies* 66, no. 277 (2015): 936–953.

———. "'Well Observed by the Poet': Elias Brand and Richardson's British Ancients." *Eighteenth-Century Fiction* 24 (2012): 597–622.

Donato, Clorinda, and Nicholas D. Nace, eds. "*Fanny Hill* Now: Papers Occasioned by the 50th Anniversary of the 1966 Supreme Court Decision Allowing Publication of *Fanny Hill*." Special issue, *Eighteenth-Century Life* 43, no. 2 (2019).

Doody, Margaret Anne. "George Eliot and the Eighteenth-Century Novel." *Nineteenth-Century Fiction* 35, no. 3 (1980): 260–291.

———. *A Natural Passion: A Study of the Novels of Samuel Richardson.* Oxford: Clarendon Press, 1974.

Doody, Margaret Anne, and Peter Sabor, eds. *Samuel Richardson: Tercentenary Essays.* New York: Cambridge University Press, 1989.

Doyle, Laura. *Freedom's Empire: Race and the Rise of the Novel in Atlantic Modernity, 1640–1940.* Durham, NC: Duke University Press, 2007.

During, Lisabeth. *The Chastity Plot.* London: University of Chicago Press, 2021.

Dussinger, John. "Fabrications from Samuel Richardson's Press." *Papers of the Bibliographical Society of America* 100 (2006): 259–279.

———. "Samuel Richardson's 'Elegant Disquisitions': Anonymous Writing in the *True Briton* and Other Journals?" *Studies in Bibliography* 53 (2000): 195–226.

———. "'Stealing in the Great Doctrines of Christianity': Samuel Richardson as Journalist." *Eighteenth-Century Fiction* 15 (2003): 451–506.

Dworkin, Craig, and Kenneth Goldsmith, eds. *Against Expression: An Anthology of Conceptual Writing.* Evanston, IL: Northwestern University Press, 2011.

Eagleton, Terry. *The Rape of Clarissa: Writing, Sexuality and Class Struggle in Samuel Richardson.* Oxford: Blackwell, 1982.

Earle, Peter. *The Making of the English Middle Class: Business, Society, and Family Life in London, 1660–1730.* London: Methuen, 1989.

Ellis, Markman. *The Politics of Sensibility: Race, Gender, and Commerce in the Sentimental Novel.* New York: Cambridge University Press, 1996.

Ellman, Maud. *The Hunger Artists: Starving, Writing, and Imprisonment.* Cambridge, MA: Harvard University Press, 1993.

Fairchild, Paul. "Kryptonite Is Crap." *The Atlantic*, June 20, 2013. https://www.theatlantic.com/technology/archive/2013/06/kryptonite-is-crap/276984/.

Fanning, Christopher. "'On Sterne's Page': Spatial Layout, Spatial Form, and Social Spaces in *Tristram Shandy*." *Eighteenth-Century Fiction* 10, no. 4 (1998): 429–450.

Ferguson, Frances. *Pornography, the Theory: What Utilitarianism Did to Action.* Chicago: University of Chicago Press, 2004.

———. "Rape and the Rise of the Novel." *Representations* 20 (1987): 88–112.

Flint, Christopher. "The Anxiety of Affluence: Family and Class (Dis)order in *Pamela: Or, Virtue Rewarded*." *Studies in English Literature, 1500–1900* 29, no. 3 (1989): 489–514.

———. *The Appearance of Print in Eighteenth-Century Fiction.* Cambridge: Cambridge University Press, 2011.

———. "The Material Book." In *Samuel Richardson in Context*, edited by Peter Sabor and Betty A. Schellenberg, 119–127. Cambridge: Cambridge University Press, 2017.

Flynn, Carol Houlihan. *Samuel Richardson: A Man of Letters.* Princeton, NJ: Princeton University Press, 1982.

Foucault, Michel. *The History of Sexuality.* Vol. 1: *The Will to Knowledge.* Translated by Robert Hurley. London: Penguin, 1998.

———. *The History of Sexuality.* Vol. 4: *The Confessions of the Flesh.* Translated by Robert Hurley. London: Penguin, 2022.

Fowler, James. *The Libertine's Nemesis: The Prude in "Clarissa" and the roman libertin.* Cambridge: Legenda, 2011.

Freeman, Elizabeth. *Time Binds: Queer Temporalities, Queer Histories.* Durham, NC: Duke University Press, 2010.

Friedman, Emily. "The End(s) of Richardson's *Sir Charles Grandison*." *Studies in English Literature 1500–1900* 52, no. 3 (2012): 651–667.

Frow, John. *Character and Person.* Oxford: Oxford University Press, 2014.

Fuentes, Marisa J. *Dispossessed Lives: Enslaved Women, Violence, and the Archive.* Philadelphia: University of Pennsylvania Press, 2016.

———. "Genres of History and the Practice of Loss: Attending to Silence in Hazel Carby's *Imperial Intimacies*." *Small Axe* 25, no. 1 (2021): 167–174.

Fysh, Stephanie. *The Work(s) of Samuel Richardson.* Newark: University of Delaware Press, 1997.

Gabaldon, Diana. *Virgins: An Outlander Short Story.* London: Century, 2016.

Gallagher, Catherine. *Nobody's Story: The Vanishing Acts of Women Writers in the Marketplace, 1670–1820.* Berkeley: University of California Press, 1994.

———. "The Rise of Fictionality." In *The Novel*, vol. 1: *History, Geography and Culture*, edited by Franco Moretti. Princeton, NJ: Princeton University Press, 2006.

Gates-Markel, Lindsey. "In Celebration of Old-School LiveJournal." The Toast, April 1, 2015. https://the-toast.net/2015/04/01/in-celebration-old-school-livejournal/.

Gevlin, Rachel. "Adulterous Austen: Educating the Rake in *Sense and Sensibility* and *Mansfield Park*." *English Literary History* 87, no. 4 (2020): 1055–1078.

Goldsmith, Kenneth. "Paragraphs on Conceptual Writing." Poetry Foundation, May 10, 2007. https://www.poetryfoundation.org/harriet-books/2007/05/paragraphs-on-conceptual-writing/.

Griffiths, Paul. *Youth and Authority: Formative Experiences in England, 1560–1640*. Oxford: Clarendon Press, 1996.

Gwilliam, Tassie. *Samuel Richardson's Fictions of Gender*. Stanford, CA: Stanford University Press, 1995.

Haggerty, G. E. "Female Abjection in Inchbald's *A Simple Story*." *Studies in English Literature, 1500–1900* 36, no. 3 (1996): 655–671.

Hall, Douglas. *In Miserable Slavery: Thomas Thistlewood in Jamaica 1750–86*. Kingston, Jamaica: University of the West Indies Press, 1999.

Harol, Corinne. *Enlightened Virginity in Eighteenth-Century Literature*. Basingstoke, UK: Palgrave Macmillan, 2006.

Harris, Jocelyn. *Jane Austen's Art of Memory*. Cambridge: Cambridge University Press, 1989.

———. *Samuel Richardson*. Cambridge: Cambridge University Press, 1987.

Harris, Jocelyn, and Lisa Zunshine, eds. *Approaches to Teaching the Novels of Samuel Richardson*. New York: Modern Language Association of America, 2006.

Harvey, Karen. *The Little Republic: Masculinity and Domestic Authority in Eighteenth-Century Britain*. Oxford: Oxford University Press, 2012.

Havens, Hilary. *Revising the Eighteenth-Century Novel: Authorship from Manuscript to Print*. Cambridge: Cambridge University Press, 2019.

Hayles, N. Katherine. *Postprint: Books and Becoming Computational*. New York: Columbia University Press, 2021.

Hernandez, Alex Eric. "Tragedy and the Economics of Providence in Richardson's *Clarissa*." *Eighteenth-Century Fiction* 22, no. 4 (2010): 599–630.

Hershinow, Stephanie Insley. *Born Yesterday: Inexperience and the Early Realist Novel*. Baltimore: Johns Hopkins University Press, 2019.

Hilliard, Raymond F. "*Pamela*: Autonomy, Subordination, and the 'State of Childhood.'" *Studies in Philology* 83, no. 2 (1986): 201–217.

Hinton, Laura. "The Heroine's Subjection: *Clarissa*, Sadomasochism, and Natural Law." *Eighteenth-Century Studies* 32, no. 3 (1999): 293–308.

Honan, Park. "Richardson's Influence on Jane Austen." In *Samuel Richardson: Passion and Prudence*, edited by Valerie Grosvenor Myer, 165–177. London: Vision Press, 1986.

Horne, Gerald. *The Apocalypse of Settler Colonialism: The Roots of Slavery, White Supremacy and Capitalism in Seventeenth-Century North America and the Caribbean*. New York: Monthly Review Press, 2017.

Ibsen, Charles A., and Patricia Klobus. "Fictive Kin Term Use and Social Relationships: Alternative Interpretations." *Journal of Marriage and Family* 34, no. 4 (1972): 615–620.

Johnson, Claudia L. *Jane Austen: Women, Politics and the Novel*. Chicago: University of Chicago Press, 1990.

Judson, Barbara. "The Psychology of Satan: Elizabeth Inchbald's *A Simple Story*." *English Literary History* 76 (2009): 599–624.

Kasey Marks, Sylvia. *Sir Charles Grandison: The Compleat Conduct Book*. Cranbury, NJ: Associated University Presses, 1986.

Kelleher, Paul. *Making Love: Sentiment and Sexuality in Eighteenth-Century British Literature*. Lewisburg, PA: Bucknell University Press, 2015.

Kerfoot, Alicia. "Virtuous Footwear: Pamela's Shoe Heel and Cinderilla's 'Little Glass Slipper.'" *Eighteenth-Century Fiction* 31, no. 2 (2019): 343–371.

Keymer, Thomas. "Epistolary Writing in the Long Eighteenth Century." In *A Companion to British Literature*, edited by Robert DeMaria Jr., Heesok Chang, and Samantha Zacher, 159–173. Chichester, UK: John Wiley, 2014.

———. *Richardson's "Clarissa" and the Eighteenth-Century Reader.* Cambridge: Cambridge University Press, 1992.

———. "Richardson's Meditations: Clarissa's Grandison." In *Samuel Richardson: Tercentenary Essays*, edited by Margaret Anne Doody and Peter Sabor, 89–109. New York: Cambridge University Press, 1989.

Keymer, Thomas, and Peter Sabor, eds. *"Pamela" in the Marketplace.* Cambridge: Cambridge University Press, 2005.

King, Thomas A. *The Gendering of Men, 1660–1750.* Vol. 1: *The English Phallus.* Madison: University of Wisconsin Press, 2004.

Kinkead-Weekes, Mark. *Samuel Richardson: Dramatic Novelist.* Ithaca, NY: Cornell University Press, 1973.

Koehler, Martha J. "The Problem of Suspense in Richardson's *Sir Charles Grandison*." *The Eighteenth Century* 54, no. 3 (2013): 317–338.

Kraft, Elizabeth. "'Happy the Man': The Eighteenth-Century Novel and the Pursuit of Happiness." *The Eighteenth Century* 57, no. 11 (2016): 151–155.

Krahn, Daniel. "Secrets and Selves: Theorizing a 'Grandisonian' Self." *Philological Quarterly* 96, no. 1 (2017): 55–76.

Kramnick, Jonathan. *Actions and Objects from Hobbes to Richardson.* Stanford, CA: Stanford University Press, 2010.

Lamb, Jonathan. *The Rhetoric of Suffering: Reading the Book of Job in the Eighteenth Century.* Oxford: Clarendon Press, 1995.

Lander Johnson, Bonnie. *Chastity in Early-Modern Stuart Literature and Culture.* Cambridge: Cambridge University Press, 2015.

Latimer, Bonnie. "'Apprehensions of Controul': The Family Politics of Marriage, Choice and Consent in *Sir Charles Grandison*." *Journal for Eighteenth-Century Studies* 32, no. 1 (2009): 1–19.

———. *Making Gender, Culture, and the Self in the Fiction of Samuel Richardson: The Novel Individual.* Burlington, VT: Ashgate, 2013.

Lee, Wendy Anne. *Failures of Feeling: Insensibility and the Novel.* Stanford, CA: Stanford University Press, 2019.

Le Faye, Deirdre. *Jane Austen: A Family Record.* 2nd ed. Cambridge: Cambridge University Press, 2004.

LeWitt, Sol. "Paragraphs on Conceptual Art" (1967). In *Conceptual Art: A Critical Anthology*, edited by Alexander Alberro and Blake Stimson, 12–16. Cambridge, MA: MIT Press, 1999.

Lipsedge, Karen. *Domestic Space in Eighteenth-Century British Novels.* Basingstoke, UK: Palgrave Macmillan, 2012.

Lubey, Kathleen. *Excitable Imaginations: Eroticism and Reading in Britain, 1660–1760.* Lewisburg, PA: Bucknell University Press, 2012.

———. "Sexual Remembrance in *Clarissa*." *Eighteenth-Century Fiction* 29, no. 2 (2016–2017): 151–178.

Lupton, Christina. *Reading and the Making of Time in the Eighteenth Century.* Baltimore: Johns Hopkins University Press, 2018.

Lycett, Andrew. *The Man Who Created Sherlock Holmes: The Life and Times of Sir Arthur Conan Doyle.* New York: Free Press, 2007.

Lynch, Deidre. *The Economy of Character: Novels, Market Culture, and the Business of Inner Meaning.* Chicago: University of Chicago Press, 1998.

———. "'Nothing of Body:' Our *Clarissa* Quarantine." *The Rambling*, June 11, 2021. https://the-rambling.com/2021/06/11/issue11-lynch/.

Macey, David. "'Business for the Lovers of Business': *Sir Charles Grandison*, Hardwicke's Marriage Act and the Specter of Bigamy." *Philological Quarterly* 84, no. 3 (2005): 333–355.

Mackie, Erin. *Rakes, Highwaymen, and Pirates: The Making of the Modern Gentleman in the Eighteenth Century.* Baltimore: Johns Hopkins University Press, 2009.

Macpherson, Sandra. *Harm's Way: Tragic Responsibility and the Novel Form.* Baltimore: Johns Hopkins University Press, 2010.

Maslen, Keith. *Samuel Richardson of London, Printer: A Study of His Printing Based on Ornament Use and Business Accounts.* Christchurch, NZ: University of Otago, 2001.

McGirr, Elaine. "Manly Lessons: *Sir Charles Grandison*, the Rake and the Man of Sentiment." *Studies in the Novel* 39, no. 3 (2007): 267–283.

McKee, Patricia. *Heroic Commitment in Richardson, Eliot, and James.* Princeton, NJ: Princeton University Press, 1986.

McKeon, Michael. *Origins of the English Novel.* Baltimore: Johns Hopkins University Press, 1987.

———. *The Secret History of Domesticity: Public, Private and the Division of Knowledge.* Baltimore: Johns Hopkins University Press, 2005.

McKillop, Alan D. *Samuel Richardson: Printer and Novelist.* 1936. Reprint, Chapel Hill: University of North Carolina Press, 1960.

———. "Samuel Richardson's Advice to an Apprentice." *Journal of English and Germanic Philology* 42 (1943): 40–54.

McMaster, Juliet. "*Sir Charles Grandison*: Richardson on Body and Character." *Eighteenth-Century Fiction* 1, no. 2 (1989): 83–102.

Mello, Patrick. "'Piety and Popishness': Tolerance and the Epistolary Reaction to Richardson's *Sir Charles Grandison*." *Eighteenth-Century Fiction* 25, no. 3 (2013): 511–531.

Mills, Charles. *The Racial Contract.* Ithaca, NY: Cornell University Press, 1997.

Moretti, Franco. *The Way of the World: The Bildungsroman in European Culture.* New York: Verso, 1987.

Morgan, Jennifer. *Laboring Women: Reproduction and Gender in New World Slavery.* Philadelphia: University of Pennsylvania Press, 2004.

Morillo, John. "Editing Eve: Rewriting the Fall in Austen's *Persuasion* and Inchbald's *A Simple Story*." *Eighteenth-Century Fiction* 23, no. 1 (2010): 195–223.

Morse, Jack. "Was LiveJournal Ever Actually Any Good? A Nostalgia-Tinged Investigation." *Mashable*, May 13, 2018. https://mashable.com/2018/05/13/was-livejournal-ever-good/.

Nace, Nicholas D. "Unprinted Matter: Conceptual Writing and *Tristram Shandy*'s 'Chasm of Ten Pages.'" *The Shandean* 24 (2013): 31–58.

Newton, John. *The Works of the Rev. John Newton.* 4 vols. New Haven, CT: Nathan Whiting, 1824.

Ngai, Sianne. *Ugly Feelings.* Cambridge, MA: Harvard University Press, 2005.

Norton, Brian Michael. *Fiction and the Philosophy of Happiness: Ethical Inquiries in the Age of Enlightenment.* Lewisburg, PA: Bucknell University Press, 2012.

Nussbaum, Felicity. *The Limits of the Human: Fictions of Anomaly, Race, and Gender in the Long Eighteenth Century.* Cambridge: Cambridge University Press, 2015.

———. *Torrid Zones: Maternity, Sexuality and Empire in Eighteenth-Century English Narratives.* Baltimore: Johns Hopkins University Press, 1995.

Oliver, Kathleen. *Samuel Richardson, Dress, and Discourse.* Basingstoke, UK: Palgrave Macmillan, 2008.

Orange, Michael. "Prudes, Lusciousness and Joseph Andrews." *Sydney Studies* 17 (1991): 46–66.

Oyěwùmí, Oyèrónkẹ́. *The Invention of Women: Making an African Sense of Western Gender Discourses.* Minneapolis: University of Minnesota Press, 1997.

Park, Julie. "I Shall Enter Her Heart: Fetishizing Feeling in *Clarissa*." *Studies in the Novel* 37, no. 4 (2005): 371–393.

Parker, Kate, and Norbert Sclippa, eds. *Sade's Sensibilities.* Lewisburg, PA: Bucknell University Press, 2015.

Pascoe, Judith. "Before I Read *Clarissa* I Was Nobody: Aspirational Reading and Samuel Richardson's Great Novel." *The Hudson Review* 56, no. 2 (2003): 239–253.

Perloff, Marjorie. *Unoriginal Genius: Poetry by Other Means in the New Century.* Chicago: University of Chicago Press, 2010.

Perry, Ruth. *Novel Relations: The Transformation of Kinship in English Literature and Culture, 1748–1818.* Cambridge: Cambridge University Press, 2004.

Place, Vanessa, and Robert Fitterman. *Notes on Conceptualisms.* Brooklyn, NY: Ugly Duckling Presse, 2009.

Porter, Roy. *Enlightenment: Britain and the Creation of the Modern World.* London: Penguin, 2001.

Potkay, Adam. *The Story of Joy: From the Bible to Late Romanticism.* Cambridge: Cambridge University Press, 2011.

Praz, Mario. *The Romantic Agony.* Translated by Angus Davidson. Cleveland: Meridian,1956.

Price, Leah. *The Anthology and the Rise of the Novel from Richardson to George Eliot.* Cambridge: Cambridge University Press, 2000.

Raff, Sarah. "Ghost of the Guardian in *Sir Charles Grandison* and *Bleak House*." In *The Afterlives of Eighteenth-Century Fiction*, edited by Daniel Cook and Nicholas Seager, 91–110. Cambridge: Cambridge University Press, 2015.

Reed, Brian. *Nobody's Business: Twenty-First Century Avant Garde Poetics.* Ithaca, NY: Cornell University Press, 2013.

Rivero, Albert J. "The Place of Sally Godfrey in Richardson's *Pamela*." *Eighteenth-Century Fiction* 6, no. 1 (1993): 29–46.

———, ed. *The Sentimental Novel in the Eighteenth Century.* Cambridge: Cambridge University Press, 2019.

Rule, John. "Employment and Authority: Masters and Men in Eighteenth-Century Manufacturing." In *The Experience of Authority in Early Modern England*, edited by Paul Griffiths, Adam Fox, and Steve Hindle, 286–317. Basingstoke, UK: Palgrave Macmillan, 1996.

Sabor, Peter. "'A Safe Bridge over the Narrow Seas': Crossing the Channel with Samuel Richardson." In *All Before Them: Attitudes to Abroad in English Literature, 1660–1780,* edited by John McVeagh, 159–170. London: Ashfield Press, 1990.

Sabor, Peter, and Betty Schellenberg, eds. *Samuel Richardson in Context.* 2 vols. Cambridge: Cambridge University Press, 2017.

Sales, Roger. *Jane Austen and Representations of Regency England.* London: Routledge, 1996.

Schellenberg, Betty A. "Authorship." In *Samuel Richardson in Context*, edited by Peter Sabor and Betty A. Schellenberg, 102–104. Cambridge: Cambridge University Press, 2017.

———. *The Conversational Circle: Re-reading the English Novel, 1740–1775.* Lexington: University Press of Kentucky, 1996.

———. "Using 'Femalities' to 'Make Fine Men': Richardson's *Sir Charles Grandison* and the Feminization of Narrative." *Studies in English Literature, 1500–1900* 34, no. 3 (1994): 599–616.

Seymour, Miranda. *A Ring of Conspirators: Henry James and His Literary Circle.* Boston: Houghton Mifflin, 1988.

Sharpe, Christina. *In the Wake: On Blackness and Being.* Durham, NC: Duke University Press, 2016.

Sharpe, J. A. "Disruption in the Well-Ordered Household: Age, Authority, and Possessed Young People." In *The Experience of Authority in Early Modern England*, edited by Paul Griffiths, Adam Fox, and Steve Hindle, 187–212. Basingstoke, UK: Palgrave Macmillan, 1996.

Shepherd, Lynn. *Clarissa's Painter: Portraiture, Illustration, and Representation in the Novels of Samuel Richardson.* Oxford: Oxford University Press, 2009.

Smith, Chloe Wigston. *Women, Work, and Clothes in the Eighteenth-Century Novel.* Cambridge: Cambridge University Press, 2013.

Smith, Hazel. "Experimental Confessionalism: The Personal Turn in American Post-conceptual Poetry." *Cordite Poetry Review* 87 (2018). http://cordite.org.au/essays/experimental-confessionalism/.

Smith, James. *Samuel Richardson and the Theory of Tragedy: "Clarissa"'s caesuras.* Manchester: Manchester University Press, 2016.

Smith, Steven R. "The London Apprentices as Seventeenth-Century Adolescents." *Past and Present* 61 (1973): 149–161.

Sollors, Werner. *Neither Black nor White yet Both: Thematic Explorations of Interracial Literature.* New York: Oxford University Press, 1999.

Soni, Vivasvan. *Mourning Happiness: Narrative and the Politics of Modernity.* Ithaca, NY: Cornell University Press, 2010.

———. "Trials and Tragedies: The Literature of Unhappiness (a Model for Reading Narratives of Suffering)." *Comparative Literature* 59, no. 2 (2007): 119–139.

Southam, Brian. *Jane Austen's "Sir Charles Grandison."* Oxford: Clarendon Press, 1980.

Spacks, Patricia Meyer. *Boredom: The Literary History of a State of Mind.* Chicago: University of Chicago Press, 1995.

———. *Imagining a Self: Autobiography and Novel in Eighteenth-Century England.* Cambridge, MA: Harvard University Press, 1976.

Spånberg, Sven-Johan. *"The Ordeal of Richard Feverel" and the Traditions of Realism.* Uppsala: Uppsala Offsetcenter AB, 1974.

Spillers, Hortense J. "Mama's Baby, Papa's Maybe: An American Grammar Book." *Diacritics* 17 (Summer 1987): 64–81.

Spivak, Gayatri Chakravorty. "Three Women's Texts and a Critique of Imperialism." *Critical Inquiry* 12 (1985): 243–261.

Stedman, John Gabriel. *Narrative of a Five Years Expedition against the Revolted Negroes of Surinam.* Edited by Richard Price and Sally Price. London: Open Road, 2016.

Stephen, Leslie. *English Men of Letters: George Eliot.* Edited by John Morley. New York: Macmillan, 1906.

Siltanen, Elina. "Conceptual Confession: Asymmetrical Emotion in Writer-Reader Relations in Trisha Low's *The Compleat Purge.*" *Journal of Modern Literature* 43, no. 4 (2020): 108–126.

Stone, Lawrence. *The Family, Sex and Marriage in England, 1500–1800.* London: Penguin, 1977.

Stuart-Buttle, Tim. *From Moral Theology to Moral Philosophy: Cicero and Visions of Humanity from Locke to Hume.* Oxford: Oxford University Press, 2019.

Suárez, Angelo V. "Appropriative Resistance." *Jacket2*, February 5, 2016. http://jacket2.org/article/appropriative-resistance.

Suzuki, Mihoko. "The London Apprentice Riots of the 1590s and the Fiction of Thomas Deloney." *Criticism* 38, no. 2 (1996): 181–217.

Tadmor, Naomi. *Family and Friends in Eighteenth-Century England: Household, Kinship, and Patronage.* Cambridge: Cambridge University Press, 2001.

Taylor, E. Derek. *Reason and Religion in "Clarissa": Samuel Richardson and "The Famous Mr. Norris, of Bemerton."* Burlington, VT: Ashgate, 2009.

Thompson, Helen. *Ingenuous Subjection: Compliance and Power in the Eighteenth-Century Domestic Novel.* Philadelphia: University of Pennsylvania Press, 2005.

———. "Secondary Qualities and Masculine Form in *Clarissa* and *Sir Charles Grandison.*" *Eighteenth-Century Fiction* 24, no. 2 (2011–2012): 195–226.

Thurlow, Michelle. "Marble under a Strange Spell: St. John Rivers' 'Long-Cherished Scheme' to Wed Jane Eyre." *Journal of Popular Romance Studies*, September 19, 2017. https://www.jprstudies.org/2017/09/marble-under-a-strange-spell-st-john-rivers-long-cherished-scheme-to-wed-jane-eyreby-michelle-thurlow/.

Todd, Janet. *Sensibility: An Introduction.* London: Methuen, 1986.

Trumbach, Randolph. *The Rise of the Egalitarian Family.* New York: Academic Press, 1978.

———. *Sex and the Gender Revolution.* Vol. 1: *Heterosexuality and the Third Gender in Enlightenment London.* Chicago: University of Chicago Press, 1998.

Voogd, Peter de. "*Tristram Shandy* as Aesthetic Object." *Word and Image: A Journal of Verbal/Visual Enquiry* 4, no. 1 (1988): 383–392.

Wall, Cynthia. *Grammars of Approach: Landscape, Narrative, and the Linguistic Picturesque.* Chicago: University of Chicago Press, 2019.

Wallace, Miriam. "Wit and Revolution: Cultural Resistance in Elizabeth Inchbald's *A Simple Story.*" *European Romantic Review* 12, no. 1 (2001): 92–121.

Wallis, Patrick. "Apprenticeship and Training in Premodern England." *Journal of Economic History* 68, no. 3 (2008): 832–861.

Wallis, Patrick, Cliff Webb, and Chris Minns. "Leaving Home and Entering Service: The Age of Apprenticeship in Early Modern London." *Continuity and Change* 25, no. 3 (2010): 377–404.

Watt, Ian. *The Rise of the Novel.* Berkeley: University of California Press, 2001.

Webster, Jeremy W. "Sentimentalizing Patriarchy: Patriarchal Anxiety and Filial Obligation in *Sir Charles Grandison.*" *Eighteenth-Century Fiction* 17, no. 3 (2005): 425–442.

Williams, Eric. *Capitalism and Slavery.* Richmond, VA: William Byrd Press, 1944.

Williams, Helen. *Laurence Sterne and the Eighteenth-Century Book.* Cambridge: Cambridge University Press, 2021.

Winnubst, Shannon. "The Many Lives of Fungibility: Anti-Blackness in Neoliberal Times." *Journal of Gender Studies* 29, no. 1 (2020): 102–112.

Wohlcke, Anne. *The Perpetual Fair: Gender, Disorder, and Urban Amusement in Eighteenth-Century London.* Manchester: Manchester University Press, 2014.

Woloch, Alex. *The One vs. the Many: Minor Characters and the Space of the Protagonist in the Novel.* Princeton, NJ: Princeton University Press, 2003.

Yates, Mary V. "The Christian Rake in *Sir Charles Grandison.*" *Studies in English Literature 1500–1900* 24, no. 3 (1984): 545–561.

Zacek, Natalie A. *Settler Society in the English Leeward Islands, 1670–1776.* Cambridge: Cambridge University Press, 2015.

NOTES ON CONTRIBUTORS

REBECCA ANNE BARR is an associate professor in the Faculty of English at the University of Cambridge in the United Kingdom and a fellow of Jesus College. She specializes in gender, narrative, and sexuality in eighteenth-century fiction.

SARAH BERKOWITZ received her PhD from the University of Virginia in 2020. Her research focuses on character and masculinity in the mid-eighteenth-century novel.

AMELIA DALE is the author of *The Printed Reader: Gender, Quixotism, and Textual Bodies in Eighteenth-Century Britain* (Bucknell University Press) and a lecturer in English at the Australian National University in Canberra.

DECLAN KAVANAGH is a senior lecturer in eighteenth-century studies at the University of Kent in the United Kingdom. He is the author of *Effeminate Years: Literature, Politics, and Aesthetics in Mid-Eighteenth-Century Britain* (Bucknell University Press) and has published numerous articles and book chapters on queerness, masculinities, and disability in Anglophone eighteenth-century literature and culture.

HEATHER LADD is a lecturer (below the bar) in English (long eighteenth century) at the University of Galway in Ireland and was recently an instructor in the Department of English at Kwantlen Polytechnic University in British Columbia, Canada. She has written a variety of pieces on eighteenth-century fiction and drama and is coeditor of *English Theatrical Anecdotes, 1660–1800.*

BONNIE LATIMER is a professor of Restoration and eighteenth-century literature at the University of Southampton in the United Kingdom. She has published on Richardson and other authors of the period.

SAMUEL ROWE's articles on eighteenth-century and Romantic literature have appeared in *ELH*, *Eighteenth-Century Studies*, and *Studies in Romanticism*. He teaches in the Chicago Public Schools in Illinois.

KERRY SINANAN is an assistant professor in global pre-1800 literature and culture at the University of Winnipeg in Canada. She specializes in the Black Atlantic, Caribbean slavery and race, and the global dimensions of Black resistance and abolition up to the present.

E. DEREK TAYLOR is a professor of English at Longwood University in Farmville, Virginia. He is coeditor, with Melvyn New and Elizabeth Kraft, of Richardson's *The History of Sir Charles Grandison*, part of the Cambridge Edition of the Works of Samuel Richardson series.

INDEX